D1612542

EAST SUSSEX COUNTY COUNCIL
WITHDRAWN
14 AUG 2024
35

04322518

THE MODERN CASTRATO

# The Modern Castrato

GAETANO GUADAGNI AND THE COMING OF A
NEW OPERATIC AGE

*Patricia Howard*

OXFORD
UNIVERSITY PRESS

# OXFORD
UNIVERSITY PRESS

Oxford University Press is a department of the University of Oxford.
It furthers the University's objective of excellence in research, scholarship,
and education by publishing worldwide.

Oxford    New York
Auckland    Cape Town    Dar es Salaam    Hong Kong    Karachi
Kuala Lumpur    Madrid    Melbourne    Mexico City    Nairobi
New Delhi    Shanghai    Taipei    Toronto

With offices in
Argentina    Austria    Brazil    Chile    Czech Republic    France    Greece
Guatemala    Hungary    Italy    Japan    Poland    Portugal    Singapore
South Korea    Switzerland    Thailand    Turkey    Ukraine    Vietnam

Oxford is a registered trademark of Oxford University Press
in the UK and certain other countries.

Published in the United States of America by
Oxford University Press
198 Madison Avenue, New York, NY 10016

© Oxford University Press 2014

All rights reserved. No part of this publication may be reproduced, stored in
a retrieval system, or transmitted, in any form or by any means, without the prior
permission in writing of Oxford University Press, or as expressly permitted by law,
by license, or under terms agreed with the appropriate reproduction rights organization.
Inquiries concerning reproduction outside the scope of the above should be sent to the
Rights Department, Oxford University Press, at the address above.

You must not circulate this work in any other form
and you must impose this same condition on any acquirer.

Library of Congress Cataloging-in-Publication Data
Howard, Patricia, author.
The modern castrato : Gaetano Guadagni and the coming of a new operatic age / Patricia Howard.
pages ; cm
Includes bibliographical references and index.
ISBN 978–0–19–936520–3 (hardback)—ISBN 978–0–19–936521–0 (electronic text)—
ISBN 978–0–19–936522–7 (online content)    1. Guadagni, Gaetano,
1728–1792.    2. Castrati--Italy--Biography.    I. Title.
ML420.G9158H69 2014
782.1092--dc23
[B]
2013036715

9  8  7  6  5  4  3  2  1
Printed in the United States of America
on acid-free paper

*In loving memory of Lucy Howard (1962–2004)*

# Contents

List of Illustrations  ix

List of Tables  xi

Acknowledgements  xiii

Recommended Listening  xv

About the Companion Website  xvii

*Introduction*  1

1. *From Lodi to London (1728–1748)*  16

2. *A London Apprenticeship (1748–1749)*  27

3. *Guadagni and Handel (1749–1755)*  42

4. *Guadagni the Actor*  65

5. *Building a Career on the European Stage (1755–1762)*  78

6. *Guadagni in Vienna (1762–1765)*  93

7. *Return to the Veneto (1765–1769)*  110

8. *Success and Scandal in London (1769–1771)*  123

9. *Guadagni the Composer*  137

*10. At Home in Padua (1771–1782)* 155

*11. The Last Decade (1782–1792)* 183

*12. Guadagni the Singer* 192

*Conclusion* 211

APPENDIX A: GUADAGNI'S DRAMATIC ROLES 213
APPENDIX B: GUADAGNI'S SALARY AT THE SANTO 219
APPENDIX C: A SELECTION OF DOCUMENTS 221
BIBLIOGRAPHY 225
INDEX 235

# List of Illustrations

0.1   Guadagni on trial before Sir John Fielding  4

0.2   'Parnassus', engraving after Antonio Fedi, c. 1790  5

0.3   Detail from Fedi  6

1.1   Baptismal record  17

1.2   From the libretto of *Cesare in Egitto*, Venice 1746  24

4.1   Garrick as Richard III by Hogarth  72

9.1   Guadagni, 'Pensa a serbarmi', Verona score, p. 1  148

9.2   Guadagni, 'Pensa a serbarmi', Bologna score, p. 1  148

9.3   Verona score, bars 36–39  149

10.1  Guadagni's house in Padua  166

10.2  Eighteenth-century marionette theatre  174

11.1  Record of Guadagni's death  190

# List of Tables

3.1    Guadagni's engagements in spring 1753  57

9.1    The key structure of *Orfeo* Act II scene 1 in the scores of 1762, 1769 and 1770  141

9.2    Content of Act II in the Paduan pasticcio  146

10.1   Orpheus operas performed by Guadagni  177

10.2   A comparison of Calzabigi's stage directions and Guadagni's scenery  178

12.1   Handel's oratorios and odes performed by Guadagni between 1750 and 1755  203

A.1    Guadagni's dramatic roles  213

B.1    Guadagni's salary at the Santo  220

*Acknowledgements*

THIS BOOK HAS been many years in the making, in which time I have accumulated debts to a number of institutions and individuals. First and foremost, the project would not have been possible without the award of a Visiting Research Fellowship from the Open University. Among the many excellent libraries, galleries and museums who have helped me are the Bodleian Library, Oxford, the University Library, Cambridge, the British Library, London, the National Archives at Kew and the Metropolitan London Archives. In addition, the Bibliothèque Nationale in Paris, the Biblioteca da Ajuda in Lisbon, the Hauptstaatsarchiv in Stuttgart, the Österreichische Nationalbibliothek in Vienna and the University of Salzburg have been particularly hospitable. But the focus of my work has been in Italy, and the following institutions have provided a wealth of archival resources: the Civico Museo Bibliografico Musicale in Bologna, the Diocesan Archive in Lodi, the Biblioteca Nazionale Braidense in Milan, the Teatro Regio in Turin, the Museo Correr and the Museo Casa di Goldoni in Venice and the Conservatorio di Musica F. E. dall'Abaco in Verona. In Padua I have enjoyed the hospitality of the Biblioteca Antoniana and the Centro Studi Antoniani, the Museo Civico and the Archivio di Stato.

In addition, a number of individual scholars have shared information, handed out advice, helped with translation problems, and facilitated my entry to private archives. I am particularly grateful for the generosity of Graydon Beeks, Lorenzo Bianconi, Irene Brandenburg, Bruce Alan Brown, Donald Burrows, Gerhard Croll,

Kerry Grant, Luca de Paolis, Brian Robins, Ian Woodfield and Eva Zöllner. Brian Baldry provided me with an elegant translation of a sonnet by Gasparo Gozzi, and Antony Bye has worked his editorial magic on the music examples. Several singers have helped me to explore Guadagni's repertory, notably James Laing, in a memorable pasticcio of pasticcios in London 2010, and Iestyn Davies in his CD *Arias for Guadagni*, referred to constantly throughout the text.

I have not hesitated to exploit the varied talents of my family, and would like to record my particular gratitude to my brother, James Lowe, for a solving a multitude of IT problems, my daughter, Charlotte Goddard, for Latin translations, my grandson, Freddie Howard Whitaker, for some creative photography, and most of all to my husband, David, for constant support and encouragement along the way.

# Recommended Listening

A REPRESENTATIVE SAMPLE of Guadagni's repertory has been recorded by Iestyn Davies on *Arias for Guadagni*, Hyperion, CDA 67924. Tracks from this disc that are discussed in the text are identified in the footnotes. The following link accesses the contents of the disc:

http://www.hyperion-records.co.uk/dc.asp?dc=D_CDA67924&vw=dc

*About the Companion Website*

**www.oup.com/us/moderncastrato**

OXFORD UNIVERSITY PRESS has created a website to accompany this book. Here readers will find the scores of three complete pieces composed by Guadagni: 'Men tiranne', 'Che puro ciel', and 'Pensa a serbarmi, o cara', and be able to listen to a recording of 'Men tiranne', sung by James Laing. There is also a short introduction to Guadagni and the part he played in the new operatic age.

The examples that appear on the website are signalled in the text with the icon .

THE MODERN CASTRATO

# Introduction

## INTRODUCING GUADAGNI

WHO WAS GUADAGNI? Where does he take his place in the glittering pantheon of eighteenth-century operatic castrato soloists? Their names are familiar enough: Bernacchi, Caffarelli, Carestini, Farinelli, Gizziello, Guadagni, Marchesi, Manzuoli, Pachierotti, Rauzzini, Senesino, Siface, Tenducci and a dozen more, characterised by their outstanding vocal abilities, eccentric personalities and extravagant conduct. Between them they shaped a century of opera. In this context, Guadagni's significance is clear. If Farinelli dominated the generation of castratos whose skills propelled *opera seria* into its dominant role in the first half of the century, Guadagni bids fair to be considered the most influential singer in the second half: a new kind of singer for a new operatic age. Gifted with what all commentators declared to be an exceptional voice, he was also intelligent, and more than usually involved with the theory of his art. Unlike the majority of the singers named above, Guadagni was an innovator: by happy accident, his career flourished during the 1760s and 1770s, the decades in which great upheavals in taste, technique and dramatic aims, widely referred to as the reform of opera, took place. Guadagni not only coincided with the reform, he was an active agent in bringing it about, collaborating with the prime movers—the theatre director Durazzo, the composers Gluck, Traetta, and Jommelli, the librettists Calzabigi and Coltellini—devising his own independent contribution to the development of singing and acting, and attempting to forge a new relationship between a singer and his audience.

In many senses Guadagni's life and career were not typical of the general run of castratos. Unusually for a castrato, he came from a family of professional musicians. Three sisters and a brother were opera singers. The operation that defined his career was undertaken not, as was so often the case, as an act of desperation by an impoverished family hoping for eventual riches,[1] but must have been an informed choice by parents who knew the profession from the inside, and to whom it might have seemed of little more significance than choosing an instrument for a child—and in effect it was precisely that. Guadagni attended no conservatory and was apprenticed to no singing teacher. As far as we can tell, he received his instruction at home from his father, a member of the choir at Lodi cathedral. And although his path from church musician to operatic soloist was conventional for a successful castrato, and the range of his activities—from Venice to London and including seasons in Dublin, Paris, Lisbon, Stuttgart, Vienna and Munich besides extensive engagements throughout Italy—was typical of many leading singers, one aspect of his repertory was unusual: no other castrato played so many roles in Handel's oratorios under the composer's direction. This influence, coming at an early stage in his career, helped to form his singing style, directing his attention to expression and declamation rather than to virtuosity and display.

Once his operatic career was established, Guadagni was unique in being, for more than two decades, identified with a single role, that of Orpheus in Gluck's seminal reform opera *Orfeo ed Euridice*. Although a few earlier singers took their stage names from their most famous roles (notably Francesco Grossi, known as Siface because of his portrayal of that character in Cavalli's *Scipione Africano*), having once adopted the name, they might never sing the role again. Before the advent of repertory opera, to repeat an opera over a decade or more was rare. Guadagni not only reprised *Orfeo* in London, Munich and Italy, but re-created the part in other settings of the same libretto, so that in the last decade of his career he sang little other than the role of Orpheus. His involvement with Gluck's *Orfeo* is remarkable. Calzabigi attributed the opera's initial success specifically to him: '*Orfeo* went well because we discovered Guadagni…in other hands it would have fared disastrously',[2] and he was credited with the subsequent diffusion of the opera, even when the title role was entrusted to other singers: '[Gluck's] famous opera of *Orfeo*…with Guadagni's admirable action, succeeded so well, that it was soon after attempted in other parts of Europe'.[3] His tendency towards eccentricity involved him in other distinguishing activities: while he was not, perhaps, the only singer to appear before the formidable Bow Street magistrate Sir John Fielding, he was almost certainly the only castrato to have a race-horse named after him.

---

[1] Patrick Barbier, *Histoire des Castrats* (1989), tr. Margaret Crosland as *The World of the Castrati*, Chapter 2, London: Souvenir Press, 1996.

[2] 'L'Orfeo andò bene, perchè s'incontrò quell Guadagni…sarebbe riuscito malissimo in altra mano', Calzabigi to Kaunitz, 6 Mar. 1767, in Vladimir Helfert, 'Dosud Neznámý Dopis Ran. Calsabigiho z r. 1767', *Musikologie* 1 (1938): 114–22.

[3] Charles Burney, *A General History of Music,* ed. Frank Mercer, ii, New York: Dover, 1957, p. 942.

We have little information about his appearance but what there is is remarkably consistent. On his arrival in London in 1748, a colleague described him as 'a handsome young soprano'. Mid-career assessments praised his 'elegant figure' and 'his countenance replete with beauty, intelligence and dignity'. Towards the end of Guadagni's life, Michael Kelly judged him 'the handsomest man of his kind I ever saw', and his obituary remembered him as being 'without those bodily defects that are usually seen in castratos'.[4] It is all the more to be regretted that no formal portrait has survived, and the lack of any such portrait in the detailed inventory of his belongings at the time of his death suggests that it is unlikely that one was ever painted. Two images are known to have been made in his lifetime. In the anonymous satirical cartoon of his appearance in the Bow Street magistrates' court, the portrayal is sufficiently anodyne to confirm that he was without the bodily defects that often afflicted castratos—unusual height, for example, or a barrel chest. (See Figure 0.1.) But this chubby figure has nothing in common with the sharply aquiline features of the medallion in Antonio Fedi's tribute to the most celebrated singers of his age. (See Figures 0.2 and 0.3.) Fedi's engraving was made around 1790.[5] While there is no firm evidence that Fedi ever met Guadagni, it is more than probable that he did so, since he was working in Padua in 1788. And as all the other medallion images bear a detectable resemblance to surviving portraits of the singers named, it is reasonable to take Fedi's portrait of Guadagni as a faithful representation: the sharp, intelligent features shown in the engraving may indeed be those of the singer.

About the singer's personality much more is known. It was full of contradictions. Guadagni was popular with his colleagues but a trial to managements; generous to a fault, and consequently both improvident and acquisitive. He was attractive to men and to women. If fewer scandalous stories are told about his amorous liaisons than is the case with many of the castratos, nevertheless his first season in London ended with one particularly colourful occasion.[6] By the time he revisited the capital some twenty years later he was the target of hysterical adulation among young women; a literary satire depicts one alarmed mother deploring her daughter's infatuation with the singer, whom she categorised as 'this mock fellow': 'She is always talking about the sweet fellow Guadaini, or some such name, then chaunts a bit of song, then

---

[4] 'Un soprano bello, giovane', Franz Pirker to Jozzi, 1 Oct. 1748, *ms* in Hauptstaatsarchiv, Stuttgart (see Chapter 2 of this volume); 'bella figura', Benedetto Croce, *I teatri di Napoli, secolo XV–XVIII*, Naples: L. Pierro, 1891, p. 749; Burney, *General History*, ii, p. 876; Michael Kelly, *The Reminiscences of Michael Kelly*, i, London, 1826, p. 151; 'senza que' difetti nel corpo che ne' castrati ordinariamente si vedono', Giuseppe Gennari, *Notizie giornaliere di quanto avvenne specialmente in Padova*, ed. Loredana Olivato, ii, Cittadella: Rebellato, 1982, p. 683.

[5] See Michael Schwarte, 'In des Fedi Parnass…Bildnisse des Sängers Anton Raff (1714–1797)', *Traditionen-Neuensätze: für Anna Amalie Abert (1906–96)*, Tutzing: Schneider, 1997, pp. 587–618.

[6] See Chapter 2.

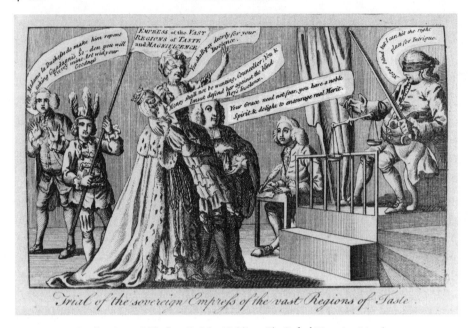

FIGURE 0.1 Guadagni on trial before Sir John Fielding, *The Oxford Magazine*, March 1771.

falls into raptures, and calls upon that sweet angelic creature'.[7] There are numerous instances of his close relationships with female singers, both as protégé and protector. Giulia Frasi mentored his London debut in 1748, introducing him to Burney and Handel and no doubt also establishing him in the circle of his compatriots in a city still suspicious of foreigners and Catholics in the wake of the Jacobite rebellion. Later in his career Guadagni advised and protected his female colleagues, notably the famously temperamental Caterina Gabrielli. He seems to have formed a close friendship with the husband and wife couple Rosa and Giuseppe Tibaldi, and his relationship with his own family, especially with his elder sister Angiola, is a recurrent theme throughout his life.

His generosity is well documented, particularly during the years he spent in Padua. One of his first acts on taking up permanent residence there in 1768 was to help settle the debts of one of the town's leading nobles, Tomaso degli Obizzi.[8] He manifested liberality on a smaller scale when he helped to pay the extra salary demanded by an orchestral soloist for accompanying an obbligato aria to be sung not by himself but by his leading lady.[9] He funded many Paduan feasts and extravaganzas and paid

---

[7] 'W' to the Duchess of [Northumberland], 20 Feb. 1771, in *The Oxford Magazine*, 6 (1771), p. 98.

[8] See P. E. Obizzi to Tomaso Obizzi, 21 Oct. 1783, in Bruno Brunelli, *I teatri di Padova dalle origini alla fine del secolo XIX*, Padua: Draghi, 1921, pp. 233–34.

[9] See Chapter 8.

FIGURE 0.2 'Parnassus', engraving after Antonio Fedi, c. 1790. (Photography F. M. Howard Whitaker)

FIGURE 0.3 Detail from Fedi. (Photography F. M. Howard Whitaker)

for the building of one of the elegant bridges that provide access to the city's large public square, the Prato della Valle.

Castratos had a reputation for arrogance. This is unsurprising; to a certain extent it went with the job. The career of a free-lance singer, having to prove himself over and over again as each season unfolded in a new town, required a high degree of self-confidence that could appear as vanity. Sometimes quirky preferences were adopted as a method of self-advertisement. Stendhal described two examples, alleging that Marchesi, 'during the latter part of his career, refused point-blank to sing at all unless his first entry in the opening scene of the opera were made either on horseback, or else on the top of a hill. Furthermore, which-ever alternative was eventually agreed upon, the cascade of plumes which sur-mounted his helmet was required to be at least six feet high. In our own time, Crivelli still refuses to sing his opening aria, unless the librettist agrees to provide him with the words *felice ornora* ['ever happy'], which are particularly convenient for the execution of certain series of roulades.'[10]

Some castratos were especially sensitive to matters of rank; dependent on the patronage of royal or noble sponsors, they asserted their sense of self-worth by refusing to be seen as grateful for favours or constrained by their subservient status. Caffarelli rejected a snuff box presented to him by Louis XV, saying he had finer ones at home; Siface defied the ruler of more than one country by refusing to sing when summoned.[11] Guadagni was no exception. It is impossible to ignore the occasional bouts of temperamental behaviour attributed to him. The epithet 'capricious' appears often.[12] He is accused of laziness[13] and undefined 'roguery'.[14] This might manifest itself as a refusal to sing. Examples abound: his 'absolute refusal' to sing at a Lenten academy in Vienna in 1763, his absence from the services in San Marco on Christmas Day 1765, and his failure to turn up for an oratorio arranged specially for him in London in February 1771. These incidents are, however, no more frequent with Guadagni than with many of his contemporaries. Not only Siface, but Senesino, Matteuccio, and Velluti all declined to sing before royalty; Caffarelli refused to sing duets with singers he disapproved of; Carestini, on the other hand, insisted on singing even when requested to stop, on the occasion of the sudden death of Pope Benedict XIII.[15]

It is sometimes possible to infer an explanation for Guadagni's acts of apparent arrogance: his shortcomings in connection with two Gluck operas, *Ezio* and *Telemaco*, were probably the result of a professional disagreement with the composer; Guadagni rebelled against what he saw as unreasonable demands on his technique. He had thought that Gluck understood his preferred style, so sympathetically provided for in *Orfeo*, and was affronted at being taken beyond it. His behaviour in London in 1770 was particularly extreme, famously described by Burney as 'so much [offending] individuals, and the opera audience in general, that, at length, he never appeared without being hissed'.[16] Although Burney appears to have been personally wounded by Guadagni's 'high notions of his own importance... which revolted many of his warmest friends', the singer's behaviour is amenable to a benign explanation: Guadagni's

---

[10] Stendhal [pseudonym of Henri Beyle], *Vie de Rossini* (1823), tr. Richard Coe as *A Life of Rossini*, 2nd ed., London: Calder and Boyars, 1970, p. 117.

[11] Angus Heriot, *The Castrati in Opera*, London: Calder, 1960, p. 151, and pp. 132–33.

[12] For example, Croce, *I teatri di Napoli*, p. 749.

[13] Elizabeth Harris to James Harris, 8 Mar. 1771, in Donald Burrows and Rosemary Dunhill, *Music and Theatre in Handel's World: The Family Papers of James Harris 1732–1780*, Oxford: Oxford University Press, 2002, p. 626.

[14] 'Guadagni [era] un birbante', Calzabigi to Kaunitz, 6 Mar. 1767, loc. cit. n. 2.

[15] An abundant supply of these and other anecdotes are to be found in Barbier, *The World of the Castrati*, chapter 5, pp. 82–121.

[16] Burney, *General History*, ii, p. 877.

offence was to refuse to interrupt the performance of *Orfeo* to acknowledge applause or to give encores; this attitude was at odds with the conventions of his age, but was entirely in the spirit of Gluck's reform, and demonstrates the singer's artistic intelligence and awareness of the changing operatic practice of his day (Guadagni the 'modern castrato'). Perhaps it was this willingness to take a principled stand that explains Burney's praise of Guadagni's courage; in a discussion on the effects of castration on the moral fibre of the victim, Burney concludes firmly on the side of the 'unfortunate persons': 'I think Guadagni and Pacchierotti were so far from pusillanimous, that they would *seek* danger rather than *shun* it, if called upon or irritated'.[17]

Elsewhere, Burney was less willing to endorse Guadagni's behaviour. No appeal to artistic principles can disguise the fact that the singer was notoriously touchy and quick to pick a quarrel: 'He had a strong party in England of enthusiastic friends and adherents of whom, by personal quarrels and native caprice, he contrived to diminish the number very considerably before his departure', wrote Burney, whose qualified endorsement of Guadagni's singing in the London productions of *Orfeo* may indicate that he had suffered personally from the singer's capricious behaviour: 'He had strong resentments and high notions of his own importance and profession, which revolted many of his warmest friends'.[18] He summed up the singer's faults in a telling scene: 'Guadagni was allowed to be the finest billiard player in Europe; but his antagonists discovering his irritability, used, when he was playing for large sums, to dispute, as unfair, something that was clearly otherwise, by which he was so agitated, as not to be a match for a child'.[19] After Guadagni's death, Burney felt free to be even more judgemental. A strange, wayward article he contributed to Rees's *Cyclopaedia; or, Universal Dictionary of Arts, Sciences, and Literature* ends with the following sour little paragraph:

> The declension of a great singer, who has not had prudence to realize an independence during prosperity, seems the most humiliating that a fallen favourite can feel. And the proud and lofty minded Guadagni, bereaved of his talents and public favour, by age, infirmities, and caprice, spent the last ten years of his life in indigence and mortification![20]

The change of tone between this note and the less barbed comments on Guadagni in both his *Present State of Music in Germany*[21] and his *General History* needs some

---

[17] Ibid., ii, p. 530.

[18] Ibid., ii, p. 876.

[19] Ibid., ii, p. 877, n.(t).

[20] Abraham Rees (ed.), *The Cyclopaedia; or, Universal Dictionary of Arts, Sciences, and Literature*, London, 1802–1820, 39 vols. The article on Guadagni appears in vol. 17, pub. 1811.

[21] Charles Burney, *The Present State of Music in Germany, the Netherlands, and United Provinces*, 2 vols., 2nd ed., London, 1775.

explanation. Burney compiled his entries for Rees's *Cyclopaedia* towards the end of his life. His method and motives have been scrutinized by Roger Lonsdale, who points out that although the bulk of the articles were compiled by cobbling together biographical material from the *General History*, after the death of a subject Burney felt free to add a more candid assessment of the artist concerned, 'rebuking pomposity and expressing frank views on the moral characters of his subjects'.[22] Guadagni, dead a decade or more before Burney wrote his assessment for the *Cyclopaedia*, became one among many candidates for his 'frank views'.

### THE SOURCES

An outline of Guadagni's professional career can be mapped from the surviving librettos in which he is named, the majority of which are listed in Sartori's index of *I libretti italiani a stampa dalle origini al 1800*.[23] Such a catalogue, however, will inevitably be incomplete. If the libretto contains no cast list, a singer's participation is not recorded, and if no libretto was printed, or if no copy has survived, it is difficult to prove a singer's presence in a given town, troupe or work. Additional information is found in the *Almanacco dramattico* [sic], a register of the formation of opera companies and their repertories, which unfortunately does not cover the period before 1764, when most of the lacunae persist.[24] The impossibility of establishing Guadagni's involvement in a production of *La fiametta* [sic] in Parma in 1747 is an example of the inadequacy of the sources.[25] His repertory can sometimes be established from newspaper notices, including *The Public Advertiser* in London, *The Salisbury Journal* and *The Bath Journal* in the provinces, *Faulkner's Journal* in Dublin, *La Gazette* and the *Mercure de France* in Paris. Theatre archives can also help to fill the gaps; among these, the most useful have been the 'Libri della Nobile Società dei Cavalieri' in the Archivio Storico in Turin, and Philipp Gumpenhuber's 'Répertoire de Tous les Spectacles, qui ont été donné au Theatre de la Ville' for the Viennese theatres between 1758 and 1763.[26] Letters and diaries provide sparse fare, but are occasionally crucial in establishing Guadagni's participation in a performance when other

[22] Roger Lonsdale, 'Dr Burney's "Dictionary of Music"', *Musicology Australia* 5.1 (1979), p. 167. I am grateful to Kerry Grant for bringing this article to my attention.

[23] Claudio Sartori, *I libretti italiani a stampa dalle origini al 1800*, 7 vols. Cuneo: Bertola and Locatelli, 1990–1994.

[24] *Un almanacco dramattico* [sic]: *Indice de' teatrali spettacoli*, ed. Roberto Verti, Pesaro: Fondazione Rossini, 1996.

[25] See Chapter 1.

[26] The three collections in the Archivio Storico are identified as 'Libri ordinati' and 'Libri conti della Nobile Società dei Cavalieri' and 'Carte sciolti'. The relevant volumes of Gumpenhuber's 'Répertoire' are Band b: 1762, and Band c: 1763, in the Österreichische Nationalbibliothek, Vienna. (I consulted a photocopy of this source at the University of Salzburg.)

sources are silent. The correspondence of the Harris family is sometimes the only means we have of proving his contribution to one or another Handel oratorio, for example, since neither the press notices nor the wordbooks routinely gave performers' names.[27] Mrs Delany's *Autobiography and Correspondence* contains the only surviving account of Guadagni's Dublin debut.[28] Giuseppe Gennari's *Notizie giornalieri* is an unrivalled source for his Paduan years.[29] Ortes' voluminous correspondence with Hasse provides informed evidence of the singer's reception in Venice.[30] But, disappointingly, Metastasio barely notices Guadagni in his letters, nowhere mentions him by name and refrains from giving an evaluation of his talents; while the root cause of his reticence may have been concern for the interests and prejudices of his chief correspondent, Farinelli, it is hard to believe that Metastasio had no opinion on the singer who took so many leading roles in his operas.

No diarist or letter-writer knew Guadagni half as well as Burney. As is already apparent, Burney's reminiscences in both his *General History* and his *Present State of Music in Germany* provide many details of Guadagni's life and career unrecorded in any other source. Burney first met the singer in London at the outset of his career, during the season of 1749–50, when Frasi introduced Guadagni to him as a new pupil sadly in need of lessons in English pronunciation. Burney was enthusiastic, praised his intelligence ('quickness of parts') and found his voice 'refined and judicious'.[31] When he renewed contact with Guadagni on the occasion of his second London visit in 1769–71, their relationship had soured. Burney was as critical of the singer's social and professional behaviour as he was of his singing, where 'neither his voice nor execution contributed much to charm or excite admiration'.[32] A year later, though, he was gratified to claim acquaintance with him on a visit to Munich in the process of collecting material for his *General History*: Burney's cameo portrait of Guadagni in the household of the Dowager Electress of Saxony, an indulged celebrity who was never allowed to forget he was a servant, is vivid and convincing. Besides recording details of repertory and reception, Burney added shrewd assessments of the singer's voice and acting ability. This is particularly valuable information since, in an age when musical criticism was in its infancy, there are few newspaper reports of

[27] Burrows and Dunhill, *Music and Theatre in Handel's World*.

[28] *The Autobiography and Correspondence of Mary Granville, Mrs Delany*, ed. The Right Honourable Lady Llanover, London: Richard Bentley, 1861.

[29] Gennari, *Notizie giornaliere*.

[30] Ms. in the Cicogna Collection in the Museo Correr in Venice. A selection of the letters to Hasse and his family is published in Livia Pancino, *Johann Adolf Hasse e Giammaria Ortes: lettere (1760–1783)*, Turnhout: Brepols, 1998. The text of the letters quoted in this book is taken from the Cicogna Collection.

[31] Burney, *General History*, ii, p. 876.

[32] Ibid.

the operas he took part in, and none that attempted seriously to describe let alone to evaluate his performance. We owe to Burney an unparalleled insight into the quality of Guadagni's voice. Where most writers, like the anonymous critic of the *Mercure de France*, praised in general terms his 'pleasing and expressive' voice,[33] only Burney gave a precise account of his technique. He analysed the singer's celebrated *messa di voce* and related it to his lack of vocal power: 'after beginning a note or passage with all the force he could safely exert, [he] fined it off to a thread, and gave it all the effect of extreme distance'.[34] But Burney is never an entirely reliable narrator. He confused names and mistook dates; his national bias, his prejudice in favour of artists he knew personally and his desire to flaunt his connection with the most distinguished musicians of his age, combine to require us to take his opinions with a large pinch of salt. Moreover, his sincerity is sometimes suspect. His aspiration to secure royal patronage made him fearful of endorsing modern developments (such as Guadagni's stand on encores) which he might otherwise have supported. On the other hand, his first-hand knowledge was prodigious, his instinctive judgement sound and the scope of his ambition to form the taste of the nation commands respect.

The insights scattered throughout Burney's writing constitute the fullest contemporary biography of Guadagni. There is nothing to compare with it for intimate knowledge of the subject and detailed, specific fact. The only other attempt to write a complete biography in his own lifetime is the entry in Gerber's *Historisch-biographisches Lexicon der Tonkünstler*.[35] The passage is short enough to give in full:

Guadagni (Gaetano), Knight of St Mark's, a contralto castrato from Padua, famed equally for his art and for his magnanimity and generosity. As early as 1754 he sang with great success in Paris. After building his reputation [in Italy], in 1766 he left his native country for a second time, and in London, through his skill in delivery and acting, proved that his nation did not lack for a model of excellence in these fields. In 1770 he joined the choir of St Anthony's Church in Padua, where, for a salary of 400 ducats, he was required only to sing at the four major festivals.

In 1771 in Verona, he came to the notice of the widowed Electress of Saxony, Maria Antonia, who brought him with her to Munich. Here the Elector

---

[33] 'Agréable et touchante', *Mercure de France*, May 1754, p. 184.

[34] Burney, loc. cit.

[35] Ernst Ludwig Gerber, *Historisch-biographisches Lexicon der Tonkünstler* (Leipzig, 1790), ed. Othmar Wessely, Graz: Akademische Druck un Verlagsanstalt, 1977, s.v.

Maximilian Joseph took him into his service and honoured him with exceptional confidence and favour for the remainder of his life.

In 1776 Guadagni journeyed to Potsdam to sing for King Frederick II, in recognition of which, the king presented him with a golden snuffbox set with diamonds, more valuable, it was said, than any gift he had ever bestowed on any private individual. Since then he has returned to his native country where he has resumed his former position in Padua.

All those who know him and who have heard him affirm that he stands at the head of his profession in appearance, in taste, in expression and in action. What is more, he is a composer, in that he himself set his role of Orfeo to music.

It is said that he is so wealthy that, on the occasion of giving a banquet, he did not have the used silverware cleared away, but left it lying in a corner of the room, to show he was not short of it, however much were needed.[36]

Gerber ends by referring his readers to other anecdotes appearing in Cramer's *Magazin der Musik* and Forkel's *Musikalischer Almanach* that tell of Guadagni's alleged indifference to worldly possessions.[37]

Quite apart from the anecdote, the shortcomings of Gerber's account are obvious. Almost every date he gives is wrong and the events he picks out are not the obvious highlights of Guadagni's career; he repeats the curious rumour, widely current in

---

[36] 'Guadagni (Gaetano), Ritter vom St Markuskreuze, ein Contraltist und Castrat von Padua, eben so sehr wegen seiner Kunst, als wegen seiner Großmuth und Freygebigkeit berühmt; sang schon im J. 1754 mit großem Beyfalle zu Paris. Hierauf kam er um 1766 zum zweytenmale aus seinem Vaterlande, wo er bereits seinen Ruhm gegründet hatte, nach London und bewies daselbst durch seine Kunst im Recitiren und in der Aktion, wie wenig es seiner Nation noch an Mustern der Vortrefflichkeit hierinne mangele. Im Jahr 1770 stand er an dem Musikchore der Antoniuskirche zu Padua als Sänger, wo er für einen Gehalt von 400 Dukaten nur an den vier Hauptfesten zu singen gehalten war.

Um das Jahr 1771 lernte ihn die verwitwete Churfürstin von Sachsen, Maria Antonia, zu Verona kennen und nahm ihn mit nach München. Hier nahm ihn der Churfürst Maximilian Joseph in seine Dienste und beehrte ihn mit seinem außerordentlichen Zutrauen und seiner Gnade bis an seinen Tod.

Noch im Jahr 1776 that Guadagni eine Reise nach Potsdam zum König Fridrich II. und ließ sich vor selbigem hören. Der König beschenkte ihn darauf mit einer goldenen mit Brillanten besetzten Dose von so hohem Werthe, als sich noch keine Privatperson rühmen konnte, von ihm erhalten zu haben. Seit dieser Zeit hat er sich wieder nach seinem Vaterlande gewendet, wo er zu Padua wieder seine alte Stelle eingenommen haben soll.

Alle diejenigen, welche ihn kennen und gehöret haben, versichern: das ser in Ansehung der Gestalt, des Geschmacks, des Ausdrucks und der Aktion, in seiner Profession obenanstehe. Er ist überdies auch Komponist, indem er sich seine Rolle zum Orfeo selbst in Musik gesetzt haben soll.

Er ist so reich, das ser, wie man sagte, bey einem Gastmahle, das gebrauchte Silberservice nicht abtragen, sondern in einem Winkel des Zimmers stellen ließ, um zu zeigen: es fehle ihm nicht daran, man brauche auch noch so viel.' Gerber ed. Wessely, op. cit.

[37] Carl Friedrich Cramer, ed., *Magazin der Musik*, p. 376, Hamburg, 1786; Johann Nicolaus Forkel, *Musikalischer Almanach für Deutschland*, Leipzig, 1783, p. 160.

Paris in the 1770s and 1780s, that Guadagni himself composed the bulk of his role in Gluck's *Orfeo*. Nevertheless, Gerber's account provides evidence of Guadagni's Europe-wide status, and suggests that his eccentricities—only benign ones are mentioned—were as widely known as his musical talent. Only a few singers were noticed in the biographical dictionaries that began to appear towards the end of the eighteenth century. Gerber devotes a column to Guadagni; by comparison, Farinelli receives three columns, Caffarelli one and a half, and Pacchierotti half a column. There is no consensus among dictionary editors as to their relative importance: in Fétis's *Biographie universelle des musiciens*, published in 1835–44, Guadagni's entry occupies three-quarters of a column, Farinelli one and a half, Pacchierotti one and three quarters, and Caffarelli a princely three and a half.

Gerber concluded his sketch with the often-repeated tale of the discarded silverware. For most eighteenth-century singers (and particularly the castratos) there exists a substantial body of anecdotal narratives, praising, mocking and vilifying in equal measure. The sheer quantity of material makes it impossible to ignore this type of source, however improbable the individual episodes. Besides giving a general indication of celebrity—anecdotes are not created about nonentities—each story illustrates a single character trait, and can tell us how a singer was perceived by his contemporaries. The episode of Guadagni and his tableware suggests an interesting parallel that, if it does not validate the anecdote, at least explains how it may have originated. Agostino Chigi, a wealthy Renaissance banker, built a great palace on the banks of the Tiber in Trastevere in Rome (now called the Villa Farnesina), the location for lavish banquets, at the conclusion of which Chigi used to demonstrate his wealth by having all his silverware thrown into the Tiber; he had, however, taken the precaution of hanging nets along the banks, so that after the feast his treasure could be retrieved.[38] Some reference, conscious or unconscious, to this story may have contributed to the legend of Guadagni's silver. That only a few silver items are mentioned in the inventory of his goods taken at his death neither proves nor disproves the tale. More suggestive are the pawnshop tickets for a number of silver items listed in the inventory.[39]

Guadagni provided a rich fund of material, the majority of the stories falling into one of two categories, illustrating either his magnanimity or his arrogance. So we read that when he lost a large sum of money to a German prince who cheated at cards, spurning the advice of his friends, he paid the debt in full, claiming that, 'He

---

[38] See Ingrid D. Rowland, 'Render unto Caesar the Things That Are Caesar's: Humanism and the Arts in the Patronage of Agostino Chigi', *Renaissance Quarterly* 39.4 (1986): 673–730.
[39] See Chapter 11.

has acted like a rogue; I shall treat him like a prince'.[40] On another occasion he was said to have given a good deal of money to an impoverished nobleman, who nevertheless protested that he regarded it as a loan which he would repay when his fortunes recovered; 'If I'd expected you to do that', said Guadagni, 'I wouldn't have lent it to you'.[41] The nobleman in the anecdote was German, but the incident could well have reflected Guadagni's generous gift (perhaps in the guise of a loan) to the young Tomaso degli Obizzi in 1768.

As an example of his arrogance, it was related that he once kept a king waiting in his antechamber while he entertained his mistress; when informed that the king was waiting, Guadagni was said to have replied 'coolly', 'Let him wait until I've finished!'[42] A similar episode was told about his stay in Munich, when the Elector allegedly surprised him in bed with a singer; Guadagni reproved the singer for not having taken the precaution of securing the door against 'tiresome interruptions'.[43] Yet another tale is set in London; Guadagni had accepted a hundred guineas to sing a duet with 'a certain Mylady', but because he had exhausted himself the previous night singing two or three long arias with another young lady, he could not do himself justice; he gave back the money, promising to return when he was in better form.[44] There are salacious overtones to some of these anecdotes: perhaps the

---

[40] 'Von eben diesem Guadagni erzehlt man, daß er einst an einen deutschen Prinzen, welcher falsch spielte, eine ansehnliche Summe Geld verloren habe. Man sagte ihm, daß er betrogen worden sey, und rieth ihm, den prinzen nicht zu bezahlen. Er antwortete aber, er hat an mir als Schurke gehandelt, ich will an ihm als prinz handeln. Und er bezahlte dis ganze Summe.' Forkel, *Musikalischer Almanach für Deutschland*, Leipzig, 1783, p. 160.

[41] 'Er theilte wohl auf seinen Reisen in Deutschland an verarmte Edelleuten Allmosen bisweilen von hundert Zechinen auf einmal aus. Einer von diesen, der so eine Summe empfangen hatte, und dabey zu stolz war, dafür danken zu wollen, sagte zu ihm: erborgte sie nur, und würde sie ihm zu rechter Zeit wiedererstatten. Wenn das meine Absicht wäre, versetzte Guadagni, so würde ich Sie ihnen nicht leihen.' Cramer, *Magazin der Musik*, Hamburg, 1783, p. 440.

[42] 'Unter die Merkwürdigkeiten von den berühmten Sänger Guadagni gehört auch diese, daß er einmal einen König im Vorzimmer auf sich warten ließ. Er war nehmlich mit seiner Maitresse alein, als man ihm sagte, Ihro Majestät sey im Vorzimmer, worauf er kaltblütig antwortete, che aspetti, quand avro finito, entrerà.' Forkel, op. cit., p. 160.

[43] 'Einandermal ward er des Nachts in dem Bette der berühmten Cori von dem Prinzen von Monac überrascht, der einen Hauptschlüssel zu dem Zimmer hatte. Guadagni sagte nichts weiter zu ihr als: Madam, wenn man bey einer Mansperson schläft, so muß man den Schlüssel in der Tasche haben, sonst lauft man Gefahr, zur Unzeit lästige Besuche zu bekommen.' Cramer, op. cit., p. 439.

[44] 'Es war übrigens gut gebildet und eine gewisse Mylady in London, die mit ihm Tete a Tete ein Duett singen wollte, bezahlte ihm einst für diese Übungsstunde hundert Guineen in voraus; allein weil die Nacht vorher zwey oder drey sehr groß e Arien mit einer Gewissen jungen Damen gesungen, so war seine Stimme so schwach, daß er seine Parthie von einem Ende bis zum andern verfehlte. Er ging weg, verdrieslich daß es ihm mislungen, gab der Mylady die Summe zurück, und sagte ganz Kalt: da ist Ihr Geld wieder, Madame; einen schlechten Sänger müssen Sie nicht so theur bezahlen, ich will wiederkommen, wenn ichs besser werde machen können.' Cramer, op. cit., pp. 439–40.

point of the joke of the king kept waiting in the antechamber was that, as a castrato, Guadagni might be capable of giving a good deal of pleasure to his mistress without ever 'finishing'; the last incident suggests the probability that his activities with neither lady related to singing duets.

Such ambiguities helped the stories to circulate. Before dismissing the anecdotal literature out of hand, it is prudent to remember that at least some of the stories are grounded in fact. Cramer relates an episode in Venice when Guadagni was commanded to sing at the Doge's Christmas-day banquet; he refused, protesting that he was not accustomed to entertain at dinner. His punishment was to be compelled to kneel before the Doge and sing from that humble position.[45] Durazzo, who was present at the banquet, relates almost the same story, with plenty of authenticating detail.[46]

My intention in undertaking this investigation was to address two questions: how far was Guadagni's career typical of a high-ranking opera singer in the second half of the century, and what made Guadagni unique, ground-breaking, or modern? By tracking the events of Guadagni's professional life from season to season, I have tried to show a career path typical of many itinerant singers of the period. This narrative runs throughout the book, and is as complete an account as the presently available biographical sources allow. From time to time the chronology is interrupted to focus on topics, many of them specific to Guadagni (his celebrated acting skills in the context of the changes to acting technique introduced during the century, his singing technique, insofar as it can be deduced from the repertory of roles he created and from his own slender portfolio of compositions), but also more generally relevant matters such as the perception of the castrato in society. There are newly discovered or newly transcribed documents such as his baptismal and death certificates, his will and the inventory of his goods at death. The appendices include a list of the dramatic roles he undertook, a record of his salary at the Santo, and documents from his life in their original language.

---

[45] 'In Venedig ist es gewöhnlich, daß der erste Sänger im Teatro nobile von S Benedetto am Weihnachtstag in der Markuskirche, und dann bey dem Banket des Doge singt. Dafür erhälte er eine Medaille, einige Zechinen werth. Guadagni schenkte diese sogleich dem Diener der Fürstinn, der sie ihm überreichte, und sagte zugleich: Er sey nicht gewohnt, bei einer Mahlzeit zu singen—er bediente sich des Wortes disnar—dafür mußte er bei dem Banket kniend dem Fürsten abbitten, und auch in dieser Stellung singen. Nie soll er schöner gesungen haben, als bey dieser Gelegenheit'. Cramer, *Magazin der Musik,* 1786, p. 376.

[46] See Chapter 7.

# 1

## From Lodi to London (1728–1748)

⁓————————————————————————————————

GUADAGNI WAS BORN 16 February 1728 at Lodi, a small town some twenty miles southeast of Milan. The baptismal record reads:

> Cosimo Guadagni
>
> In the year of Our Lord 1728, on Monday the 16th of February, I, Camillo Boni, parish priest of the cathedral church of Lodi, baptised an infant born this morning to Sebastiano Guadagni and Caterina Maura, husband and wife of the greater parish, to whom was given the name Cosimo Gaetano.[1]

The place and date of his birth were unknown until recently.[2] In an early biographical sketch, Burney referred to the singer as 'Gaetano Guadagni of Vicenza'.[3] This threw subsequent biographers off the scent, even though it is not clear whether Burney ever intended to imply that Guadagni had been born in Vicenza. Gerber's dictionary entry, the only other biography written in the singer's lifetime, offered Padua, the place of his death, as the birthplace.[4] It was probably Fétis who, without citing his source, first identified Lodi.[5] But Burney's authority was too strong for later biographers

---

[1] Cosmus Guadagnus. Anno Domini millesimo septingentesimo vigesimo octavo, die lune, decima sexta mensii Februarii. Ego Camillus Bonius canonicus parochus ecclesie Cathedralis Laude baptizavi infantem hodiem manem natus ex Sebastiano Guadagno et Catharina Maura coniugibus huius parochie maiorii cui impositum fuit nomen Cosmus Caetanus. *Liber baptismatorum ab anno 1719 usque ad anno 1732,* xii, Archivio Parrocchio, Lodi, p. 106r.

[2] See Patricia Howard, 'Happy birthday, Cosimo Gaetano Guadagni!' *Musical Times,* 148 (2007): 93–96.

[3] Burney, *General History,* ii, p. 875.

[4] Gerber, ed. Wessely, *Historisch-biographisches Lexicon,* 1997.

[5] François-Joseph Fétis, *Biographie universelle,* Paris, 1835.

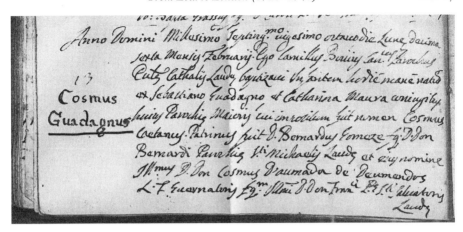

FIGURE I.I Guadagni's baptismal record, Archivio Parrocchio, Lodi

who, through to the twenty-first century, hedged their bets with the cautious phrase 'Vicenza or Lodi', without, apparently, thinking it worthwhile to establish which. The wrong birthdate (1725) was stated by Fétis and copied in all biographies until 1987, when Paolo Cattelan discovered an inaccurate entry in the register of deaths in Padua and mistakenly inferred a birthdate of 11 December 1729.[6] However, a scrutiny of the baptismal registers of the seventeen parishes in eighteenth-century Lodi settled a matter which had been needlessly elusive for some 280 years.

Nothing is known of the next eighteen years of Guadagni's life, and indeed the early life of a castrato is rarely documented. Childhood in the eighteenth century was not generally a state to be celebrated in anything but the intimacy of the family circle, and the special circumstances of a castrato's boyhood added a degree of shame and fear that tended to obliterate records. Many castratos came from humble families who would have no reason to preserve for posterity their memories of the childhood of just another little boy, and the fact of their having handed their child over for castration was further cause for reticence. The practice was often concealed behind lies or evasions. Even the word 'castrato' is surprisingly rare in eighteenth-century Italian texts, which prefer to identify such a singer as '*musico*' or '*primo uomo*'; French writers were less prudish, and frequently specified '*castrats*' or '*eunuques*'; English satirical literature sometimes referred to 'capons'. Describing his fruitless search for information on the subject, Burney famously wrote of the secrecy with which the process was hedged about:

> I enquired throughout Italy at what place boys were chiefly qualified for singing by castration, but could get no certain intelligence. I was told at Milan that it was at

---

[6] Paolo Cattelan, 'La musica della "omnigena religio": accademie musicali a Padova nei secondo Settecento', *Acta musicologica* 59.2 (1987), p. 162, n. 34.

Venice; at Venice that it was at Bologna; but at Bologna the fact was denied, and I was referred to Florence; from Florence to Rome, and from Rome I was sent to Naples. The operation is most certainly against the law in all these places, as well as against nature; and all the Italians are so much ashamed of it, that in every province they transfer it to some other.... It is said to be death by the laws to all those who perform the operation, and excommunication to everyone concerned in it, unless it be done, as is often pretended, upon account of some disorders which may be supposed to require it.[7]

A colourful history of the long and anatomically varied practice of castration is given in Nicholas Clapton's biography of Alessandro Moreschi.[8] The legality of the operation in the eighteenth century is unclear. Roman law, as codified by the emperor Justinian in the sixth century AD, forbade the practice except for urgent medical reasons, and that prohibition was still valid throughout Italy in the eighteenth century. No such proscription operated in ecclesiastical law. Castration was sanctioned and even tacitly encouraged by the Catholic Church, which welcomed castratos into its choirs as a more reliable alternative to choirboys, and indirectly promoted the castrato's career in opera by banning women from the stage in the Papal states. The Church, however, paid the price for this when it found that its choirs were denuded of castratos in the opera season.[9] Pope Leo XIII, who held office from 1878 to 1903, allegedly put an end to the employment of castratos in the Vatican; Moreschi, however, whose singing was recorded in 1902 and 1904, continued to be a member of the choir until 1913.[10]

The act of castration often distanced a child from his family. For a poor family, it was seen as an investment: if the child should turn into an opera star it could bring untold wealth to the whole family, and even if the voice proved less exceptional, it offered a good chance of secure employment in the church.[11] Adult castratos could

---

[7] Charles Burney, *The Present State of Music in France and Italy*, London, 2nd ed., 1773, pp. 312–13.

[8] Nicholas Clapton, *Moreschi: The Last Castrato*, London: Haus, 2004, especially chapter 1.

[9] Burney wrongly declared castration to infringe canon law. On the distinction between civil illegality and ecclesiastical tolerance, see John Rosselli, 'The Castrati as a Professional Group and a Social Phenomenon, 1550–1850', *Acta musicologica* 60 (1988), pp. 150–51. On the eighteenth-century edict by Pope Benedict XIV forbidding members of the papal choir who were clerics to sing in opera during Carnival, Rosselli, op. cit., p. 167. For a brief and graphic history of castration, see 'La mutilazione crudele: note storiche su castratori e castrati', Carla Serarcangeli and Gennaro Rispoli, *Medicina nei secoli* 13.2 (2001): 441–54.

[10] See Joe K. Law, 'Alessandro Moreschi Reconsidered: A Castrato on Records', *The Opera Quarterly* 2.2 (1984): 1–12.

[11] On the acute poverty in Italy in the seventeenth century and its contribution to the culture of the castrato, see John Rosselli, *Singers of Italian Opera*, Cambridge: Cambridge University Press, p. 35.

conceal such mercenary motivation by claiming that the operation had been necessary to save them from an illness such as cholera, a condition such as hernia, or an
accident—a fall from a horse or being gored by a wild boar is often mentioned.[12] But
even with these available excuses, few mature singers volunteered an explanation for
their enforced career, and biographers were reluctant to question them.[13] The only
castrato to write his autobiography was silent on the reasons for and process of his
castration. Filippo Balatri, who recorded his life in a picaresque verse narrative, disposed of the first fifteen years of his life in four lines addressed to Fate:

> I was born. Until the age of knowledge you left me alone to a life of harsh
> monotony; but as soon as I was fifteen years old you came with your net and
> fished me out.[14]

Many castratos understandably came to resent what had been done to them,
and retained scant affection for their families. The story is told of Loreto Vittori
who, at the height of his fame, was approached by an old man claiming to be his
father, begging for money. Vittori allegedly handed the man an empty purse, saying that he would pay him back in his own coin.[15] On the other hand, the musical
training that followed castration often provided the young singer with a surrogate
family. The process of apprenticing a young boy to a music teacher or institution
bound boy and teacher in a close relationship. Some singers took a diminutive of
their teacher's name—for example Caffaro's pupil Caffarelli, Gizzi's pupil Gizziello,
Porpora's pupil Porporino—which they were unlikely to have done if the relationship had been anything but a warm one. Guadagni, however, was a family name,
and Gaetano's brother, the tenor Giuseppe Guadagni, and three sisters, the sopranos
Anna, Angiola and Lavinia Guadagni, all became opera singers.

It was presumably Sebastiano and Caterina Guadagni who nurtured the talents
of their musical children. From the efficient way all five embarked on their careers,

[12] 'A farrago of notions drawn from ancient authors such as Hippocrates [alleged that] castration cured or pre-
vented gout, elephantiasis, leprosy, and hernia.' Ibid., p. 33.

[13] Ibid., p. 32.

[14] 'Nacqui. Fin all'età di cognizzione/ah, mi lasciasti star in aspra quiete;/ ma appena ebbi tre lustre, con la
rete/venisti a far di me la pescagione.' Filippo Balatri's verse autobiography, "Frutti del mondo esperimen-
tati da F.B. nativo dell'Alfea in Toscana", exists in manuscript in Bayerische Staatsbibliothek, Munich, cod. It.
39. A substantial extract from this has been published as *Frutti del mondo*, ed. Karl Vosser, Naples: Sandron,
1924, n.p. See also Martha Feldman, 'Strange Births and Surprising Kin: The Castrato's Tale', in Paula Findlen,
Wendy Ryworth and Catherine Sama (ed.), *Italy's Eighteenth Century: Gender and Culture in the Age of the
Grand Tour*, Stanford: Stanford University Press, 2009, pp. 175–202.

[15] Cornelio Parolari, 'Giambattista Velluti', *Rivista musicale italiana* 39 (1932): 265.

it seems likely that Sebastiano had professional skills to pass on; he probably sang in the choir of Lodi cathedral, where Gaetano was baptised. Guadagni left no account of his childhood, and as there is no record of his musical training, we can presume he drew on the resources of his home town and his musical family. The lives of the siblings intersected constantly. Anna and Giuseppe made their debut together in Venice in 1744. Giuseppe also managed the early stages of the careers of his two younger sisters, taking the opportunity of his early venture as impresario to launch them in chorus roles at Este in 1749, when Lavinia was not quite fourteen years old. While Anna's career faded early, perhaps because of marriage, Angiola and Lavinia flourished. The family was close-knit, and the siblings had an endearing tendency to perform together whenever circumstances permitted (though their closeness cannot rival that of some of the large singing families characteristic of buffo troupes, for example the Baglioni clan[16]). Giuseppe followed Gaetano into the Cappella di Sant'Antonio at Padua (the Basilica del Santo, invariably known as the Santo), as did Angiola's future husband, Antonio Nasolini, both remaining on the books of the Cappella while pursuing successful careers in opera buffa. Angiola and Lavinia sang in the same company as Giuseppe in Modena in 1756, and in Brescia in 1761. Angiola shared the stage with Gaetano in Vicenza in 1756 and Venice in 1767. Lavinia, exclusively a buffa singer, never sang in the same company as her more famous brother, but coincided with him in Vienna in 1764, in Venice in 1767, and in London in 1769, where Guadagni's dispute with George Hobart, the manager of the King's Theatre, was exacerbated by Hobart's dismissal of Lavinia in favour of his mistress.[17]

After the baptismal record, the next surviving source is a document that records Guadagni's entry into the choir of the Santo in July 1746, aged eighteen.[18] Described as a contralto-register singer, Guadagni was elected unanimously into the choir with a salary of 150 ducats per annum, and awarded travelling expenses for his journey from Cremona to Padua. How long Guadagni had been in Cremona is unknown.

---

[16] Franco Piperno, 'State and market, production and style: an interdisciplinary approach to 18th-c Italian opera history', in *Opera and Society in Italy and France from Monteverdi to Bourdieu*, ed. Victoria Johnson, Jane F. Fulcher and Thomas Ertman, Cambridge: Cambridge University Press, 2007, pp. 148–56.

[17] See Patricia Howard, '"Mr Justice Blindman" and the "Priestess of Fashion"', *Il saggiatore musicale*, 7.1 (2000): 51.

[18] 'Sentito in prova sugli Organi il Signor Gaetano Guadagni contralto, che desidera esser assunto al s ʳᵛ ᵒ della V[eneran]da Arca, ed essendo stato riconosciuto idoneo per parere anche del Maestro di Cappella, fu proposta parte di assumerlo in Cappella come contralto con uno stipendio di ducati 150 annui, e di rimborsagli le spese di viaggio da Cremona a Padova. La parte fu approvata all'unanimità' (5 July 1746). Archivio Antico della Veneranda Arca del Santo, *Atti e Parti*, vol. 30, fo. 124v–125r. The *Atti e Parti* are held in the Centro studi antoniani, Padua. They have been excerpted, with commentary and notes, by Lucia Boscolo and Maddalena Pietribiasi, in *La cappella musicale antoniana*, Padua: Centro studi antoniani, 1997. For ease of access, reference is made to Boscolo and Pietribiasi where relevant; for the above passage, see p. 184.

He could have had some training there, though there was no conservatory. He might have had a church position, but he is unlikely to have obtained theatrical experience. Cremonese musical life was dominated by two societies, the Accademia degli Arcadi and the Accademia Musicale; just as Guadagni was leaving (or passing through) the town a new theatre was being planned by a consortium of noblemen known as the Casino di Conversazione; the theatre opened in 1747 and hosted a predominantly opera buffa repertory. But by then Guadagni had both entered the choir of the Santo, and been expelled from it.

It would be interesting to know why, in contrast to his siblings, Guadagni's first career choice was to be a church musician. His father, if he were a member of the choir of Lodi cathedral, would have seen the advantages and disadvantages of the job at first hand. By 1746 Guadagni would also have had the operatic experiences of two siblings to learn from, and while the alacrity with which he left the Santo as soon as a theatre opening presented itself might indicate that he saw the church position as no more than a stepping stone, his return to Padua at the height of a successful stage career argues otherwise. The advantages of church over opera house included a regular salary and greater social status.

The Santo was a major institution in Paduan musical life. A centre of intense creative and theoretical activity, it provided Guadagni with a lifelong education. When he joined the choir, the musical director was the priest, composer and theorist Francesco Antonio Vallotti, who presided over a choir of sixteen singers and an orchestra of sixteen string players. An active and intelligent musician, Vallotti interested himself in many debates of the mid-eighteenth century, devising a system for tuning keyboard instruments that challenged equal temperament,[19] and developing a theory of chord inversions independently of Rameau's contemporaneous work in the same area.[20] He was better known, however, for his conservatism, for both preaching and practising the *stile antico*, transcribing Palestrina's masses and employing the old contrapuntal style in his own sacred music. It is impossible to define what Guadagni learned from his brief initial period under Vallotti, but their relationship on a personal level was warm and enduring. Despite his early dismissal from the choir, and the intermittent nature of his later association with the Santo (he was back on the payroll in 1768, but with frequent, negotiated absences for opera engagements), Guadagni retained an affection for his old mentor, paying homage by singing at Vallotti's funeral service in 1780.[21]

[19] Francesco Antonio Vallotti, *Della scienza teorica e pratica della moderna musica*; only Book 1 was published in his lifetime (Padua: Stamperia del Seminario, 1779). This was reissued together with the remaining three books in 1950 as *Trattato della moderna musica,* ed. G. Zanon and B. Rizzi, Padua: Biblioteca Antoniana, 1950.
[20] Jean-Philippe Rameau, *Traité de l'harmonie*, Paris, 1722.
[21] On Guadagni's readmission to the Santo, see Cattelan, 'La musica della "omnigena religio"', p. 158. On Vallotti's funeral, see Leonida Busi, *Il Padre G. B. Martini*, Bologna: Zanichelli, 1891, p. 333.

The orchestra at the Santo was led by Giuseppe Tartini.[22] While it is difficult to establish any specific trace of Vallotti's influence on Guadagni's career, one aspect of Tartini's musicianship made a lasting impression. On a visit to the Elector of Saxony in 1772, Burney described hearing Guadagni, with fellow castrato Rauzzini, taking advantage of the resonance of a bathroom to work 'successfully through all Tartini's experiments, in order, by sustaining with their voices two consonant intervals, to produce a *third sound*, which is generated in the air'.[23] Although Tartini did not publish his work on difference tones till 1754,[24] he began work on their use as a practical means of ensuring exact intonation some ten years earlier,[25] so that in 1746 he may well have put Guadagni through his 'experiments'. The only permanent influence that can be securely attributed to Guadagni's brief early period at the Santo was a concern for accurate tuning—he is among a minority of eighteenth-century singers who were never criticised for their intonation.[26]

### SEASON OF 1746–1747

In the autumn of 1746, within six months of obtaining his place at the Santo, Guadagni joined an opera company. It was understood that his engagement at the Santo permitted external work as long as permission was obtained. This concession caused the authorities a good deal of trouble over the years, with musicians leaving the Cappella several times a year, often for many months at a time. To attempt to deal with this instability, the Arca (the governing body of the Santo) devised a system of annual appraisals, called a *riballottazione*, in which all members of the Cappella, including Vallotti, had to submit to re-election by the seven governors of the Arca. A musician who failed to secure a majority vote might make an appeal (*una supplica*) in which he begged for readmission, which was usually granted. Stricter rules

---

[22] Daniel Heartz asserts that it was Tartini who 'lured' Guadagni to Padua (*Music in European Capitals*, New York: Norton, 2003, p. 228), but I have found no evidence of any such invitation.

[23] Burney, *The Present State of Music in Germany, the Netherlands, and United Provinces*, i, 2nd ed., London, 1775, pp. 139–40.

[24] Giuseppe Tartini, *Trattato di musica secondo la vera scienza dell'armonia*, Padua: Stamperia del Seminario, 1754.

[25] Pierluigi Petrobelli, *Giuseppe Tartini: Le fonte biografiche*, Venice: Fondazione Giorgi Cini, 1968, p. 125.

[26] Writing of the previous generation, Pier Francesco Tosi judged that 'modern intonation is very bad'; in *Opinioni de' cantori antichi e moderni* (1723), tr. Mr. Galliard as *Observations on the Florid Song* (1743), ed. Michael Pilkington, London: Stainer and Bell, 1987, p. 4. Guadagni's contemporaries fared little better, with Giambattista Mancini, *Pensieri e riflessioni pratiche sopra il canto figurato*, Vienna: Gehlen, 1774 (revised as *Riflessioni pratiche sul canto figurato*, Milan: Galeazzi, 1777), and Domenico Corri, *The Singer's Preceptor*, London, 1810, criticising current practice and devoting many pages of their treatises to the acquisition of exact intonation. On the evidence of Wilhelm Cramer, even Guadagni's great rival Pacchierotti was 'apt to sing too flat'; see Philip Olleson, *The Journals and Letters of Susan Burney*, Farnham: Ashgate, 2012, p. 94.

were drawn up in an edict of 29 December 1746, as a result of which members of the Cappella were able to apply for leave of absence (*accordata la licenza*) but could not expect their permanent posts to be kept vacant for them, though more often than not they were.[27] On 5 October, the Arca granted Guadagni permission to sing 'this autumn and the following Carnival in Venice'.[28]

One factor in this move must surely have been the influence of Anna and Giuseppe Guadagni, who had given their first professional performances in Venice at the Teatro San Moisè two years earlier. In the season of 1744–45, Giuseppe and Anna both sang in Avossa's *Don Saverio* and the pasticcio *Emira*; Anna also took the title role in Palella's *Origille*. Our Guadagni's career began in the same theatre, where he took the subsidiary role ('terzo uomo') of Achilla in *Cesare in Egitto*, with music by the local composer Antonio Colombo to an old libretto by Giacomo Francesco Bussani. The company's second production was *Zenobia*, with music by Girolamo Michieli to a libretto by Metastasio; Guadagni again took the third male role in the part of Mitrane. The librettos for both the Venice and Treviso productions of *Cesare in Egitto* and for the Venice production of *Zenobia* list the singer as 'Il Signor Gaetano Guadagni di Lodi'.[29] (See Figure 1.2.) The music of both operas is now lost. Before the end of the season, *Cesare in Egitto* transferred to near-by Treviso at the small Teatro Dolfin (where Angiola and Lavinia were to sing in 1753).

It was customary for smaller towns in the Veneto to mount only one opera each season and these were often repeats of Venetian productions.[30] Little more than a hundred years after the first public opera opened in Venice, Italy was well provided with theatres. Every town aspired to have its own opera house, usually owned by a noble family or an accademia and managed on a day-to-day basis by an impresario with a team of artistically and financially interested parties. Theatres varied enormously in prestige, from the grandest, which included the San Benedetto in Venice, the San Carlo in Naples and the Teatro Regio in Turin, to smaller, poorer houses; the Dolfin in Treviso and the San Moisè in Venice were in the latter category. A contemporary description of the San Moisè emphasised its restricted size: 'It was the most graceful little theatre one could imagine, seating at most seven hundred spectators; it was really small, with narrow boxes which were nevertheless decorated

---

[27] See Boscolo and Pietribiasi, op. cit., pp. 184–85.

[28] 'Fu accolta all'unanimità la supplica con cui Gaetano Guadagni chiede di poter andare a recitare quest'autunno e il prossimo carnevale a Venezia.' 5 Oct. 1746, see ibid., p. 184.

[29] Both librettos published in Venice by Modesto Fenzo in 1746; copies in Biblioteca Nazionale Braidense, Milan (*Cesare* and *Zenobia* at San Moisè) and Civico Museo Bibliografico Musicale, Bologna (Treviso production of *Cesare in Egitto*).

[30] See Eleanor Selfridge-Field, *Song and Season: Science, Culture and Theatrical Time in Early Modern Venice*, Stanford: Stanford University Press, 2007.

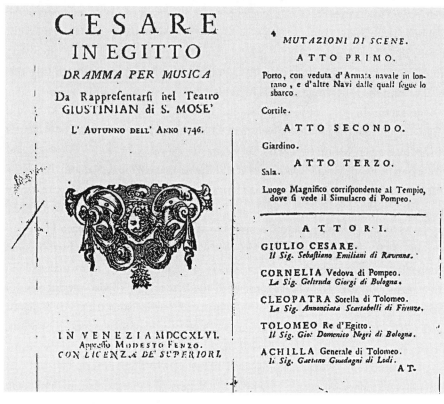

FIGURE 1.2 From the libretto of *Cesare in Egitto*, Venice 1746

gaily—everything was done with little loss of elegance; both voices and orchestra could be easily heard; modest voices were adequate and the orchestra was through necessity scaled down in proportion'.[31]

While the prestigious theatres gave mostly premières, usually new settings of Metastasian texts, houses like San Moisè concentrated on revivals. Colombo's *Cesare in Egitto* was one such; Bussani's libretto had originally been set by Sartorio in 1676 and adapted by Haym for Handel in 1724; Colombo's setting was first given in 1744. Michieli's *Zenobia*, on the other hand, was a première, a new setting of an old libretto, first set by Predieri in 1740; Mitrane was the first operatic role written for Guadagni.

---

[31] 'Era il più grazioso teatrino ch'immaginar si potesse, capace di settecento spettatori al più, piccolo in vero, con palchetti angusti, ma internamente di gaio aspetta. Tutto vi faceva con poco bella comparsa: niente perdevasi della declamazione e della musica: voci discrete diventavano sufficienti; a proporzione era necessariamente formata l'orchestra', Giovanni Rossi, *Storia delle leggi e costumi veneziani*, mss. in Biblioteca Nazionale Marciana, Venice, in Nicola Mangini, *I teatri di Venezia*, Milan: Mursia, 1974, pp. 106–7.

The librettos for *Cesare in Egitto* and *Zenobia* indicate that the works were performed 'in the autumn of 1746'. It is often impossible to establish the exact dates of an opera season or the first performance of a run; librettos rarely recorded a date. (Most exceptional is a libretto for Traetta's *Nitteti* in which Guadagni sang in Reggio Emilia in 1757, which contains the handwritten dates of the 26 performances that followed the first night, which would itself be a *prova generale*, or public dress rehearsal, to add to the confusion).[32] Sometimes librettos indicate a specific occasion such as 'the Feast of Ascension', but more often they identify a season such 'autumn', 'spring', or 'Carnival'. The latter designation can mislead, since, although it generally ran from 26 December to the beginning of Lent, Carnival was identified by the year in which the majority of the performances fell, so that although the first opera of a Carnival season usually had its *prova generale* on 26 December, it would be listed under the following year. Dates can sometimes be inferred from theatre archives, playbills, newspaper announcements, diary references and letters, though there are many cases in which none of these is available. The wording of Guadagni's *licenza* ('autumn and the following Carnival') implies that *Cesare* and *Zenobia* may have been expected to run on from the autumn into the Carnival season or that he hoped to obtain a new engagement early in 1747.

The authorities at the Santo soon became aware that Guadagni's ambitions lay in opera. His employment was suspended on 25 February 1747, 'because he did not turn up on 21 February for the feast of the Santa Lingua', one of the compulsory attendances required by his contract.[33] He was not formally reinstated until 11 October.[34] Reluctant to separate himself from the security of a church appointment, he made regular petitions for leave of absence and reinstatement during 1747 and 1748 that reflect an uneasy relationship with the authorities. He finally received permission to travel to England on 7 December 1748—some three months after he had left the country.[35] It is ironic in the circumstances that his departure was authorised under the condition that on his return he would be required to undertake a new audition: when, twenty years later, Guadagni returned to the Santo it was as an international celebrity and any thought of a re-audition was waived. Just as he was leaving the Santo, Guadagni's brother, Giuseppe Guadagni, joined the Cappella as

---

[32] In Biblioteca Nazionale Braidense, Milan, Racc. Dram., 4582.

[33] 'Perché Gaetano Guadagni non è venuto il 21 febbraio scorso, giorno della festa della S. Lingua, benché siano terminate le recite dell'autunno e del carnevale a Venezia, periodo nel quale era stato dispensato dal servizio della V. Arca, si ritenga licenziato', 25 Feb. 1747; see Boscolo and Pietribiasi, op. cit., p. 186. The compulsory attendances were the feasts of S. Lingua, Easter, Pentecost, S. Antonio, and Christmas; see ibid., p. 249.

[34] '…la V. Congregazione…decise all'unanimità di concedegli di continuare il suo impiego in Cappella, nonostante la parte presa il 25 febbraio in merito alla sua presunta mancanza'; ibid., p. 187.

[35] 'Licenzia per partenza di Gaetano Guadagni per Inghilterra', 7 Dec. 1748, ibid., p. 188.

an unpaid supernumerary; he was admitted as a full member in 1750 and remained on the payroll until his death in 1770.[36]

It seems probable that Guadagni either had or was trying to obtain an opera engagement in the Veneto for the 1747–48 season. If he succeeded, nothing is known of the appointment. There is some suggestion that he performed in Parma during this period: Fétis, with his customary lack of sources, noted that 'Guadagni began to make himself known in 1747 at the theatre in Parma';[37] this information was copied by many subsequent biographers, but the statement, which ignores the fact that Guadagni had already made his debut in Venice in the 1746–47 season, is impossible to substantiate. Only one opera libretto was published in Parma in 1747, the comic opera *La fiametta* [sic] and the libretto contains no cast list. But the balance of probability lies with Fétis. It is likely that Guadagni found operatic employment during the 1747–48 season, and engagement with a comic troupe is plausible, given that his brother and sister were active in that field. More significantly, his next known engagement was in comedy. In the autumn of 1748 Giovanni Francesco Crosa took a company of established buffo singers to England, recruiting Guadagni as *primo uomo serio*, the young romantic lead.

[36] Ibid., p. 194.

[37] 'Guadagni commença à se faire connaître en 1747, au théâtre de Parme.' Fétis, *Biographie universelle*, Paris, 1835, s.v.

# 2

## A London Apprenticeship (1748–1749)

We do not know how and where Guadagni met the impresario Giovanni Francesco Crosa (John Francis Croza). He joined Crosa's *buffa* troupe after the end of the 1747–48 season, travelling with them to England, and arriving towards the end of September 1748. He missed his future mentor Gluck by a mere two years, though his seven-year stay in England coincided almost exactly with that of his compatriot Canaletto. On 23 September, the *General Advertiser* carried an announcement of the arrival in London of a 'company of Italian performers, who are to entertain the town…with operas of a new kind, entitled BURLETTAS'. Quite by accident, at this early stage in his career Guadagni opened his account as an innovator.

A valuable source for Guadagni's first London season is the correspondence between the violinist Franz Pirker and his wife, the soprano Marianne Pirker. Both Pirkers had been employed at the King's Theatre in 1747–48, but when Marianne joined the Mingotti troupe in Hamburg in the summer of 1748, Franz remained in London. They wrote frequently to each other and to their colleague, the castrato Giuseppe Jozzi, who at this period was on the move throughout the continent.[1] The first mention of Guadagni's arrival was on 24 September, when Pirker noted that 'the impresario for the buffa operas is expected daily; he has left the company in

---

[1] The Pirker correspondence is in the Hauptstaatsarchiv, Stuttgart, A 202 Bü 2839–2842. I am grateful to Gerhard Croll and Irene Brandenburg at the University of Salzburg for allowing me to read photocopies of the correspondence. Pirker wrote in German to his wife and in Italian to Jozzi.

Dover till he has arranged lodgings etc. He is bringing a castrato with him'.[2] A week later, Pirker recorded the troupe's arrival in London: 'The new company has finally arrived: first, a handsome young soprano, 17 [recte: 20] years of age, from Lodi; I have forgotten his name... second, Laschi and his wife, whom they say will be the prima donna in the style of Frasi.'[3]

Crosa's company was well-established and had toured successfully in Italy since 1742.[4] A vivid picture of the impresario is given in a notice published in the *London Evening Post* in 1750, on the occasion of his absconding from a jail sentence for bankruptcy:

> The said John Francis Croza is a thin man about five feet and five inches high, of a swarthy complexion, with dark brown eye-brows, pitted with the small-pox, stoops a little in the shoulders, is about fifty years of age, and takes a remarkable deal of snuff; walks sideling, with his head inclining to his right shoulder, which is a little higher than his left; has a hitch in his gait, and is of a pensive aspect; he talks Italian and French, but very little English.[5]

The company owed its success to its two leading *buffo* singers, the tenor Filippo Laschi, and the versatile Pietro Pertici, who sang tenor and bass roles; their wives Anna Querzoli and Caterina Brogi were also members of the troupe. The musical director was Vincenzo Ciampi. Horace Walpole, a lively and acerbic but generally reliable witness, assessed the uneven talents of the company: 'Pertici is excessively admired; Garrick says he is the best comedian he ever saw; but the women are execrable; not a pleasing note among them.'[6] Crosa's troupe brought with them a repertory of seven *opere buffe*. It is surprising to find Guadagni in such company. His debut in Venice was in heroic opera, and he was eventually to make his mark as one of the most noted exponents in Europe in serious roles. He had, of course, his older brother and sister as role models in the field of comic opera, and there is the possibility, discussed above, that he sang in *La fiametta*, but he must have been eager for any

---

[2] Franz to Marianne Pirker, 24 Sept. 1748: 'Der Impresario für die "Buffa Opern" wird täglich erwartet und läßt die Compagnie in Dohvres, bis er hier die Quartiere etc geregelt hat. Er bringt einen Castraten mit'.

[3] Pirker to Jozzi, 1 Oct. 1748: 'La nuova compagnia e finalmente arrivata: 1° un soprano, bello, giovane, da 17 anni, Lodesano, ho scordato il nome... 2° Laschi e la sua moglie che si dice che farà la prima donna a la Frasi.' Pirker repeats his error over Guadagni's age in a letter to Marianne dated 3 Oct.

[4] Crosa's career is examined in Richard G. King and Saskia Willaert, 'Giovanni Francesco Crosa and the First Italian Comic Operas in London', *Journal of the Royal Musical Association* 118 (1993): 246–75.

[5] *London Evening Post*, 17–19 May, 1750.

[6] Horace Walpole, patron, politician, novelist, historian and indefatigable correspondent: letter to Horace Mann, 2 Dec. 1748, *The Yale Edition of Horace Walpole's Correspondence*, ed. Wilmarth Sheldon Lewis, xx, New Haven: Yale University Press, 1937–1983, p. 4.

stage engagement to take employment among performers who were actors first and foremost and singers by necessity.

Much was made in the press of the novelty of Crosa's repertory. *Opera buffa*, which emerged in Italy in the 1730s, had not previously been given in England, and the management of the King's Theatre, always on the edge of financial disaster, was hopeful that the innovation might prove popular. Founded in 1705 by members of the Kit-Cat Club, an association with literary ambitions and Whig sympathies, the King's Theatre was the only London theatre licensed to give Italian opera—a curious and accidental development in the light of the fact that one of the aims of the club was to foster a sense of national identity.[7] The monopoly on Italian opera put the theatre in both a privileged and a precarious position. The attraction of *opera seria* for the English could never be taken for granted, and there were many failures. After a series of commercially disastrous seasons, the management announced the new repertory, stressing its novelty, as 'Burletta or Comic Opera…Being the first of this Species of Music Drama ever exhibited in England.'[8] Burney gave an overview of the season:

> In the autumn of this year, serious operas being discontinued, a new company of comic singers was brought hither from Italy, for the first time, by Signor Croza. These performers, consisting of *Pertici, Laschi*, and *Guadagni*, then very young, for first man; Frasi, and afterwards Mellini, for serious women, and the comic female parts by the wives of Pertici and Laschi, the two best buffo actors I ever saw, formed a very good troop; and in the comic operas of *La Comedia in Comedia*,[9] *Orazio, Don Calascione, Gli tre Cicisbei ridicoli*, etc. composed by Latilla, Natale Resta, and Ciampi, who came over as maestro to the company, and filled the theatre, very successfully, during the whole season.[10]

In a footnote, he added:

> Of the first three *opere buffe*, which have been mentioned, the Music of *Don Calascione*, by Latilla, was much the best; the whole being truly characteristic and charming… *Gli tre Cicisbei ridicoli* had likewise great comic merit; but this species of composition was now so new, and the acting of Pertici and Laschi,

---

[7] See Ophelia Field, *The Kit-Cat Club: Friends Who Imagined a Nation*, London: Harper Press, 2008. For the intricacies of the licensing of London theatres, see V. J. Liesenfeld, *The Licensing Act of 1737*, Madison: University of Wisconsin Press, 1988.

[8] *General Advertiser*, 3 Nov. 1748.

[9] Always given with this spelling in the eighteenth century.

[10] Burney, *General History*, ii, p. 848.

so excellent, and so fully engaged the attention, that critics had little leisure left
for a severe examination of the Music.

Burney found the remaining repertory, the pasticcios *La finta frascatana* (performed
once only, on 31 December 1748), *Il giramondo* (given twice, 14 and 18 February
1749) and the serenade *Peace in Europe*, written to celebrate the peace of Aix-la
Chapelle (29 April 1749) 'of little merit'[11]; another failure, *La maestra*, received only
one performance on 28 February 1749.

   Crosa's repertory in England comprised tried and tested operas that had already
proved successful on the continent. Rinaldo da Capua's *La comedia in comedia*, which
opened the season at the King's Theatre on 8 November, was a well-constructed satirical opera, with a libretto by Vanneschi, first performed in Rome in 1738. It enjoyed
moderate success in London, being judged sufficiently popular to justify as commercially viable the publication of its *Favourite Songs*.[12] The burlettas were designed to
display the talents of actors rather than singers: Pertici attracted enthusiastic notices
as 'one of the greatest comedians of his age and country'.[13] The music was undemand-
ing, and the simple, largely syllabic airs hardly gave Guadagni the chance to make
an impression as a singer. Pirker gave a cautious welcome to the production: 'At last
the opera has opened. I liked the men, but the women not so much… the castrato
pleased greatly.… All in all it was well rather than poorly received, though there was
no lack of those who spoke very badly of it. There was both hissing and applause,
and some of the arias were encored. Only time will tell'.[14] He repeated his approval
of Guadagni in a letter to Marianne, adding, 'The castrato Gaetano Guadagni is a
charming boy with somewhat clumsy feet'.[15]

   The next production, on 29 November was *Orazio* by Pietro Auletta with a
libretto by Antonio Palomba. The opera, premièred in Naples in 1737, had been
repeated throughout Europe in pasticcio form, incorporating items by Pergolesi
and Jommelli among others.[16] It appears to have been successful. Pirker noted that
Guadagni sang 'pretty well' but there was obviously something amiss with his acting: 'The castrato Gaetanino sang in *Orazio*; his arm movements are wretched; he

---

[11] Ibid., p. 848. Walpole described *Peace in Europe* as 'a wretched performance'; letter to Mann, 3 May 1749,
*Correspondence*, xx, p. 49.

[12] *The Favourite Songs in the Opera call'd La Comedia in Comedia*, London: Walsh, 1749.

[13] *Daily Advertiser*, 17 Nov. 1749.

[14] Pirker to Jozzi, wrongly dated 5 Oct. 1748 [?8 Nov.]: 'Finalmente l'Opera è andato in scena. L'uomini mi piac-
cino ma le Donne non tanto… il Musico piacce di molto… Tutto insieme è più gradito che sprezziato, benche
non manchino chi dicono male assai. Furono fischi ed applausi e repliche d'arie. Il resto decidera il tempo.'

[15] Franz to Marianne Pirker, 18 October: 'Der castrat ist ein charmante Bub Gaetano Guadagni, etwas dicke Füße'.

[16] Two editions of the libretto were published: that of London: Woodfall, 1748, *The Favourite Songs in the Opera
call'd Orazio* was announced by Walsh on 20 December.

pleased nevertheless, but his success owed much to the advocacy of Frasi, whose faction and influence made itself heard both in the gallery and in the pit.'[17] The soprano Giulia Frasi seems to have taken Guadagni under her wing from the start.

After the failure of *La finta frascatana*, the company turned to another trusted favourite, *Don Calascione*. This opera, by Gaetano Latilla, with a libretto by Gennaro Antonio Federico, was originally titled *Il Gismondo* when first produced in Naples in 1737, revised as *La finta cameriera* for Rome and finally took the name of its most popular character as its title for the production in London, which opened on 21 January 1749. Guadagni's contribution failed to catch the attention of one keen opera-goer: 'Went to see *Don Calascione*; Laski & Pertici & their wives the best of the set. Full of drollery. The music here and there well adapted to the words.'[18] It was followed by another success, *I tre cicisbei ridicoli* by Ciampi, with a libretto by Carlo Vasini, premièred on 14 March. It is not possible to be certain about which of the operas Guadagni took part in: playbills, librettos and *Favourite Songs* name his participation only in *La comedia* (as Celindo), *Orazio* (as Leandro) and *Don Calascione* (as Filando).

Guadagni also sang outside the opera house in his first London season. In January 1749 Pirker recorded that he sang in churches.[19] He also began to make his mark in secular concerts. The two most prevalent types of concert in mid-eighteenth-century London were charity concerts and benefit performances. Subscription series were also beginning to feature, though they did not form a regular part of the concert provision for some years. The main musical charity was the Fund for the Support of Decayed Musicians and their Families; this benevolent organization, of which Handel was a founder member, gave a grand concert every spring with a wide variety of popular items. The programmes were built to a formula: beginning with an overture or symphony, vocal and instrumental items then alternated, as did the contributions from male and female soloists; a duet between the latter was often included. The whole event represented domestic family music-making on a large scale. The vocal solos provide an interesting insight into what was popular at the time. For the concert at the King's Theatre on 21 March 1749, Guadagni sang 'Pupille amabili' by Jommelli and 'Ah! non lasciarmi' by Bertoni, composers who were to play an important part in his later career. The programmes of benefit concerts were less

---

[17] Literally, 'both in the gallery and among the servants'; Franz to Marianne Pirker, 17 Dec. 1748: 'Der castrat Gaetanino macht den Orazio, sein portement de bras ist elend; er gefällt demnach ziemlich, wobey aber die Protection der Frasi vieles contribuiret, welche in der Gallerie, und unter den Laquais ihr faction und pouvoir hören läßt'.

[18] Diary of George Harris, 10–11 Feb. 1749, in Donald Burrows and Rosemary Dunhill, *Music and Theatre in Handel's World*, p. 254.

[19] Franz to Marianne Pirker, 7 Jan. 1749: 'Abende der castrat hat gesungen in der Kirchen'.

predictable, and could range in scale from a recital of chamber proportions to the performance of a complete opera. Guadagni (identified as 'Guadanno') took part in a benefit recital for Margherita Giacomazzi at the Little Theatre in the Haymarket on 17 April 1749. At the end of his first season in London, without attracting any particular notice, Guadagni was quietly integrating into musical life in the capital.

Off-stage was another matter. An incident, related by Walpole, provides the first episode in an alternative biography of Guadagni—a biography that could be constructed from the colourful anecdotes, most of them possible, many of them probable, that attached themselves to the singer throughout his career. Horace Walpole, the youngest son of Sir Robert Walpole, was one of the polymaths of the century: wit, historian, letter-writer, novelist, publisher and architect of the Gothic fantasy villa at Strawberry Hill. His mordant comments, scattered throughout his prolific correspondence, provide lively insights into the society of his time. He was a regular opera-goer, and seems to have been fascinated by Guadagni to the extent of naming a racehorse after him, possibly with the intention of drawing a tasteless comparison between the castrato and the gelding.[20] His references to the singer are rarely favourable. Ever hungry for scandalous anecdotes and eager to disseminate gossip, the bi-sexual Walpole clearly relished the following incident:

[Francis Blake] Delaval, a wild young fellow, keeps an Italian woman, called the Tedeschi. He had notice one day that she was actually then in bed with Guadagni, a handsome young eunuch, who sings in the burlettas. The injured cavalier takes one of his chairmen and a horsewhip, surprises the lovers, drags them out of bed, and makes the chairman hold Mars, while he flogged Venus most unmercifully. After that execution, he takes Guadagni, who fell on his knees and cried and screamed for mercy—'No, Sir,' said Delaval, 'I have another sort of punishment for you,' and immediately turned up that part, which in England indeed is accustomed to be flogged too, but in its own country has a different entertainment— which he accordingly gave it. The revenge was a little particular!'[21]

Walpole's anecdote is only one among many to portray Guadagni in a sexual relationship.[22] It is, to say the least, a curious circumstance. While there is an abundance of evidence to suggest that castratos held a powerful appeal for women, it is less clear

---

[20] It ran at Bellewstown near Drogheda on 28 Aug. 1751. *Faulkener's Dublin Journal*, 31 August–3 September.

[21] Horace Walpole to Horace Mann, 23 Mar. 1749, *Correspondence*, xx, p. 41. Caterina Tedeschi sang as third woman at the King's Theatre in 1741–42, but is not known to be employed in England in 1748–49.

[22] Angus Heriot, a valuable repository of anecdotal literature, observed that, 'Many of the castrati were famous lady-killers'. *The Castrati in Opera*, London: Calder, 1960, p. 55.

whether they were able to take advantage of it. Modern medical opinion is divided about the extent to which a castrato could function sexually. His infertility was beyond doubt (despite Tenducci's assertion that he had fathered two children[23]) but there is considerable confusion as to whether a degree of potency might have been possible. Opposing points of view are argued by Enid and Richard Peschel, who maintain that castratos 'could not have had any normal male sexual function', and Wendy Heller, who asserts that 'there is no evidence to suggest that many castrati weren't capable of performing sexually'.[24] The most complete survey of the physiological evidence to date has been undertaken by Meyer Melicow, who concludes that 'we have no way of knowing':

There was a consensus that bilateral orchiectomy properly performed on boys between the ages of five to seven years should result in *permanent sterility and impotence*....Boys castrated at a later stage, i.e., from nine to 12 years of age, should have been rendered sterile, but potency need not have been compromised because the interstitial cells that manufacture testosterone had probably functioned and induced erections and, once begun, erectability may have continued because of testosterone-producing cells along the cords and in the retroperitoneum.[25]

There are no known cases of boy singers castrated as young as five or six years of age. Even seven would normally be considered too soon to be sure that the voice was sufficiently promising to take such an irrevocable step. 'Nine to 12 years of age' was the normal window for the operation; Paoluccio was ten years old and Caffarelli was twelve when they underwent the operation.[26] But Haydn was fourteen or fifteen, with his voice on the point of breaking, when he was allegedly saved in the nick of

---

[23] See Dora Tenducci, *A True and Genuine Narrative of the Marriage and Subsequent Proceedings of Mr and Mrs Tenducci*, London: Pridden, 1768, and Helen Berry, *The Castrato and His Wife*, Oxford: Oxford University Press, 2011.

[24] Enid Rhodes Peschel and Richard Peschel, 'Medicine and Music', *The Opera Quarterly* 4.4 (1986), p. 33; Wendy Heller, 'Varieties of Masculinity: Trajectories of the Castrato from the Seventeenth Century', *British Journal for Eighteenth-Century Studies* 28 (2005), pp. 307–8. See also Roger Freitas, *Portrait of a Castrato: Politics, Patronage, and Music in the Life of Atto Melani*, Cambridge: Cambridge University Press, 2009, p. 135; C. d'Ollincan, *Traités des eunuques* (Berlin, 1707), tr. Robert Samber as *Eunuchism Display'd*, London, 1718. For further medical insights, see Carla Serarcangeli and Gennaro Rispoli, 'La mutilazione crudele: note storiche su castratori e castrati', *Medicina nei secoli arte e scienza*, 13.2 (2001): 441–54; Peter W. Vogelaar, 'Castrati in Western Art Music', *Medical Problems of Performing Artists* 13.3 (1998): 94–99 and 13.4 (1998): 146–54.

[25] Meyer M. Melicow, 'Castrati singers and the lost cords', *Bulletin of New York Academy of Medicine*, 59.8 (1983): 749, 754. My own conversations with urogenital specialists lead me to conclude, in agreement with Melicow, that castratos were probably no more and no less potent than a twelve-year-old boy today.

[26] Vogelaar, 'Castrati in Western Art Music', p. 152.

time from a similar fate.[27] (Castration after puberty, as practised in myth by the followers of Cybele and in fact as recently as the last century by the Russian Skopecs, is clearly irrelevant to this issue.[28]) For castrated choirboys with mature but unbroken voices, Melicow's conclusions appear to fit the case. Historical debate founders on uncertain terminology. Discussions in the seventeenth and eighteenth centuries often confuse the issue of potency with fertility. The unspoken assumption was that they came to the same thing, since it was a requirement of the Catholic church (and some other denominations) that the infertile were barred from marriage—still a live issue today in the current theological debate over gay marriage.

In the eighteenth century, what mattered more than physiological accuracy was the widely held belief that castratos *might* be potent, and the ambiguity surrounding their physical nature only heightened their appeal. Castratos were seen as a real moral danger to both men and women. This was particularly true in England, where they were suspect on two counts: they were perceived to be effeminate and known to be foreign—a double threat to manhood and nationhood. They were also charged with sins against religion and the economy. The castrato was an 'Amphibious Animal...only fit to enervate the Youth of Great Britain by the pernicious Influence of his Unnatural Voice',[29] and regularly described as one who 'weakens that roughness whereby we are characterised the bravest nation in Europe'.[30]

By no means all the alarms related to sexual dangers. In London in the 1730s, the attacks focussed on one particular import, Farinelli, who joined the Opera of the Nobility in 1734 for three seasons. His impact on the capital was described as amounting to sacrilege:

> Unheeded now the Bells to worship call
> In empty Churches, Clerks and Curates bawl,
> Whilst the *Beau Monde* adore an Eunuch Shrine
> Their Morning Prayer, o Far—i—llo's thine,
> One G—d, one Songster, they alike partake,
> But for the Songster, they their G—d forsake.[31]

---

[27] Georg August Griesinger, *Biographische Notizen über Joseph Haydn*, Vienna: Breitkopf und Härtel, 1810, p. 11. Rosemary Hughes discusses further sources for this incident in *Haydn* (The Master Musicians Series), London: Dent, 1974, p. 15, note 1.

[28] Ionel Florian Rapaport, *La castration rituelle: l'état mental des Skoptzy*, Paris: Lipschutz, 1937.

[29] *The Prompter*, no. 37, 14 Mar. 1735. The French, too, regarded the castratos as 'invaders...corrupting the French nation with their foreign usages' (Ange Goudar, *Le Brigandage de la Musique Italienne*, Paris, 1777, p. 148), but there were fewer complaints against the singers than in England because they never obtained a toehold as soloists on the professional stage in France.

[30] Thomas Wilkes, *A General View of the Stage*, 2nd ed, London: Williams, 1762, p. 70.

[31] The Lady of Taste: or F——'s Levee, 1737, in *A Collection of Miscellany Poems,* London, 1737, p. 152.

He was also held responsible for impoverishing the nobility and draining money into foreign coffers:

> My Lord has money—well—we grant it true
> It is for FARINELLI—not for you.
> The Op'ra, too, will Ready Money take,
> His Lordship must subscribe, his Rep's at stake:
> Shou'd he imprudently his Tradesman pay,
> Where wou'd the Gold be had to keep up Play?[32]

Most of the literature, however, charged castratos with being a sexual threat. Some twenty years before Guadagni's arrival in London, the satirical press was obsessed first with Senesino and later Farinelli, attributing to them both over-familiar behaviour towards their leading ladies, and cruel rejection of them. A curious series of verse epistles, examined in detail by Thomas McGeary, purported to define the charges and provide the accused's response.[33] The satirists delighted to stimulate male anxieties about sexual control, implying that the castrato was a better lover:

> Well knowing Eunuchs can their wants supply,
> And more than Bragging Boasters satisfy;
> Whose Pow'r to please the Fair expires too fast,
> While F——lli stands it to the last.[34]

They also advanced one very real benefit of such a liaison:

> They know that safe with Thee they may remain;
> Enjoy Love's Pleasures, yet avoid the Pain;
> Each, blest in thee, continue still a Maid;
> Nor of a Tell-Tale Bantling be afraid…
> Eunuchs can give uninterrupted Joys,
> Without the shameful Curse of Girls and Boys:
> The violated Prude her shape retains,
> A Vestal in the Publick Eye remains.[35]

---

[32] Joseph Dorman, *The Rake of Taste*, London: Mrs Dodd, Mrs Nutt, 1735, p. 7.

[33] Thomas McGeary, 'Verse Epistles on Italian Opera Singers', *Royal Musical Association Research Chronicle*, 33 (2000): 29–88.

[34] Anon., 'The Happy Courtezan: or The Prude demolish'd. An Epistle from Mrs C—P—[Teresia Constantia Phillips] to the Angelick Signor Far—n—li'. London, 1735, p. 6.

[35] 'The Happy Courtezan', pp. 5–6.

The sex appeal of the castrato seems to have surprised some of their contemporaries. Their physical appearance was often savagely lampooned: 'They have the look of a crocodile, the grin of an ape, the legs of a peacock, the paunch of a cow, the shape of an elephant, the brains of a goose, the throat of a pig, and the tail of a mouse.'[36] The motivation for such a caricature may have been to defuse the threat, to 'assuage the anxieties raised by the castrated body', and the rumours of its superior potency.[37] But even dispassionate modern writers paint a grotesque and freakish portrait:

> Emasculating a boy before puberty causes primary hypogonadism, a condition characterized by a number of abnormalities in development.... These include an infantile penis; an underdeveloped prostate; a lack of beard growth; a lack of the usual distribution of axillary hair and of hair on the extremities; pubic hair distributed in the female instead of the male pattern; more developed subcutaneous fat than in the normal male...fatty deposits that occurred sometimes in the lateral portions of the eyelids, creating facial distortions; and skin that often appeared swollen and wrinkled.[38]

Eighteenth-century reactions to male beauty, however, are often surprising. There is a body of writing describing women's reactions to the male nude in classical sculpture (the only context in which a respectable woman could contemplate the masculine form) that establishes a very definite prejudice in favour of effeminate characteristics. Chloe Chard has assembled a selection of opinions from women undertaking the Grand Tour, viewing both the rugged masculinity of the Farnese Hercules and the smooth and hairless Apollo Belvedere, devoid of visible musculature.[39] One such traveller, Lady Miller, reacted to the Hercules with distaste: 'It may be very beautiful, and the most perfect model of a man in the world; but I am insensible enough to its charms to own, that if all mankind were so proportioned, I should think them very disagreeable and odious'. Her female companion made a direct comparison with the Apollo: 'The muscles of this Hercules...are like craggy rocks compared with the Belviderean Apollo.'[40] Male writers were equally ready to prefer the more feminised physique, but tended to excuse their judgement by pretending to

[36] *The Remarkable Trial of the Queen of Quavers and Her Associates, for Sorcery, Witchcraft, and Enchantments*, London, [1777?], pp. 7–8.

[37] See Berta Joncus, 'One God, so many Farinellis: Mythologising the Star Castrato', *British Journal for Eighteenth-Century Studies* 28 (2005), p. 440.

[38] Peschel and Peschel, 'Medical Insights into the Castrati in Opera', *American Scientist* 75 (1988): 582.

[39] Chloe Chard, 'Effeminacy, pleasure and the classical body', in *Femininity and Masculinity in Eighteenth-century Art and Culture*, ed. Gill Perry and Michael Rossington, Manchester: Manchester University Press, 1994, pp. 142–61.

[40] Lady Miller, *Letters from Italy*, London, 1776, ii, p. 86.

speak for women: 'If I was a woman, I should be more in love with the APOLLO than I am with the VENUS. For I have seen many women whom I should prefer to the VENUS; but never such a beautiful graceful sublime figure of a man as the APOLLO is'.[41] By hypothesising a female viewer, male critics could indulge their appreciation of graceful male beauty without incurring the charge of effeminacy.

If the more feminine aspects of their appearance were no barrier to their desirability—and Guadagni, as we have seen, was reportedly handsome, and 'without those bodily defects that are usually seen in castratos'[42]—the special quality of their voices reinforced rather than detracted from their seductive appeal. The fullest and most explicit account we have of the sexual effect of the castrato voice comes from the diaries of Fanny Burney, and relate to her experience of listening to Giuseppe Millico in the spring of 1773. She dismissed his physical attractions in a phrase: 'He is an immense Figure, and not handsome *at all, at all*'.[43] Her reaction to his singing was outspoken, and plainly implies sexual attraction:

> I have no Words to express the delight which his singing gave me. More, far away, than I have ever received—even at the Opera—for his Voice is so sweet, that it wants no Instruments to cover it.... For my own part, the mere recollection fills me with *rapture*—my terms are strong, & yet they but weakly express my meaning.[44]

When, a month later, she continued her ecstasies, she was clearly aware of the forbidden fruits she was tasting:

> The Voice of Millico seems continually sounding in my Ear, & harmonizing my Soul. Never have I known pleasure so exquisite, so Heartfelt, so *divinely penetrating*, as this sweet singer has given me. He is ever present to my imagination, his singing & his songs, are the constant Companions of my recollection.... I express myself in very strong terms, but all terms, all words are unequal & inadequate to speak of the extreme Delight which Millico's singing affords me. If this Journal was not *sacred* to myself, I am not ignorant that *any* other Reader would immediately give me credit for either affectation or some degree of Craziness: but I am too much my own friend, ever to expose my *Raptures* to

---

[41] Lancelot Temple, *A Short Ramble Through Some Parts of France and Italy*, London, 1771, pp. 34–35.

[42] Gennari, *Notizie giornaliere di quanto avvenne specialmente in Padova*, ii, p. 683.

[43] *The Early Journals and Letters of Fanny Burney*, ed. Lars E Troide, Oxford: Oxford University Press, 1988, I, p. 234.

[44] Ibid., p. 235.

those who cannot simpathize in them, though I have never written my feelings with more honesty.[45]

If the combination of bodies that, in at least some cases, harmonised with an eighteenth-century taste in male beauty, with voices regularly described as angelic, guaranteed the castratos a certain appeal, their attraction was only intensified when they were heard on the operatic stage. In the theatre, education, taste, career-structure, local custom and church law conspired to create a situation of infinite options in matters of sex and gender. The circumstance that introduced castratos into opera in the first place was their outstanding vocal skill, the result of an extended period of training, typically twice as long as that of any female singer. Their availability also happened to coincide with a taste for high-register melodic lines, especially two equal high 'voices' moving in parallel, intertwining, or chasing suspensions above an independent bass. Susan McClary has interpreted the trio sonata texture favoured in seventeenth-century opera, and memorably featured in the love duet 'Pur ti miro' in Monteverdi's *L'incoronazione di Poppea*, as a specifically sexual sound image.[46] A few decades later, other considerations applied. In seventeenth-century Venetian opera a castrato had not automatically assumed the role of 'first man': that was as often given to a female singer. A catalyst for their rise to stardom was the spread of public opera houses in the eighteenth century. The castratos' well-drilled vocal technique and the extraordinary quality of their voices pleased the paying audiences, even if the moralists disapproved. Singers happily cultivated celebrity and began to command fees that at first equalled and then outstripped those earned by female singers.[47]

In the course of the eighteenth century, in most European opera houses castratos became, from the point of view of casting, interchangeable with women. Many castratos took female roles at the outset of their careers (though Guadagni did not). Caffarelli was one who made his debut in this way, taking the usual course of moving on to male roles as his voice matured; Andrea Martini, on the other hand, allegedly with a thin voice of little power, sang exclusively female roles. Martini spent the whole of his career in Rome where, by law, all female roles had to be taken by male singers. Outside the papal states, women were available and accustomed to represent

---

[45] Ibid., p. 236.

[46] Susan McClary, 'Constructions of gender in Monteverdi's dramatic music', *Cambridge Opera Journal* 1.3 (1989): 203–23.

[47] Rosselli, 'The Castrati as a Professional Group', pp. 158–167; Wendy Heller, 'Reforming Achilles: gender, *opera seria* and the rhetoric of the enlightened hero', *Early Music*, 26.4 (1998): 562–81; Susan McClary, 'Gender Ambiguities and Erotic Excess in Seventeenth-Century Venetian Opera', in *Acting on the Past: Historical Performance across the Discipline*, ed. Mark Franko and Anne Richards, Hanover, N.H.: Wesleyan University Press, 2000, pp. 177–200.

characters of either sex. At this distance in time, it seems curious that castratos and women shared the same male heroic roles, so that a soldier, lover or villain was as likely to be sung by a woman as by a man. Silke Leopold has argued persuasively that composers selected vocal register rather than the sex of the singer when portraying a character.[48] In Handel's operas, the roles of the soldier Cleone in *Alessandro*, the lover Medoro in *Orlando* and the arch villain Polinesso in *Ariodante* were all created by women. When, in subsequent productions, a woman was replaced by a man (for example when Margherita Durastanti, who created the title role in *Radamisto*, later ceded it to Senesino), the exchange appears to have attracted no comments relating to the singer's sex.

To add confusion upon confusion, many opera plots involved cross-dressing. With a nod to the old theatrical tradition that regularly contrived plots that got stage characters as rapidly as possible into the costume appropriate to the actor's sex (as happens, for example, to Shakespeare's cross-dressing heroines, invariably played by boys), in Handel's last opera, *Deidamia*, the young hero Achilles was played by a woman, who spends much of the opera disguised—as a woman. There is some evidence that women in 'trouser roles' were particularly attractive to male audiences, who found the revealing costumes more titillating than they found the soprano-register voices disconcerting.[49]

It was inevitable that the prevailing air of ambiguity should fuel rumours of homo-sexuality among the castratos, an assumption implicit in Walpole's anecdote and noted by several writers. Casanova once admitted to having been sexually attracted to a singer he thought to be a castrato in women's clothing, only to discover that she was a woman.[50] Goethe, too, was susceptible to the charms of castratos taking women's roles.[51] Montesquieu described his own reactions:

> While I was in Rome, there were two little castratos, Mariotti and Chiostra, dressed as women, who were the most ravishing creatures I had ever seen, and who would have inspired a taste for Gomorrah in those with the least depraved tendencies in this respect. A young Englishman, believing one of the pair to be

[48] Silke Leopold, ' "Not Sex but Pitch": Kastraten als Liebhaber—einmal über der Gürtellinie betrachtet', in *Provokation und Tradition: Erfahrungen mit der Alten Musik*, ed. Hans-Martin Linde and Regula Rapp, Weimar: Metzler, 2000, pp. 219–40.

[49] Katharine Maus, 'Playhouse Flesh and Blood: Sexual Ideology and the Restoration Actress', *English Literary History* 46 (1979): 595–617.

[50] See the episode of Bellino/Thérèse in Casanova de Seingalt, *Histoire de ma vie*, Paris: La Sirène, 1924, ii, chapters 1–2.

[51] Heriot, *The Castrati in Opera*, p. 26.

a woman, fell madly in love with her and continued in this state for more than a month.[52]

In one of the most sympathetic and least prurient accounts of the castratos' relationships, Rosselli has argued that much apparently scandalous behaviour was in fact a bid for companionship.[53] Castratos were often lonely. It was usual, and understandable, for them to reject their parents, and some invoked the law to get rid of importunate family members who tried to claim a portion of their earnings.[54] Colleagues provided a surrogate family, and ties were reinforced when, as often happened, a castrato would help to train a female singer as, according to Alessandro Ademollo, Guadagni had coached the seventeen-year-old Caterina Gabrielli in his brief season in Venice in 1747.[55] His romp with Signora Tedeschi could well have originated in a similar relationship.

The aptness of the castrato to undertake the role of a lover was rarely questioned. As Roger Freitas has shown, the roles allotted to castratos in Baroque opera are often those of *young* lovers, the 'beardless boy', or 'golden youth', with all the sexual ambiguity those terms imply.[56] And though, by the mid-eighteenth century, notably in Metastasian operas, a composer might cast a castrato in a power role—as god (Apollo), king (Siroe), prince (Farnaspe), or general (Ezio), he is a *young* divine, ruler or soldier, and his dramatic function is, more often than not, to woo rather than to command. The conflict between love and duty that shapes the majority of Metastasian plots, and the aria-based structure of *opera seria*, conspired to ensure that the hero spent more time displaying emotion than taking decisive action. Guadagni's roles often feature a misunderstood youth wrongly accused of treason or betrayal, a lover who suffers much before the inevitable happy ending (Arbace, Orazio, Megacle). Even in a more mature role as husband (Orfeo), he spends most of the opera lamenting the loss of his wife. In his role as Hercules in Handel's *The Choice of Hercules* he is as far removed from the muscular hero who repelled Lady Miller as can be imagined. His two arias depict the choice offered him, between the delicious pleasures represented in 'Yet can

---

[52] 'Il y avoit de mon temps à Rome deux petits châtrés, Mariotti et Chiostra, habillés en femmes, qui étoient les plus belles créatures que j'aye vues de ma vie, et qui auroient inspiré le goût de Gomorrhe aux gens qui ont le goût le moins dépravé à cet égard. Un jeune Anglois, croyant qu'un de ces deux étoit une femme, en devint amoureux à la fureur, et on l'entretint dans cette passion plus d'un mois.' Charles de Montesquieu, *Voyages*, Bordeaux: Gounouilhou, 1894, p. 220.

[53] Rosselli, 'The Castrati as a Professional Group', pp. 176–78.

[54] Avanzati, Elisabetta. "The unpublished Senesino." In *Handel*, ed. David Vickers, Farnham: Ashgate, 2011, pp. 305–9.

[55] Ademollo, Alessandro. *La più famosa delle cantanti italiane nella seconda metà del secolo XVIII: Caterina Gabrielli*, Milan: Ricordi, 1890, pp. 10, 27.

[56] Roger Freitas, 'The Eroticism of Emasculation: Confronting the Baroque Body of the Castrato', *Journal of Musicology*, 20 (2003): 196–249.

I hear that dulcet lay', and the rocky path of virtue in 'Lead, goddess, lead the way'. When he decides for Virtue, he not only follows in the more vigorous footsteps of a woman, albeit a divinity, but receives as his reward the crown of 'immortal youth'—a condition in which his body has already imprisoned him.

There is no indication that verisimilitude—the enactment of a young lover by a castrated man—was perceived as a problem by eighteenth-century audiences. Nor was the soprano register considered a bar to the expression of masculine sentiments. This has proved much more of an issue for recent opera companies that, for a limited period in the twentieth century, practised the downward transposition of castrato roles. The art historian Oskar Hagen prepared a series of editions of Handel's operas in the 1920s for the Göttingen Handel Festival, which consistently transposed castrato roles down an octave.[57] (The transpositions were the least of his violations of the scores, which included excising *da capo* repeats and reassigning arias to different characters.) Hagen's motivation was nationalism: he was less concerned with pitch and gender than with reclaiming Handel as a German composer, forcing his male protagonists into roles comparable with the heroic roles in Wagner's operas. Hagen's first transgressive scores were *Rodelinda* (1920) and *Giulio Cesare* (1922). The practice of octave transposition resurfaced in Germany in the 1960s, again in connection with *Giulio Cesare*, with the bass Walter Berry in the title role in 1965, and the baritone Dietrich Fischer-Dieskau in 1969. The German bass Norman Treigle imported the practice to the New York Opera in 1966. That this usage is now in abeyance can be attributed to two causes: the historically-informed performance movement, that has inculcated a desire to reconstruct the pitches, tones and timbres (though sadly not the production values) inherent in the original work, and an abundant supply of excellent countertenors to undertake castrato roles—not, to be sure, claiming to reproduce the unique quality of the castrato voice, but offering an alternative remote and special vocal timbre, removed from everyday life.

Guadagni escaped much of the controversy surrounding the castrato's on- and off-stage persona. His generation of castratos was never ridiculed for undertaking heroic or romantic roles. Audiences had long accustomed themselves to the sound, and if they had any complaints, these were directed at the fact that, as the product of the reform of opera, Guadagni rejected the extremes of virtuosity associated with the castratos of Farinelli's generation. Offstage the enigma remains: as Melicow sagely concluded, 'We have no way of knowing'. Guadagni was renowned for his friendships with both men and women. His capacity for a physical relationship seems the least important aspect of his personality.

---

[57] 'Revival, Revision, Rebirth: Handel Opera in Germany, 1920–1930', Abbey E. Thompson, MA thesis, University of North Carolina, Chapel Hill, 2006. See also comments on 'the unfortunate Göttingen reconstructions' in Paul Henry Lang, *George Frideric Handel*, New York: Norton, 1966, p. 672.

# 3

## Guadagni and Handel (1749–1755)

CROSA'S TROUPE HAD spent the summer of 1749 at the Théâtre de la Monnaie in Brussels, where they repeated the most successful operas of the previous season. Laschi was much lauded in the press.[1] Pertici and his wife, however, left the company soon after its arrival in Brussels. This was a serious loss to the company, since Pertici was regarded as one of the outstanding comic performers in Europe. It is likely that Guadagni did not stay for the whole two-month summer tour: although he sang his role of Filando in *Don Calascione*, he did not take part in the other revival, *Orazio*. On his return to London, Crosa rebuilt his troupe, recruiting Giulia Frasi, Margherita Giacomazzi and Francesco Lini.

The new season in London started badly. A quarrel between Crosa and Vanneschi led Crosa temporarily to abandon the King's Theatre. According to Burney, 'At the beginning of the next season, in November 1749, upon a quarrel with the manager, Signor Croza, there was a schism at the great theatre, and the composer, with the principal singers withdrew, and erected their standard at the Little Theatre in the Hay-market, where they performed a new comic-opera set by Ciampi, called *Il Negligente*, nine times.'[2] *Il negligente*, with a libretto by Goldoni, opened at the Little Theatre in the Haymarket on 21 November 1749. It was not successful. In Colley Cibber's opinion, 'the *Italian* Burletta (which is not so well performed as last Year) had but a poor House the first Day, and, I believe, like a sickly Plant, will die, before

---

[1] *Gazette de Bruxelles,* 5 Aug. 1749.

[2] Burney, *General History*, ii, pp. 848–49. Notices in the *General Advertiser* record only eight performances.

it takes any great Root among us.'[3] In the new year, the troupe returned to the King's Theatre for their next production, Latilla's setting of Barlocci's *Madama Ciana*; it was premièred on 13 January 1750 and was given four poorly-attended performances. Crosa's response was to try a serious opera: Ciampi's *Adriano in Siria*, with a libretto by Metastasio, given on 20 February. Once again, the opera was received without enthusiasm, and to ensure respectable receipts for a benefit performance for Laschi, Crosa took the precaution of playing Pergolesi's iconic intermezzo *La serva padrona* between the acts.[4] Burney attributes some part of its failure to Guadagni's inexperience in the genre: 'ADRIANO IN SIRIA, a new serious opera by Ciampi, was attempted; but as no new serious singers were arrived, and Guadagni, then a young and wild performer, and Frasi, performed the principal parts, after six thin houses [*recte*: eight] it was superseded for the comic-operas of the preceding winter.'[5]

After revivals of *Don Calascione*, and *Il negligente*, the last new opera of the season opened on 31 March. Ciampi's *Il trionfo di Camilla* re-worked an old libretto by Silvio Stampiglia, first set by Bononcini in 1696. It received only two performances, and after repeats in late April of *Madama Ciana* and *Don Calascione*, the season was brought to a premature close with Crosa's arrest for bankruptcy. He was tried and committed in April, escaped from prison in May, and fled to Holland in the same month.

Crosa's failure was not perhaps particularly prominent in the financially-troubled history of the King's Theatre. Burney remembered the first season as filling the theatre very successfully though Walpole was more cautious: 'the burlettas are…I think not decisively liked or condemned yet'.[6] A variety of reasons has been suggested for the lack of enthusiasm. Although prejudice against foreigners in general and Roman Catholics in particular was not as rabid as in 1745 when, in the aftermath of the Jacobite Rebellion the King's Theatre was closed, there was still a lingering resistance to imported opera. Moreover, presenting comic opera at the King's Theatre, the traditional venue for *opera seria*, created its own problems. Ticket prices varied between the prestigious King's Theatre and the 'playhouses'—Covent Garden, Drury Lane and the Little Theatre—which were home to spoken drama and (English-language) ballad opera. At the King's Theatre, admission to the pit and boxes cost half a guinea (ten shillings and sixpence) and the gallery five shillings; at the playhouses the boxes cost five shillings, the pit three shillings, the galleries one and two shillings.

---

[3] Colley Cibber to Benjamin Victor, 21 Nov. 1749, in Benjamin Victor, *The History of the Theatres of London and Dublin from the Year 1730 to the Present Time*, ii, Dublin, 1761, pp. 207–8.

[4] Given on 27 March, not 27 April as Burney asserts (Burney, loc. cit.).

[5] Burney, loc. cit.

[6] Walpole to Mann, 2 Dec. 1748, *Correspondence*, xx, p. 4.

For *Il negligente* at the Little Theatre, Crosa charged eight shillings for the pit and boxes and four shillings for the gallery, and the public were disinclined to pay sums not much short of *seria* prices for *buffa* fare. (Five years later the reverse situation obtained: Walpole accounted for the success of an inferior troupe presenting comic opera at Covent Garden because lower ticket prices made the performances seem a bargain: 'There are no less than five operas every week, three of which are burlettas; a very bad company...but these being at the playhouse and at play prices, the people, instead of resenting them, call them their own operas, and I will not swear that they do not take them for English operas.'[7]) Another hurdle for Crosa's troupe was the very fact of giving comic operas in a foreign language. The provision of dual-language librettos worked well enough for slow-moving *opera seria*, but comedy, often depending on rapid repartee and double meanings, was less suited to the system. Burney shrewdly suggested an additional cause, noting that 'the productions which had obtained the greatest applause and celebrity in their own country, have had the least favour shewn them here. This may be partly ascribed to a difference of taste in things of humour; but more, I believe, to our natural aversion to the being told what we should admire.'[8] Yet another factor that affected theatre-going in general in the spring of 1750 was a series of small earthquakes that shook London, and spread a nervous disinclination to go out; the first tremor was recorded on 8 February, the last on 5 April.

Before the end of the 1749–50 season, however, Guadagni had found a new and more appropriate outlet for his abilities when 'the excellence of his voice attracted the notice of Handel.'[9] By 1750 Handel's oratorios had become a fixed and popular addition to London concert life. There were about a dozen performances each year during Lent. The oratorios, given at this period in Covent Garden, were mostly revivals of older works, though Handel continued to adapt them to changes of cast, and produced occasional new compositions.[10] His company included English and Italian singers, some of them recruited from his (now disbanded) opera troupe but with a notable influx of new blood. In the spring of 1750 Guadagni joined the company which included his old friend Giulia Frasi, the mezzo soprano Caterina Galli, the tenor Thomas Lowe and the bass Henry Theodore Reinhold.[11] These were

[7] Walpole to Mann, 28 Jan. 1754, *Correspondence*, xx, p. 410.
[8] Burney, *General History*, ii, p. 849.
[9] Ibid., ii, p. 875.
[10] For a comprehensive overview of the genre see Winton Dean, *Handel's Dramatic Oratorios and Masques*, London: Oxford University Press, 1959. For a detailed examination of Handel's adaptations of his own works, see David Vickers, 'Handel's Performing Versions: A Study of Four Music Theatre Works from the "Second Academy" Period', PhD thesis, Open University, Milton Keynes, 2008.
[11] Of the singers named, only Reinhold had sung in Handel's operas.

established artists; Guadagni was still a comparative newcomer, his only reputation being the mixed success of one and a half seasons of comic opera, and it is interesting to speculate exactly what, in the castrato's short career, had attracted Handel's attention. Crosa's burlettas gave him only a limited chance to shine, and although Handel would have had a better opportunity to assess his voice on the basis of Guadagni's contribution to concerts, such as the one given on 21 March 1749 where his performance of airs by Jommelli and Bertoni might have impressed Handel, Guadagni sang in few other concerts in 1749. It is more probable that Handel sought out Guadagni on the recommendation of other singers, and the most likely contact was Frasi. Established in London from 1742, Frasi made her debut in oratorio a year before Guadagni, singing the title role in *Susanna* in February 1749. From the moment of his arrival in London, she appears to have undertaken the role of 'protectress' to Guadagni, ensuring his success in *Orazio* despite his 'wretched arm movements'. They sang together in a number of concerts. She was responsible for bringing Guadagni to Burney's notice and indeed Burney to Handel's, so her introduction of Guadagni to Handel was inevitable. In Burney's words:

> My acquaintance with Sir Joseph Hankey during the Election of St Dionis Back Church, procured me Frasi for a scholar; and Frasi procured me Guadagni on his first arrival, to accompany him in his studies, and assist him in the pronunciation of the English words in the parts given him in the Oratorios by Handel: and even the acquaintance of Handel himself; who used to bring an Air, or Duet, in his pocket, as soon as composed, hot from the brain, in order to give me the time and style, that I might communicate them to my scholar.[12]

Handel's employment of Guadagni is the more remarkable in that he rarely used castratos in his oratorios after 1737.[13] The most recent castrato before Guadagni was Andreoni, who sang the part of David in a revival of *Saul* in 1741. Guadagni made his oratorio debut at Covent Garden on 2 March 1750 in the same role.[14] Although not written for him, the seamless legato of the expressive aria 'O Lord, whose mercies numberless' is perfectly adapted to Guadagni's preferred style, and may have prompted Handel to provide the singer with similar lyrical arias in later oratorios.[15]

---

[12] *Memoirs of Dr Charles Burney 1726–69*, ed. Slava Klima, Garry Bowes and Kerry S. Grant (winter 1749–50), Lincoln: University of Nebraska Press, 1988, p. 92.

[13] In 1737 Annibali sang in a revival of *Alexander's Feast* and Gizziello (Conti) sang in *Esther*.

[14] *Saul*, with words by Charles Jennens, was first performed at the King's Theatre on 16 Jan. 1739. There were two performances in 1750, on 2 and 7 March.

[15] This aria can be heard, sung by Iestyn Davies, on a disc devoted to Guadagni's repertory: 'Arias for Guadagni', Hyperion CDA67924.

One member of the audience identified Guadagni as 'one of the opera men that sings very well in the Farinelli style.'[16] His next parts were in *Judas Maccabaeus* as the Israelite Man and the Messenger. This popular oratorio, a setting of words by Thomas Morell, first performed on 1 April 1747, was revived at Covent Garden on 9 March 1750.[17] A week later, on 16 March, he sang Didymus in the première of *Theodora*.[18]

Didymus was the first role Handel wrote for Guadagni, and the first role created for Guadagni of which the music has survived. It is remarkable for its exploitation of those vocal characteristics for which Guadagni later became celebrated. Handel must have seen in him the potential for the rapt, contemplative delivery that, much later in his career, came to dominate his performances. It is difficult to see how Guadagni could have acquired such a style through the light, syllabic comic roles that dominated his repertory up to this point. Handel heard the possibility of something different, and composed accordingly. In 'The raptur'd soul' and 'Sweet rose and lily', he gave Guadagni expansive lyrical phrases, requiring a seamless legato as well as great flexibility in the sustained melismas.[19] Another air, 'Deeds of kindness', requires a clear and nuanced delivery of the words—for which Guadagni sought Burney's help. As Winton Dean perceptively wrote:

> It can hardly be an accident that Handel never gives [Guadagni] lively or energetic music, such as we might expect in so defiant a hero. On the contrary, he emphasizes the spiritual quality of the man by introducing both his airs in Act I with a phrase of sustained rapture in a different mood and metre from what follows. If it were an accident that Morell made Didymus a Roman where Boyle and Corneille made him a Syrian, and that Guadagni was at hand with an alto and not a tenor voice, Handel seized on the circumstances with the transfiguring greed of genius.[20]

The role of Micah in *Samson*, which Guadagni sang on 4 April, is similarly restrained and reflective.[21] One air, 'Return, O God of Hosts', originally written for

---

[16] George Harris to (his mother) Elizabeth Harris, 8 Mar. 1750, in Burrows and Dunhill, *Music and Theatre in Handel's World*, p. 266.

[17] Guadagni sang in four performances in 1750, a further one in March 1751, and possibly four more in 1753. Dean, *Handel's Dramatic Oratorios and Masques*, p. 472.

[18] Words by Thomas Morell, based on Robert Boyle's *The Martyrdom of Theodora and Didymus*, London 1687, and Corneille's *Théodore vierge et martyre*, Paris, 1645. Guadagni sang in three performances in 1750.

[19] 'The raptured soul' is also recorded on 'Arias for Guadagni'.

[20] Dean, *Handel's Dramatic Oratorios and Masques*, p. 561.

[21] Words by Newburgh Hamilton, first performed 18 Feb. 1743. There were two performances in 1750. For Handel's changes in adapting the role of Micah for Guadagni, see Dean, *Handel's Dramatic Oratorios and Masques*, p. 352.

Susanna Cibber, was already a favourite with London audiences; Guadagni sang it in a number of concerts, including six occasions between January and April 1753. In the light of Guadagni's success in these *cantabile* roles, it is all the more surprising that, for the revival of *Messiah*[22] on 12 April 1750, Handel wrote 'For He is like a refiner's fire'—the *prestissimo* middle section of 'But who may abide'—forcing Guadagni into a display of energy and agility rarely visited in the remainder of his Handelian repertory. It is difficult to understand Burney's judgement of Guadagni as a 'wild and careless singer' in this season.[23] Handel is unlikely to have written 'The raptur'd soul' for a wild singer, or 'For He is like a refiner's fire' for a careless one. Certainly Guadagni showed a remarkable range of styles at this period and it was Handel who developed in him the restrained lyricism that was to become his trademark.

It is impossible to overestimate the stimulus to his career provided by Guadagni's participation in the oratorios. Operatic roles were rigidly categorised, and the hierarchy of first, second and third man dictated a singer's status, income and career prospects. Within oratorio, there was much less formal hierarchy. As Guadagni took on, season by season, an increasing number of the alto-register roles, he was selected primarily for his vocal compass, and treated as a team member rather than a contender for stardom. In Dean's words, Handel 'trained and moulded [his singers] to his own purposes…entrusting important parts to artists who were primarily not singers at all but actresses'. Dean singles out the acting talents of Mrs Cibber, Mrs Clive and the tenor Lowe, but Guadagni, too, belongs in this list of singers valued for their 'histrionic qualities' and 'unrivalled powers of expression'.[24]

In the autumn of 1750 Guadagni's career briefly took a new direction. The early autumn afforded a chance for provincial music clubs and festivals to attract star performers from the capital. Concerts were often associated with St Cecilia, though the dates strayed some distance from 22 November, the saint's dedicated day. It is often the case that the only sources for these events are local newspapers, many of which survive in incomplete runs. Guadagni's known travels this autumn make up a sporadic programme, which either represents a deliberate holiday period or conceals a rather busier schedule. At the end of September he was in the small Wiltshire town of Devizes. The event was well-advertised in the *Salisbury Journal*:

> At Devizes, Wilts. On Tuesday and Wednesday the 25th and 26th of this instant September, will be a Grand Concert of Vocal and Instrumental Musick at the

---

[22] Words by Charles Jennens, first performed 13 Apr. 1742. Guadagni repeated the role on 1 May at the Foundling Hospital.

[23] Burney, *General History*, ii, p. 875.

[24] Dean, *Handel's Dramatic Oratorios and Masques*, p. 107.

Town Hall. There will likewise be at St John's Church each day in the Morning, a Performance of Church Musick, by some of the most eminent Opera Hands; together with the assistance of performers from Bath and Salisbury, and the principal Vocal Part by Signior Guadagni.[25]

The evening concerts invariably ended with a Ball 'for the Ladies'. It is not clear whether Guadagni sang in the church concerts as well as the Grand Concerts in the Town Hall, and there is no indication of his repertory. It is notable that even at this early stage of his career, he was announced as a celebrity, and his name was presumed to be an attraction to potential concert-goers.

A week later he was in Salisbury to take part in a St Cecilia's Festival. The structure of the festival exactly paralleled that in Devizes, with 'A Te Deum and Two Anthems of Mr Handel's each day in the Cathedral Church, and Vocal and Instrumental Musick at the New Assembly Room' in the evening. The whole programme comprised Handel's music: on the first night (4 October) the evening concert was a performance of *Messiah* and on the second night *L'Allegro ed il Penseroso*. Again Guadagni was singled out as a star attraction: 'There will … several Performers from London, Oxford and Bath, particularly Dr Hayes, Signior Guadagni and Mr Leander.'[26] The Salisbury Festival at this period was very much the concern of James Harris, whose family correspondence forms an indispensable source for the period.[27] Harris would have heard of Guadagni from his brother George, who had attended Crosa's burlettas in the spring of 1749 and Handel's oratorios in 1750.

A month later Guadagni was in Bath, where he found his compatriot Galli already engaged in concerts. On 5 November he joined her in a benefit concert for the child prodigy Cassandra Frederica, who made her debut in a series of concerts that autumn:

For the Benefit of Miss Cassandra Frederica, a Child of Seven Years of Age, at Mr Wiltshire's Great room, this present Evening, will be a Concert of Vocal and Instrumental Musick. The vocal parts by Seignora Galli, and Seignior Guadagni. Miss Cassandra will perform a Concerto and various Lessons of the celebrated masters.[28]

[25] *Salisbury Journal,* 17 Sept. 1750.
[26] *Salisbury Journal,* 1 Oct. 1750. William Hayes was professor of music at Oxford University; Leander was a horn player. See also Douglas J. Reid and Brian Pritchard, 'Some Festival Programmes of the Eighteenth and Nineteenth Centuries: 1. Salisbury and Winchester', *Royal Musical Association Research Chronicle* 5 (1965): 51–79.
[27] See Burrows and Dunhill, *Music and Theatre in Handel's World.*
[28] *Bath Journal,* 5 Nov. 1750.

Two days later he contributed to another benefit concert for the horn player Leander at the same venue. On this occasion the full programme was advertised:

> First Act
> An Overture
> A Song, 'Le dolcezze dell'amore'
> A Concerto on the Harpsichord by Miss Cassandra Frederica
> A Song, 'Se possono tanto'
> A Symphony
>
> Second Act
> A new Concerto of Sig. Hass
> A Song, 'Parto, si bella Tiranna'
> A Lesson on the Harpsichord by Miss Cassandra Frederica
> 'The Highland Laddie'
> A Concerto on the French Horn[29]

Apart from Ciampi's song 'Le dolcezze dell'amore', one of Guadagni's favourite recital pieces, the exact identity of the music is not known. The idea of Guadagni, with his imperfect English, rendering 'The Highland Laddie' is perplexing, but it must have been enjoyed because it features 'by desire' in his next Bath concert, which took place on 26 November at the same venue, another benefit concert for the indefatigable Frederica, who contributed 'a Concerto and various Lessons of the celebrated masters'. This was a smaller occasion with, presumably, no orchestra. Guadagni sang three items: 'Se tu sapessi appieno', Handel's 'Return, O God of Hosts', and 'By desire…"The Highland Laddie"'. Mrs Frederica, the mother of the prodigy, contributed a further three arias.[30] Between the two latter concerts, Guadagni fitted in a trip to Bristol to sing in a St Cecilia's Day concert, appropriately on 22 November, in the Assembly Rooms.[31]

It would be interesting to know who was Guadagni's host during this prolonged stay in the West Country. There was a widespread custom of wealthy families inviting professional musicians into their homes, sometimes for a weekend, often for a more protracted period; one particular instance of this is described by Ian

[29] *Bath Journal*, 6 Nov. 1750.

[30] *Bath Journal*, 26 Nov. 1750.

[31] Philip H. Highfill Jr, Kalman A. Burnim, and Edward A. Langhans, eds., *A Biographical Dictionary of Actors, Actresses, Musicians, Dancers, Managers & Other Stage Personnel in London, 1660–1800*, vol. 6, Carbondale and Edwardsville: Southern Illinois University Press, 1973–1993, p. 436.

Woodfield in *Salomon and the Burneys*.[32] The visiting musician might give lessons to the mistress of the household or to her children, and would certainly be required to perform at house concerts or at more public venues in the neighbourhood. When Guadagni returned to England in 1769, he enjoyed the protracted hospitality of the young Sir Watkin Williams Wynn, but there is no record of a similar house party in the 1750s.

SEASON OF 1750–1751

Following Crosa's failure, there was no Italian opera at the King's Theatre in 1750–51. Guadagni, with Frasi and Galli, joined an opportunist company at the Little Theatre in the Haymarket, where he played second man in *La forza d'amore*, announced as 'a new pastoral drama' by Vanneschi and Domenico Paradies, opening on 19 January 1751; there were five performances.[33] The same company also put on *Nerina*, another 'new pastoral opera', on 16 February, with two subsequent performances. No libretto has survived for this work and it is not known whether Guadagni sang in it, or even the composer's name, though it is likely to have been another Vanneschi-Paradies collaboration.

Guadagni sang in a benefit concert for the ageing soprano Francesca Cuzzoni at Hickford's Music Room in Brewer Street on 22 February, the first of three benefit concerts through which Cuzzoni attempted to settle her debts.[34] Meanwhile, at Covent Garden Guadagni rejoined Handel's oratorio company. On 22 February he sang Cyrus in a revival of *Belshazzar*,[35] and on 1 March he created the role of

---

[32] *Salomon and the Burneys. Private Patronage and a Public Career*, Royal Musical Association Monographs 12, Aldershot: Ashgate, 2003. See also *Concert Life in Eighteenth-Century Britain*, ed. Susan Wollenberg and Simon McVeigh, Aldershot: Ashgate, 2004.

[33] The work was probably a pasticcio; all the numbers in the *Favourite Songs* are by Paradies: *Favourite Songs*, London: Walsh, 1751; libretto, London: Woodfall, 1751.

[34] The other concerts were held at the Little Theatre on 27 April and Hickfords on 23 May. The latter was advertised with an unusual degree of importunity: 'I am so extremely sensible of the many Obligations I have already received from the Nobility and Gentry of this Kingdom that nothing but extreme Necessity, and a Desire of doing Justice, could induce me to trouble them again, but being unhappily involved in a few Debts [she had been arrested for debt the previous year and only released through the Prince of Wales's intervention], am extremely desirous of attempting every Thing in my Power to pay them, before I quit England; therefore take the Liberty, most humbly to entreat them, once more to repeat their well-known Generosity and Goodness, and to honour me with their Presence at this Benefit, which shall be the last I will ever trouble them with, and is made solely to pay my Creditors; and to convince the World of my Sincerity herein, I have prevailed on Mr Hickford to receive the Money, and to pay it to them.' *General Advertiser*, 23 May 1751.

[35] Words by Jennens, first performed 27 Mar. 1745. Guadagni sang in two performances in February 1751.

Hercules in *The Choice of Hercules*, advertised as 'an Additional New Act' and added to performances of *Alexander's Feast*.[36] On 15 March he took the role of Assuerus (Ahasuerus) in *Esther*, a revival of the version first given on 2 May 1732. He also sang in a revival of *Judas Maccabaeus*, given on 20 March, which was restricted to a single performance owing to the death of the Prince of Wales. He sang in *Messiah* at the Foundling Hospital on 18 April and 16 May. It was a thin season for Guadagni, though there was additionally a charity concert for the Decayed Musicians' Fund on 16 April when Guadagni sang arias by Resta and Ciampi and a Handel duet with Cuzzoni.

When there are no performances, Guadagni disappears from view. He is rarely mentioned in letters and diaries—Walpole's scandalous anecdote is an isolated example—and he left no account of his life and travels. There are some long gaps in the record. In the autumn of 1751 he returned to the West Country, repeating his engagements of the previous year. The St Cecilia's Festival in Salisbury was held on 26 and 27 September. The structure was similar to 1750, comprising 'a Te Deum of Mr Handel's, with Two of his Coronation Anthems' in the morning concerts, and *Alexander's Feast* and *Samson* in the evenings. No performers are identified by name: 'There will be performers, Vocal and Instrumental, from London, Oxford and the [*sic*] Bath etc'.[37] But Guadagni's participation can be assumed with reasonable safety: both *Alexander's Feast* and *Samson* were in his repertory, and he was certainly in the area, since his next concerts, in Devizes, were advertised in the same column of *The Salisbury Journal*. They took place on 10 and 11 October. These 'Grand Concerts' were to be performed 'By some of the most eminent Opera Hands; with the Assistance of several of the best Performers in the country; The principal Vocal Parts by the celebrated Italian Singer, Signior Guadagni'.[38] It is gratifying to see his name heading the bill as the main attraction, a status not yet accorded him in London. He appears to have given just one benefit concert in Bath, on 20 November, in 'Mr Wiltshire's Great Room', for 'Messrs. Lashly [a flautist] and Leander'. Guadagni contributed two items: 'He was despised' from *Messiah* and an English song, 'How pleasing is beauty'.[39]

---

[36] There were four performances in 1751. See *The Choice of Hercules,* ed. Donald Burrows, London: Novello, 1982. For Guadagni's presumed participation, see Dean, *Handel's Dramatic Oratorios and Masques*, p. 586.

[37] *Salisbury Journal*, 23 Sept. 1751.

[38] *Salisbury Journal*, 23 Sept. 1751 and *Bath Journal* 30 Sept. 1751.

[39] *Bath Journal*, 18 Nov. 1751.

SEASON OF 1751–1752

In January 1752 he travelled to Dublin. The mid-eighteenth century has been described as a golden age for music in Ireland.[40] The number of musicians of international reputation settled in Dublin included Michael Arne, Dubourg, and Geminiani; still more were regular visitors, including Thomas Arne, Lampe, Pasquali, and Handel. The concert-going public was small, educated, affluent and enthusiastic. Dublin was well-provided with theatres and concert halls, the most important of these being the Great Music Hall in Fishamble Street, which saw the first performance of *Messiah* in 1742, and the Music Hall in Crow Street, originally built 'for the Practice of Italian Music'.[41] Dublin audiences had a keen taste for Handel's oratorios and enjoyed a wide variety of instrumental music, often presented in concerts by the many charitable organisations. There were at least eight hospitals in Dublin at this period supported by charitable fundraising, in addition to causes such as the Charitable Musical Society for the Relief of Imprisoned Debtors.[42]

What drew Guadagni to Dublin is not known, but he was probably influenced by his fellow musicians in Handel's oratorio company, who would have been able to paint an attractive picture of a small and cultivated society, eager for music and well able to afford to support it. It is entirely possible that he had already visited Dublin during the empty months in the summer of 1751, though there is no record of his presence there. An earlier visit would explain the speed and efficiency with which he made his mark in Dublin's musical calendar. Even if this were his first visit, his reputation in oratorio preceded him. Arriving in the city early in 1752, he was quickly engaged to sing at a private concert on 18 January. The event was described by Mrs Delany: 'Last Saturday we were invited to the Primate's to hear music…Our music was chiefly Italian—the *Stabat Mater* sung by Guadagni (whom you heard sing in Mr Handel's oratorios) and Mrs Oldmixon; Dubourg the principal violin: it was well performed, and some of the duet parts are very pretty.'[43] The *Stabat Mater* was Pergolesi's work for soprano and alto soloists and strings, a staple of Guadagni's repertory in the 1750s. His fellow performers were local celebrities: the English violinist Matthew Dubourg, who held the post of Master and Composer of State Music in Ireland and was prominent as soloist, orchestral player and conductor, notable for having led the orchestra for the first performance of *Messiah*. Mrs [*recte*: Miss] Oldmixon was an Irish soprano who later married the conductor Giovanni Battista Marella.

[40] Brian Boydell, 'The Dublin musical scene', *Journal of the Royal Musical Association* 105 (1978–79), p. 77.

[41] Ibid., p. 83.

[42] Denis Arnold, 'Charity music in eighteenth-century Dublin', *Galpin Society Journal* 21 (1968): 162–74.

[43] Mrs Delany to Mrs Dewes, 26 Jan. 1752, in *The Autobiography and Correspondence of Mary Granville, Mrs Delany*, ed. The Right Honourable Lady Llanover, iii, London: Richard Bentley, 1861, p. 80.

It is difficult to establish the extent of Guadagni's participation in the oratorios in Dublin. No singers are named in the press advertisements or librettos. We cannot assume he walked into all the available alto roles: an obvious rival was the Irish counter-tenor Daniel Sullivan, who had sung in a number of oratorios in London, taking the roles that Guadagni later assumed in *Samson* and *Saul*. It was certainly possible for Guadagni to have sung in two performances of *L'Allegro* given in Fishamble Street on 24 January and 10 April, and *Joshua* on 3 and 7 February; both works were conducted by Dubourg, with whom he was already acquainted. Guadagni must have been sufficiently well-known in Dublin for him to risk a concert for his own benefit in Crow Street on 8 February; on this occasion he again sang with Mrs Oldmixon, perhaps repeating the *Stabat Mater*. It is probable that he took his accustomed roles in *Judas Maccabaeus* on 17 February. He sang at four concerts in March: on 11 March, together with Mrs Oldmixon, he took part in a charity concert in Fishamble Street at noon, and in the evening, in Crow Street, he contributed to a benefit concert for the horn player Mr Andrews, which advertised 'the vocal part by Signor Guadagni, who will sing several favourite English and Italian songs.'[44] On 19 March he sang in another benefit concert for the double bass player Stephen Storace; the other soloist was Daniel Sullivan. There was a concert for his own benefit in Fishamble Street on 16 April, where he again advertised 'Italian and English songs',[45] and a performance of *Samson*, conducted by Dubourg, for Mrs Oldmixon's benefit on 27 April. This meagre information is all we know of Guadagni's Dublin season.

## SEASON OF 1752–1753

Nothing is known of Guadagni in the summer and autumn of 1752. He may well have repeated his West Country engagements. At the St Cecilia Festival held in Salisbury on 27 and 28 September, the oratorio repertory comprised *Samson* and *Judas Maccabaeus*, both of which included roles he had made his own. Unfortunately no soloists are named; there was the bare statement that 'There will be Performers Vocal and Instrumental, from London, Oxford and Bath'.[46] Notices for the concerts in Devizes on 6 and 7 November are similarly uninformative: 'By several Performers from London'.[47] Very few concerts were advertised in Bath this season, and none of them named Guadagni.

---

[44] See Brian Boydell, *A Dublin Musical Calendar 1700–1760*, Dublin, Irish Academic Press, 1988, p. 163.

[45] Ibid., p. 165.

[46] *Salisbury Journal*, 25 Sept. 1752.

[47] *Bath Journal*, 23 Oct. 1752.

We next hear of him in London in January 1753. With yet again no Italian opera at the King's Theatre, his career was about to take a new turn. The spring of 1753 was to be by far the busiest period of his professional life to date—perhaps one of his busiest seasons ever—as Guadagni took advantage of renewed activity in London concert life. A catalyst for this was the recently opened Great Room at 21 Dean Street in Soho. In December 1751, the violinist Felice Giardini and oboist Thomas Vincent had joined forces to promote a series of twenty subscription concerts in a room advertised as being 'disposed in the most convenient and elegant Manner for the reception of the Company, and kept in proper Warmth by the Help of a German Stove, to prevent them from catching Cold'.[48] The dimensions and structure of the room have not been recorded, though by 1760, if not before, it was virtually a theatre, possessing a pit and gallery. In 1753 it was already an established concert venue. In March Thomas Harris reported: 'I was last Tuesday evening at the concert of the delitantis [dilettantes] in Dean Street, where the room was entirely crowded with fine people'.[49] Not fine enough, however, for another correspondent, who confessed, 'The greatest pleasure to me of this winter...has been the concert at Soho [i.e. Dean Street] which I subscribed to, and attended without failing once. It's very ungenteel to like a publick concert, but I confess I was so far vulgar as to enjoy this mightily'.[50] The room was in demand for subscription series and benefit concerts, and both types were represented in Guadagni's engagements.

Two sets of subscription concerts were given in Dean Street in 1753. A series of twelve was directed by the itinerant violinist Carlo Chiabrano (or Chabran), lately arrived in London from Paris. Six more concerts were organized by Giuseppe Passerini, a versatile singer and violinist. Both Chiabrano and Passerini married singers, and their wives took part in the concerts too. In addition to singing in all eighteen subscription concerts—a reliable measure of his popularity—Guadagni contributed to six benefit concerts. At each concert, of whichever type, he would usually sing two arias and a duet, often including music by Ciampi (director and house composer of Crosa's ill-fated troupe) and Handel. A particular favourite was 'Return, O God of Hosts' from *Samson*, which in this single season he sang twice at Chiabrano's concerts, twice at Passerini's, at a benefit concert for Marianne Davies (a prodigy who played harpsichord and flute, shamelessly advertising her age as 'a child of nine years old'), and at the concert for the Decayed Musicians' Fund, besides taking part in two further oratorio performances at Covent Garden.

---

[48] *General Advertiser*, 9 Dec. 1751.

[49] Thomas to (his mother) Elizabeth Harris, 1 Mar. 1753, in Burrows and Dunhill, *Music and Theatre in Handel's World,* p. 286.

[50] C. Gilbert to Elizabeth Harris, 21 May 1753, in Burrows and Dunhill, *Music and Theatre,* p. 291.

It is impossible to reconstruct an exact schedule of Guadagni's engagements. Some concerts were postponed or cancelled, and cancellations were not always announced in the press. Passerini's last concert, repeatedly advertised, rescheduled, and cancelled, was delayed for over a month, revealing a disastrous lack of local knowledge:

The Reasons for putting off the Concert till the above Day are the following:

The Holy Week the Concert was put off, because all Diversions were deferred in London. The following Week it was put off, because many of the Subscribers were gone to Newmarket. The last Week it was put off, because the Room was taken; for that Reason Signor Passerini did advertise, that the Concert should be on Friday: He was again obliged to put off the Concert, because some of the principal Performers were engaged.[51]

It eventually took place on 17 May. Some concerts involved more than the single evening engagement implied: the concert promoted by François-André Danican Philidor on 23 February was preceded by an open rehearsal the day before to which ticket holders were invited, and this arrangement was not uncommon.[52] Meanwhile at Covent Garden there was a successful season of oratorios in which Guadagni's presence is presumed.[53] The dates slot neatly into his diary.[54] A surprise item this season is a single charity performance of Arne's *Alfred*, Guadagni's first attempt at English-language opera.

*Alfred* has a complex history. In 1740 Arne was commissioned to set a heroic masque by James Thomson for a private performance at the country house of Cliveden, as a component in an elaborate birthday party for the three-year-old daughter of Frederick Prince of Wales. The masque was a small-scale affair, with only seven musical numbers, one of which was Arne's most enduring success, 'Rule Britannia'. *Alfred* was given in Dublin in this form in 1744, and the following year

---

[51] *Public Advertiser*, 15 May 1753.

[52] Billed as 'Mr Philidor's Concert'. Several Philidors appear in this chapter, so a brief history of a confusing section of the family tree may be required: already the third generation of a musical dynasty, André Danican Philidor the elder (c.1647–1730), instrumentalist, composer, and principal copyist to Louis XIV, lived to be over 80 and married twice. Among the many skilled musicians in his family were his eldest son, Anne Danican Philidor (1681–1728), and his youngest son by his second wife, born 45 years later, François-André Danican Philidor (1726–1795). F.-A. D. Philidor lived in London from the mid-1740s, and in his lifetime was more renowned as a chess player than as a composer.

[53] 'The oratorios were never more constantly full than this spring'. Frances Griesdale to Elizabeth Harris, 12 Apr. 1753, in Burrows and Dunhill, *Music and Theatre*, p. 289.

[54] Winton Dean doubts Guadagni's participation in this oratorio because, although Handel clearly adapted the role of Hamor for a new singer for this performance, his part in the newly-written quintet is in the soprano clef, whereas Handel normally wrote for Guadagni in the alto clef; see *Handel's Dramatic Oratorios and Masques*, p. 619. See however *Jephtha*, ed. Kenneth Nott, Hallesche Händel-Ausgabe 1.30, Kassel: Bärenreiter, 2009, p. ix, col. 1.

revised for Drury Lane with additional music. The patriotic text appealed to the mood of the moment following the crushing of the Jacobite Rebellion. (The following month Arne had another popular success with his setting of 'God save the King', sung nightly at Drury Lane 'until the danger of the Young Pretender's rebellion had passed'.[55]) In 1751, *Alfred* appeared in a new version with which Arne had little to do: Garrick, aspiring to play the part of Alfred, had David Mallet transform the work into a play with a few songs, some of them by Burney. In 1753 Arne reclaimed his score and recast it as an English heroic opera. Among the changes was the addition of a new role, Prince Edward, created for Guadagni. Arne gave him a brilliant and war-like air, 'Vengeance, O come inspire me!'. It is among the relatively few bravura arias composed for Guadagni in the course of his career—not his preferred style, but one which he was presumably able to do justice to.[56] The revised work was performed at the King's Theatre at noon on 12 May, a benefit concert for the Lying-in Hospital. It is pleasing to think of Guadagni, with his notoriously imperfect English pronunciation, joining in the concluding bars of 'Rule Britannia'.

What we know of Guadagni's crowded diary for the spring of 1753 is summarised in Table 3.1. All concerts took place in Dean Street, all oratorios at Covent Garden, with the exception of the annual performance of *Messiah* at the Foundling Hospital. Allowing even minimal time for rehearsals and note-learning (Guadagni's roles in *Jephtha* and *Alfred* were new to him), it was a very busy period.

SEASON OF 1753–1754

In the autumn of 1753, Guadagni headed for Paris. It would be interesting to know how far he was aware of the 'Querelle des Bouffons', a very public debate concerning the rival merits of French and Italian opera, fought out in pamphlets and performances between 1752 and 1754.[57] A major contribution to the debate, Rousseau's *Lettre sur la musique française*, was published within a month of Guadagni's arrival in Paris, and he could hardly have avoided hearing it discussed. Of more relevance to his future career is the fact that the librettist Calzabigi was also in Paris at this time, engaged in preparing an edition of Metastasio's collected works. Calzabigi's famous preface to this edition, 'Dissertazione su le poesie drammatiche del sig. Abate Pietro Metastasio', contains his first published views on what became, within a decade, the reform of opera—a career-changing development for Guadagni.[58]

[55] Julian Herbage, 'Arne', *The New Grove Dictionary of Music and Musicians*, London: Macmillan, 1980.

[56] The aria can be heard on 'Arias for Guadagni'.

[57] The principal documents in the case are reproduced in facsimile in Denise Launay, ed., *La Querelle des Bouffons*, Geneva: Minkoff, 1973.

[58] 'Dissertazione di Ranieri de' Calzabigi, dell'Accademia di Cortona, su le poesie drammatiche del sig. Abate Pietro Metastasio', in *Poesie del Signor Abate Pietro Metastasio*, Paris, 1755.

TABLE 3.1

Guadagni's engagements in spring 1753

| Date | Event | Notes on Guadagni's repertory |
|---|---|---|
| 9 January | Benefit concert for Mr Grosman | |
| 20 January | Chiabrano's subscription concert (1) | 'Le dolcezze dell'amore' (Ciampi); 'Non ha ragione, ingrato' (Hasse); duets with Frasi |
| 27 January | Chiabrano's subscription concert (2) | 'Non mi piacque, ingiusti' (Ciampi); 'A me, che gioia' (?); duet with Miss Turner |
| 3 February | Chiabrano's subscription concert (3) | 'Il pastor' (Ciampi), 'Return, O God of Hosts' (Handel); with Frasi, the duet 'Ah, m' ingannasti' from *La caduta de' giganti*, the first known occasion when Guadagni sang music by Gluck |
| 10 February | Chiabrano's subscription concert (4) | 'Pious orgies' (Handel); 'Destrier che all'armi usato' (Ciampi); duet with Miss Turner |
| 17 February | Chiabrano's subscription concert (5) | 'Rondinella' (Ciampi); 'Figlio se più' (?); duet with Frasi |
| 22 February | open rehearsal for Mr Philidor's concert | |
| 23 February | Mr Philidor's concert | |
| 24 February | Chiabrano's subscription concert (6) | 'Il pastor' and 'Destrier che all'armi usato' (Ciampi); duet with Miss Turner |
| 3 March | Chiabrano's subscription concert (7) | 'Return, O God of Hosts' (Handel); duet with Frasi |
| 9 March | *Alexander's Feast* and *The Choice of Hercules* | |

*(Continued)*

TABLE 3.1 (Continued)

| Date | Event | Notes on Guadagni's repertory |
|---|---|---|
| 10 March | Chiabrano's subscription concert (8) | 'O beauteous queen' (Handel); 'Le dolcezze dell'amore' (Ciampi); duet with Miss Turner |
| 12 March | Benefit concert for Mr Barbandt | |
| 14 March | *Alexander's Feast* and *The Choice of Hercules* | |
| 15 March | Passerini's subscription concert (1) | |
| 16 March | *Jephtha* | |
| 17 March | Chiabrano's subscription concert (9) | 'Son fatturato' (Ciampi); 'Se possono tanto' (?Handel); duet with Frasi |
| 19 March | Benefit concert for Miss Davies | 'Il pastor' (Ciampi); 'Return, O God of Hosts' (Handel) |
| 21 March | *Jephtha* | |
| 22 March | Passerini's subscription concert (2) | |
| 23 March | *Judas Maccabaeus* | |
| 24 March | Chiabrano's subscription concert (10) | 'Negli occhi tuoi vedo' (?);'Pious orgies' (Handel); duet with Miss Turner |
| 26 March | Benefit concert for Chiabrano | 'Rondinella' (Ciampi); 'Parto da te' (Gluck); duet with Sig.ra Chiabrano |
| 28 March | *Judas Maccabaeus* | |
| 29 March | Passerini's subscription concert (3) | 'Destrier che all'armi usato' (Ciampi); 'Return, O God of Hosts' (Handel); duet with Sig.ra Passerini |
| 30 March | *Judas Maccabaeus* | |
| 31 March | Chiabrano's subscription concert (11) | 'Destrier che all'armi usato' (Ciampi); 'Dearest Phyllis' (Ciampi); duet with Frasi |
| 4 April | *Samson* | |

(*Continued*)

TABLE 3.1 (Continued)

| Date | Event | Notes on Guadagni's repertory |
|---|---|---|
| 5 April | Passerini's subscription concert (4) | |
| 6 April | *Samson* | |
| 7 April | Chiabrano's subscription concert (12) | 'O beauteous queen' (Handel); 'Destrier che all'armi usato' (Ciampi); duet with Miss Turner |
| 11 April | *Samson* | |
| 12 April | Passerini's subscription concert (5) | 'Return, O God of Hosts' (Handel); 'Stabat Mater' (Pergolesi) |
| 13 April | *Messiah* | |
| 28 April | Benefit concert for Miss Turner | |
| 30 April | Concert for Decayed Musicians' Fund (King's Theatre) | 'Return, O God of Hosts' (Handel); 'Il pastor' (Ciampi) |
| 1 May | *Messiah* (Foundling Hospital) | |
| 2 May | Benefit concert for Sig. Ranieri | |
| 12 May | *Alfred* (King's Theatre) | |
| 17 May | Passerini's subscription concert (6) | |

Guadagni's first recorded engagement was in the private theatre at Versailles, where he sang at the invitation of the Dauphine Maria Josepha of Saxony:

On 13 [October] at Versailles, in the apartments of Madame la Dauphine, was performed the Italian opera called *Didone abbandonata*, the music of which is by Hasse.... The principal roles were sung by Caffarelli, Guadagni, Chambalante [Ciambalanti] and Albanese. Guadagni came from England.

His fine performance and the beauty of his voice have won him a great reputation.[59]

Castratos played an ambivalent role in French musical life. Louis XIV relished the voice, and admitted castratos into the Chapelle Royale from 1676. They soon established a small permanent community at court, and, as Patrick Barbier has uncovered, for more than fifty years a house was provided for their use in the Montreuil district of Versailles.[60] They continued to be represented in the Chapelle Royale up to the Revolution. Opportunities for employment were, however, limited, and their earning potential in Paris was small in comparison with the large sums available to the best of the castratos elsewhere in Europe.[61] Popular taste excluded them from appearing as soloists on the public stage, although a few were employed in the chorus at the Opéra, singing the soprano line alongside female singers, of whom there was no shortage in Paris.[62] Their only opportunity to shine as soloists was at the Concert Spirituel, for much of the eighteenth century the focus of Parisian music outside the Opéra. This prestigious concert series, founded in 1725 by Anne Danican Philidor, was held in the Salle des Suisses at the Château des Tuileries, and provided devotional Lenten fare, featuring sacred vocal works and instrumental music, while the Opéra was closed. Italian music, especially that of Pergolesi and Geminiani, was popular, and castratos took their place among a number of Italian musicians who appeared in the programmes. Although the presence of Italians in Paris was always politically sensitive, it seems that at the Concert Spirituel they met no opposition. The Concert deliberately avoided the heated Franco-Italian disputes of the 'Querelle des Bouffons'.[63] But it was at court that castratos received their warmest welcome, and the Dauphine was their most fervent admirer.

Although his other engagements are unknown, Guadagni must have remained in Paris till the end of the year, since, again at the invitation of the Dauphine, he sang at

---

[59] 'On exécuta le 13 à Versailles, chez Madame la Dauphine, l'opéra italien intitulé *Didon abandonnée*, dont la musique est du sieur Hasse….Les principaux rôles furent chantés par les sieurs Cafarieli, Guadagni, Champalante et Albanese. Le sieur Guadagni arrive d'Angleterre. Sa grande exécution et la beauté de sa voix lui ont acquis beaucoup de réputation.' *La Gazette*, 20 Oct. 1753. Two numbers from *Didone abbandonata* can be heard on 'Arias for Guadagni'.

[60] Patrick Barbier, *La maison des Italiens*, Paris: Grasset, 1998.

[61] Ibid., p. 180.

[62] Ibid., p. 230.

[63] Constant Pierre compares the 'lutte assez vive et même discourtoise' at the opera with the 'calme, sinon l'indifférence, [qui] continua de régner au Concert.' *Histoire du concert spirituel 1725–1790*, Paris: Heugel, 1975, p. 108.

Versailles on 17 and 19 December, sharing a concert of Italian arias with Caffarelli.[64] He may well have left Paris in January 1754 (at the same time as Caffarelli), returning to Paris to give seven recitals at the Concert Spirituel in April 1754. The mechanics of the contacts and patronage that prompted such invitations are hard to untangle. François-André Danican Philidor, the 'Mr Philidor' for whom Guadagni had performed in London the previous year, had just returned to the French capital, and was in the process of applying for the post of court composer. In this he was unsuccessful, but he may well have sought to enhance his international credentials by securing a visit from the increasingly celebrated castrato. The director of the Concert Spirituel at this period was Joseph-Nicolas-Pancrace Royer, a native of Turin but a naturalised Frenchman. In Holy Week (8–12 April) 1754 Guadagni gave nightly performances of Pergolesi's *Stabat Mater*; his fellow soloist was the soprano-register castrato Albanese, and the work was given in an arrangement by Royer with added choruses. In Easter week he gave another performance of the work, and sang two Italian arias at a further concert. The *Mercure de France* commented favourably: 'M. Guadagni, whom we have not heard before, sang the contralto part; his voice has a limited range, but is pleasing and touching.'[65] If Guadagni had been invited to sing at Versailles during this visit, there is no record of the fact.

SEASON OF 1754–1755

Back in London in the autumn of 1754, Guadagni joined a burletta troupe at Covent Garden as second man in a cast which included Anna Castelli, Cristiano Tedeschini Korbitz, Eugenia Mellini, Gaetano Quilici and Ninetta de Rossenaw. The company gave two settings of Goldoni's comedies: Galuppi's *L'Arcadia in Brenta* was given twice in November, and Ciampi's *Bertoldo, Bertoldino e Cacasenno all corte del re Alboino* received five performances between 9 December and 3 January. The reception was mixed: 'The burletta opera begun again last night. I was at an assembly where many people came who had been at it and consequently heard that it was very good & very bad & neither one nor t'other.'[66] The enterprise quickly failed, and the singers gave three benefit concerts to restore their finances:

> The Managers…having been engaged to come over by a Man, who pretended to associate himself with them, in order to carry on the Burlettas in the said

---

[64] Barbier, op. cit., p. 215.

[65] 'M. Guadagni que nous n'avons pas encore entendu, y a chanté le contralto ou bas dessus: sa voix n'est pas étendue, mais elle est agréable et touchante.' *Mercure de France*, May 1754, p. 184.

[66] C. Gilbert to Elizabeth Harris, 19 Nov. 1754, in Burrows and Dunhill, *Music and Theatre*, p. 298.

Theatre, who promised them great Advantages, but as the Success did not in the least answer their Expectation, the abovesaid Person has disappeared, and left them not only to pay several Debts, of which he was up to pay the Half, but has likewise involved them in the utmost Difficulties.'[67]

The three benefit concerts were given at the Little Theatre, the latter two including performances of *La serva padrona*, which was beginning to prove as popular in London as it was in Paris.

The opera-going public were soon consoled for the collapse of the burletta troupe by the appearance of a new English opera at Drury Lane: *The Fairies*, adapted from *A Midsummer Night's Dream* and set by John Christopher Smith.[68] The adaptation of Shakespeare's play has been attributed to David Garrick, and while he denied this, as theatre manager, he was the moving spirit behind the production.[69] He certainly wrote the prologue, which he delivered in a typically dramatic manner:

> The English opera went off very well last Monday, & met with great applause.—
> Just after the overture was begun, Garrick stepped in upon the stage & advancing to the orchestra bid the music stop, & then he spoke a prologue, very satyrical upon the Italian operas.... After the prologue was ended, the overture began again, and then everything went on regular.[70]

Garrick's prologue includes a routine denigration of English opera put into the mouths of two foreigners, and attempts to invest Smith with some of Handel's fame:

> Why would this rash Fool, this Englishman,
> Attempt an Op'ra 'tis the strangest Plan!
> Struck with the wonders of his Master's Art
> Whose sacred Dramas shake and melt the Heart
> Whose Heaven-born strains the coldest Breast inspire,
> Whose Chorus-Thunder sets the Soul on Fire!
> Inflam'd, astonish'd! at those magic Airs,

---

[67] *Public Advertiser*, 22 Jan. 1755.

[68] Son of Handel's treasurer and principal copyist, in 1755 Smith was organist at the Foundling Hospital, where he directed the annual performances of *Messiah* after Handel's death.

[69] Garrick to James Murphey French, 7 Dec. 1756: 'I received your letter, which indeed is no more facetious than just—for if you mean that *I* was the person who altered the *Midsummer Night's Dream*, and the *Tempest* into operas, you are much mistaken.' In *Letters of David Garrick*, ed. David M. Little and George M. Kahrl, i, London: Oxford University Press, 1963, p. 256.

[70] George Harris to (his brother) James Harris, 6 Feb. 1755, Burrows and Dunhill, *Music and Theatre*, p. 301.

When Samson groans, and frantic Saul despairs,
The Pupil wrote—his Work is now before ye.
And waits your Stamp of Infamy, or Glory![71]

The cast included the tenor John Beard (Theseus), the singer who had made the part of Samson his own, and two Italians, Guadagni, as Lysander, and Christina Passerini as Hermia. The role of Oberon was sung by the treble 'Master Reinhold', son of the Handelian bass Henry Theodore Reinhold, whose family Garrick had generously supported after the death of Reinhold senior in 1751.

Smith's setting does indeed show the influence of Handel. Guadagni's first air, 'When that gay season did us lead / to the tann'd haycock in the mead' is imbued with the lyrical pastoral idiom of *L'Allegro*. His other arias, 'Say lovely dream' and 'Do not call it sin in me / that I am foresworn for thee' are more operatic, with extensive ornamentation; both include a number of held notes on which Guadagni may have introduced the *messa di voce* (crescendo and diminuendo) for which he later became celebrated. The role exploits an exceptionally wide range. 'When that gay season' is entirely within an alto compass, from a to e″; 'Say lovely dream' treats his voice as a mezzo, taking him up to f″, and in his duet with Passerini, 'Not the silver doves that fly', he matches her soprano range, echoing phrases that take him to g″.[72]

Walpole took a somewhat jaundiced view of the whole enterprise:

Garrick has produced a detestable English opera, which is crowded by all true lovers of their country. To mark the opposition to Italian operas, it is sung by some cast [i.e., second-rate] singers, two Italians, and a French girl [Miss Poitier], and the chapel [Chapel Royal] boys; and to regale us with sense it is Shakespeare's *Midsummer Night's Dream*, which is forty times more nonsensical than the worst translation of any Italian opera-books—But such sense and such harmony are irresistible![73]

Guadagni's imperfect English was noticed:

This opera I believe, won't be considered as a capital performance.—I daren't upon only once hearing presume to criticize; but can safely say, there were some very pleasing songs, & one duette sung by Passerini & Guadagni seemed to me

[71] The Prologue is printed in the second edition of the libretto, London: J. and R. Tonson and S. Draper, 1755.
[72] The score, omitting the recitative, dances, and one chorus, was published by Walsh, 1755. 'Say lovely dream' can be heard on 'Arias for Guadagni'.
[73] Walpole to Richard Bentley, 23 Feb. 1755, *Correspondence*, xxxv, pp. 209–10.

something very elegant.—Passerini did her part extremely well.—Guadagni was defective as to his pronouncing his recitative; of which he had too large a share.—But in this respect he'll certainly mend, the oftener the piece is performed.[74]

*The Fairies* ran for nine nights and was a financial success,[75] but, according to Burney, was not revived in subsequent seasons since its success had depended on the talents of the soloists Guadagni and Passerini.[76]

The season ended with another crowded schedule of oratorios and concerts. In the Earl of Shaftesbury's opinion, 'the singers Frazi and Guadagni do incomparably this season'.[77] Guadagni probably sang in *Alexander's Feast* and *The Choice of Hercules, L'Allegro, Samson, Joseph, Theodora, Judas Maccabaeus* and *Messiah*. He may also have sung at a performance of *Esther* given as a benefit for Miss Turner in Dean Street in March. There was the usual concert at the King's Theatre for the Decayed Musicians' Fund and benefit concerts in Dean Street for Mrs Ogle (widow of the owner of the Dean Street property), Miss Davies and Frasi. Guadagni made a rare appearance at Hickford's Music Room, an older and less fashionable venue than Dean Street, for benefit concerts for a Dublin colleague Giovanni Battista Marella, and the harpist John Parry. His last engagements in England appear to be a performance of *Alexander's Feast* as a benefit for Christina Passerini at the Little Theatre on 18 April and a last *Messiah* at the Foundling Hospital on 1 May.

[74] George Harris to James Harris, 6 Feb. 1755, Burrows and Dunhill, *Music and Theatre*, p. 301.

[75] George Winchester Stone Jr, "*A Midsummer Night's Dream* in the hands of Garrick and Coleman", *Proceedings of the Modern Language Association* (June, 1939): p. 469.

[76] Burney, *General History*, ii, p. 681. Burney mistakenly names Frasi as the female lead.

[77] Letter dated 1 Mar. 1755, Earl of Shaftesbury to James Harris, in Burrows and Dunhill, *Music and Theatre*, p. 303.

# 4

## Guadagni the Actor

THE SHORT SEASON of working with Garrick had a profound effect on Guadagni's reputation. To Garrick, and Garrick alone, Guadagni's acting skills have been attributed. Every subsequent biographer has made the connection and ignored any other possible influence that might have turned the 'charming boy with somewhat clumsy feet' into an actor who had 'no equal on any stage in Europe'. The myth originated with Burney, who was motivated to exaggerate his countryman's role, and assert the superiority of the British acting tradition over continental styles. It is impossible to ignore Burney's opinion. No other professional critic observed the singer at such close quarters over so long a period of time, and few made such detailed comments about his acting, such comments being especially useful since there are no images of the singer on stage. According to Burney: 'As an actor, he seems to have had no equal on any stage in Europe: his figure was uncommonly elegant and noble; his countenance replete with beauty, intelligence, and dignity; and his attitudes and gestures were so full of grace and propriety, that they would have been excellent studies for a statuary'.[1] But Garrick was far from being the only performer whose acting influenced Guadagni.

Much was written in the eighteenth century about the technique of acting.[2] Dramatists and managers laid down prescriptions and theatre-goers contributed

---

This chapter draws extensively on my ' "No equal on any stage in Europe": Guadagni as actor', first published in *Musical Times*, 151 (2010): 9–21. I am grateful for permission to reproduce this material.

[1] Written on the occasion of Guadagni's second London visit, 1769–1771. Burney, *General History* ii, p. 876.

[2] For an invaluable survey of the sources see Dene Barnett, 'The Performance Practice of Acting: The Eighteenth Century', *Theatre Research International*, 1977–1981 (see Bibliography for individual references); also Barnett's

letters and memoirs. The reform of opera touched all theatrical practice, both in the spoken theatre and in the opera house. Just as scores and librettos underwent a process of transformation in the hands of Traetta and Gluck, Frugoni and Calzabigi, so too with scenery (the Galliari brothers), costume (Diderot) and dance (Angiolini and Noverre). There was a marked shift between the look of an opera on the stage in the first half of the eighteenth century and how it might have been produced a decade or so later. Guadagni was in the company of the modernisers. He worked with the most progressive artists of his day, and played a part in many ground-breaking productions. He involved himself deeply in the reform of acting, and even urged a further development of his own: the re-education of audience behaviour.

He was not, it seems, a natural actor. When in October 1748 Guadagni arrived in London as a member of Crosa's buffa company, Franz Pirker's immediate impression was of Guadagni's clumsy acting. A violinist in the orchestra at the King's Theatre, Pirker was well-placed to watch Guadagni as he attempted to master his craft. Since Pirker's comments are the only adverse criticism Guadagni's acting ever attracted, it is reasonable to infer he was a quick learner, though Burney waited some six years before recording an improvement in a comment that found its way into every subsequent assessment of the singer: 'His ideas of acting were taken... from Garrick, who, when he was performing in an English opera called the *Fairies*, took... much pleasure in forming him as an actor'.[3] However, by the time Guadagni met Garrick in 1755, he had already worked with Filippo Laschi and Pietro Pertici, the two actors about whom Walpole, not an easy man to please in matters of theatrical performance, enthused: 'There never were two better comedians than Pertici and Laschi'.[4] When Guadagni first appeared on the London stage he must have needed some training. Brought up to be a church musician, with only two or three *opera seria* productions under his belt and (possibly) totally inexperienced in the more demanding genre of comic opera, it is most likely to have been Laschi and Pertici who 'formed him as an actor' at this time.

The pair of them have impressive references. Joseph von Sonnenfels saw Laschi in Vienna in 1768, and praised his 'profound knowledge of both acting and music that would assure him a place among the most excellent theatrical performers of Italy'. He also described Laschi as 'never seeking applause at the expense of Nature',[5] a practice

---

*The art of gesture: the practices and principles of 18th century acting*, Heidelberg: Carl Winter University Press, 1987.

[3] Burney, *General History*, ii, p. 876.

[4] Letter to Horace Mann, 23 Mar. 1749, *Correspondence*, xx, p. 41.

[5] 'Laschi sucht nie auf Kosten der Natur das handelklatschen des Parterrs... seine tiefen Kenntnisse, sowohl in der Schauspielkunst als der Musik, versichern ihm indessen noch itzt einen Platz unter den vortrefflichsten Teatralpersonen Italiens.' *Briefe über die Wienerische Schaubühne*, ed. Hilde Haider-Pregler, letter dated 2 Mar. 1768, Graz: Akademische Druck und Verlagsanstalt, 1988, pp. 70–71.

that Guadagni came to adopt, though whether from principle or from 'high notions of his own importance'[6] it is impossible to say. In 1782 the young Michael Kelly was sent to study with Laschi:

> Lord Cowper advised me to take some lessons in acting, for which purpose he introduced me to Laschi, who had been the greatest actor of his day, but was at that time living in retirement at a country house near Florence. He undertook to instruct me, and did it *con amore*; nothing could exceed the pains he took with me, and I endeavoured by rigid attention to reap the full benefit of his instructions.[7]

Pertici, recommended to the London public as 'one of the greatest comedians of his age and country',[8] also attracted a range of endorsements. Casanova saw him on the stage in 1756, and his comments are a reminder that many *buffo* singers were active in both spoken and sung drama: 'I saw Pertici with pleasure; being old and no longer able to sing, he took part in in comedies in which he proved to be a fine actor—a rare thing, because both male and female singers, relying on the power of their voices, neglect the art of acting'.[9]

Unfortunately, for the many writers who identify an 'excellent theatrical performer' or a 'fine actor', few specify the techniques that made them great. Pertici's career affords one possible clue. He was intimately connected throughout his life with the foremost dramatist in Europe, Goldoni. He sang in Goldoni's operas and acted in his spoken comedies, and in Goldoni's opinion Pertici was admirable in both.[10] At this period of his life, Goldoni was involved in a debate about acting in the legitimate theatre, the bone of contention being the use of masks.[11] Apart from librettos for serious and comic operas, the bulk of his work was for spoken theatre. For some years he had produced examples of the popular genre of semi-improvised comedy, which used traditional *commedia dell'arte* characters who always acted in mask. Gradually, and in the face of much opposition from his audience, Goldoni turned his back on this genre, and, taking Molière for his

---

[6] Burney, *General History*, ii, p. 876.

[7] Kelly, *Reminiscences* (1826), i, p. 54.

[8] *Daily Advertiser*, 17 Nov. 1748.

[9] 'Je vis Pertici avec plaisir; étant vieux et ne pouvant plus chanter, il jouait la comédie, et est un bon acteur, ce qui est rare; car les chanteurs, hommes et femmes, se fiant sur la durée de leur voix, négligent l'art de la scène'. Jacques de Seingalt Casanova, *Histoire de ma vie*, vii, Paris: La Sirène, 1928, p. 136.

[10] 'assai noto al mondo per l'eccellente sua abilità nelle parti buffe per musica e presentemente bravissimo attore nelle commedie in prosa a Firenze.' Goldoni, Preface to *Il cavaliere e la dama*, Florence, 1749–50.

[11] See Gianni Cicali, *Attori e ruoli nell'opera buffa italiana del settecento*, Florence: Le Lettere, 2005.

model, introduced comedies of situation, featuring realistic individuals who acted unmasked. The development was surprisingly unpopular. Goldoni failed to win the argument in Italy, and withdrew to Paris for a more sympathetic reception. In his memoirs, he rehearsed the arguments he had made nearly half a century earlier:

> The mask must always hinder the performance of an actor in his expression of joy or sorrow; no matter whether he is in love, angry, or good-humoured, he must always exhibit the same features; and however he may gesticulate and vary his tone of voice, he can never show by his facial expressions, which are the interpreters of the heart, the different passions with which his soul is moved....Nowadays the actor is required to possess a soul; and the soul concealed beneath a mask is like fire under ashes.[12]

For Goldoni, facial expression was the core of successful acting. He surely would not have described Pertici as a 'bravissimo attore' had he not excelled in this aspect, and it would be surprising if Guadagni had not learned the lesson in his season of acting at Pertici's side.

There is plenty of advice in the literature as to how facial expression should be employed. At the beginning of the century, the range was limited and formulaic: 'You must lift up or cast down your Eyes according as the Nature of the Things you speak of; Thus if of Heaven, your eyes naturally are lifted up; if of Earth, or Hell, or anything terrestrial, they are naturally cast down'.[13] By the mid-century, acting required a less mechanical approach: 'The Face is the grand *Index* to the mind...Every *feature*, every *muscle*, may be made to *speak*...without the least Assistance from *Speech*'.[14]

Both of these injunctions come from essays on spoken drama. Developments in the legitimate theatre tend to precede those in opera by several decades, and by the time of Guadagni's second London visit, facial expression was held to be as essential for singers as it was for actors. Mancini's influential essay recommended that 'this knowledge of changing the face, showing now ferocity, now sweetness, then

---

[12] 'Le masque doit toujours faire beaucoup de tort a l'action de l'Acteur, soit dans la joie, soit dans le chagrin; qu'il soit amoureux farouche, ou plaisant, c'est toujours le même cuir qui se montre; e il a beau gesticuler e changer de ton, il ne sera jamais connoître, par les traits du visage qui sont les interprètes du cœur, les differentes passions dont son ame est agitée...on veut aujourd'hui que l'Acteur ait de l'ame, et l'ame sous le masque est comme le feu sous les cendres.' Goldoni, *Mémoires*, ii, Paris, 1787, p. 196.

[13] Thomas Betterton, *The life of Mr Thomas Betterton*, London, 1710, p. 71.

[14] [Roger Pickering], *Reflections upon Theatrical Expression in Tragedy*, London, 1755, pp. 40–41.

tenderness, affection, ire, disgust … is the most beautiful part of the action which the actor can use'.[15] The point was underlined in Corri's treatise *The Singer's Preceptor*:

SCHOLAR:   I never conceived any attention to the variation of countenance necessary, unless I were a professional singer.
MASTER:   You are much mistaken, for words either in speaking or singing have most effect on the heart, when accompanied with suitable expression of countenance.[16]

Significantly, Corri went on to quote Sheridan's tribute to Garrick:

> The Grace of Action—the adapted Mien
> Faithful as nature to the varied scene.

Guadagni worked with Pertici for one season, with Laschi for two; he shared the stage with Garrick for a bare six weeks, but, thanks to Burney, to this day it is Garrick's art that is always mentioned in connection with the singer. We have more precise information on Garrick's acting and the impression it made on his contemporaries than we do about Laschi or Pertici. Like Goldoni's actors, Garrick was admired for the range and truthfulness of his facial expressions. The French dramatist Charles Collé saw Garrick act the dagger scene from *Macbeth*:

> He gave us the scene where Macbeth thinks he sees a dagger in the air … it would be impossible to paint a situation better, to act it with more warmth and yet to maintain complete control over himself. His face expresses all the passions one after the other, without grimacing even though this scene is full of dreadful and turbulent action'.[17]

Garrick also won praise for his expressive voice, commended as being 'neither whining, bellowing, or grumbling, but in whatever character he assimilates, perfectly easy in its transitions, natural in its cadence, and beautiful in its elocution'.[18]

[15] Giambattista Mancini, *Riflessioni pratiche sopra il canto figurato* (Milan, 1774), tr. Edward Forman, Illinois: Pro Musica Press, 1967, p. 75.
[16] Domenico Corri, *The Singer's Preceptor*, London, 1810, p. 4.
[17] 'Il nous esquisse la scène où Macbeth croit voir un poignard en l'air … il n'est pas possible de mieux peindre une situation, de la rendre avec plus de chaleur, et de posséder en même temps davantage. Son visage exprime toutes les passions successivement, sans faire aucune grimace, quoique ce scène soit pleine de mouvements terribles et tumultueux.' 13 July 1751, Charles Collé, *Journal et mémoires*, ed. Honoré Bonhomme, i, Paris, 1868, p. 332.
[18] *Gentleman's Magazine*, 12 (1742), p. 527.

This expressive quality has obvious parallels with the declamatory singing that was Guadagni's most praised technique.

At the heart of Garrick's innovations lay his movement on stage. Before Garrick, actors in spoken tragedy had tended to deliver their speeches while holding a static pose in a predetermined spot on the stage. Garrick, however, moved about the stage while speaking. One of the most vivid accounts of the sheer novelty of his technique is given by the dramatist Richard Cumberland, who saw him act in the same play as the Irish actor James Quin:

> With very little variation of cadence, and in a deep, full tone, accompanied by a sawing kind of action…[Quin] rolled out his heroics with an air of dignified indifference, that seemed to disdain the plaudits that were bestowed on him.…Then I beheld Garrick, then young and light and alive in every feature, come bounding on the stage…heavens, what a transition!—it seemed as if a whole century had been stept over in the transition of a single scene.[19]

Acting in *opera seria* was necessarily more static than in spoken drama or comic opera, not least because of the fashion for exaggerated perspective scenery that meant that a singer could not 'bound' or even move freely up and down stage without appearing seriously distorted against the foreshortened perspective. Some singers must indeed have flouted visual credibility in this way, since Algarotti mocked 'imaginary giants' who 'dwindle by degrees as they come forward', and characters who come on stage at a point where 'the capitals of the columns rise no higher than their shoulders.'[20] Courting such ridicule must, however, have been rare: eighteenth-century engravings of opera scenes tend to show the singers well forward of the flats, confined to the front stage or *proscenio*, a placing which favoured the projection of their voices but where they would have had very little space to move freely and in a natural manner. Metastasio favoured this traditional disposition. In a much-quoted letter to the librettist Giovanni Claudio Pasquini he allotted the characters fixed stage positions in the *proscenio* (while arguing that this was a particularly liberal suggestion since he did not place his characters exclusively according to their rank or gender).[21]

Movement on the opera stage suffered a further restriction. A convention, explicit or implied in a number of eighteenth-century treatises on acting, assumed that

[19] Richard Cumberland, *Memoirs of Richard Cumberland*, London, 1806, p. 59.

[20] Francesco Algarotti, *An essay on the opera* (tr. anon., 1768), ed. Robin Burgess, Lampeter and New York: Edwin Mellen Press, 2005, p. 55.

[21] Letter dated 10 Feb. 1748. Metastasio's letter are accessible online at www.liberliber.it/mediateca/libri/m/metastasio/lettere_edizione_brunelli/pdf/letter_p.pdf. Also in vols. 3–5 of Bruno Brunelli, *Tutte le opere di Pietro Metastasio*, Verona: Mondadori, 1951–1965.

gesticulation was confined to the recitatives. In arias a singer was still expected to hold a pose, very different from Garrick's fluid action during a soliloquy. Mancini, for example, locates his instructions on 'actio' within his chapter on recitative, apparently ignoring the possibility of acting during the arias.[22]

Guadagni rejected this tradition. He may have felt free to blur the distinction between aria and recitative because so much of his repertory did just that. The quantity of accompanied recitative he was allocated increased markedly in the later decades of his career. In *Orfeo*, for example, the bulk of his role consisted in declamatory singing of various kinds, from the detached interjections in the opening chorus to the expansive arioso 'Che puro ciel'; there is no clear-cut distinction between unstructured airs such as 'Men tiranne' and measured accompanied recitative like 'Numi! barbari Numi'. We learn from Burney that Guadagni did not restrict his acting to recitative, but acted in the few genuine arias in this opera: Burney specifically commended the singer's attitudes *and action* (my italics) while singing the lyrical aria 'Che farò'.[23]

Theatrical sources from the first half of the century suggest that hand and arm gestures, like eye and facial movements, were formal and decorative rather than natural and expressive. Some writers recommended that all movement should be based on the structured positions of dance.[24] Many instruction manuals contain engravings of representative postures.[25] Some illustrations use arrows to indicate a succession of movements, showing how the passage from one hand position to another might make a harmonious pattern without necessarily conveying any identifiable emotion. The acting reforms associated with Garrick avoided stock poses, and aimed to make each gesture individual and meaningful. (A parallel reform was being made in dance, moving from geometric patterns to expressive 'pantomime' in the second half of the century.) Garrick's most innovative hand gesture, with splayed fingers to indicate extreme emotion, was captured by Hogarth in 1745. (See Figure 4.1.)

This pose was utterly different from the instructions in early eighteenth-century acting manuals to keep the second, third and fourth fingers together and gesture with thumb and index finger: 'Then let the fingers be arranged in such a way, that

---

[22] Mancini tr. Forman, p. 74. On the static delivery of arias see also Barnett, 'The Performance Practice of Acting', *Theatre Research International*, 1977, pp. 157–86; Colley Cibber, *A critical edition of An apology for the life of Mr Colley Cibber, comedian*, ed. J. M. Evans, New York: Garland, 1987, p. 225; Sven H Hansell, 'Stage Deportment and Scenographic Design in the Italian Opera of the Settecento', *International Musicological Society, Congress Report, (Copenhagen 1972)*, i, pp. 415–24; Hellmuth Christian Wolff, *Die Händel-Oper auf der modernen Bühne*, Leipzig: Deutscher Verlag, 1957, pp. 28–30.

[23] Burney, *General History*, ii, p. 877.

[24] Francesco Riccoboni, *L'art du théâtre*, Paris, 1750, cited in Wolff op. cit., p. 29.

[25] See especially Franciscus Lang, *Dissertatio de actione scenica*, Munich, 1727. For a brief but informative demonstration of gesture in early eighteenth-century opera, see www.baroquegestures.com.

FIGURE 4.1  Garrick as Richard III by Hogarth. (Courtesy National Museums, Liverpool, Walker Gallery)

as a rule the index finger is stretched out straight, the rest being curved by degrees, more and more drawn in towards the palm....It is wrong and unseemly to spread the fingers of the hands.'[26] Garrick's gesture became his trademark—literally so, since he had Hogarth's image engraved on his visiting card. It is therefore entirely possible that an anonymous artist's satirical representation of Guadagni before the Bow Street magistrates some thirty years later intended to make a connection between the actor and the singer: the banner parodies Guadagni's faulty English and the image caricatures his use of Garrick's open hand gesture (see Figure 0.1).

Garrick's very 'naturalness' pitched him into the middle of an intriguing debate. Some mid-century writers, for example the dramatist Aaron Hill, argued that the only skill an actor needed was to feel an emotion in order to portray what he felt.[27] Diderot held the opposite view, arguing that actors needed technique rather than feeling: 'Extreme emotion makes for mediocre actors...it is the complete absence of emotion that is necessary to produce sublime actors.'[28] What we know of Guadagni's attitude to his roles, notably his increasing empathy in the later stages of his career with the character of Orfeo in settings by a variety of composers, implies a degree

[26] Lang, *Dissertatio*, tr. Barnett, *Theatre Research International* 3 (1977): 6, 18.

[27] Aaron Hill, 'The art of acting', *The works of the late Aaron Hill*, iv, London, 1753, pp. 353–414.

[28] 'C'est l'extrême sensibilité qui fait les acteurs médiocres...c'est le manque absolu de sensibilité qui prépare les acteurs sublimes.' Denis Diderot, *Paradoxe sur le comédien*, Paris: Gallimard, 1966, p. 153.

of involvement with the role that would appear to endorse Hill's ('method acting') position.

At the heart of the acting reforms stirring across Europe in the second half of the eighteenth century, in both spoken and sung drama, was the concept of ensemble acting, in which characters would address their remarks to each other rather than to the audience, and react to the dialogue in which they played a part. This technique, which Planelli called 'il gesto muto' or silent acting,[29] was often expressed simply as the need for an actor to 'attend to what is done by others, and be affected accordingly'.[30] Planelli stressed that the obligation to pay attention to the speaker and react to his words was not the sole responsibility of the actor addressed, but was shared by all the characters on stage.[31] Several writers vented their disapproval of early eighteenth-century practice: 'Instead of one actor minding what another says to him and marking by the different modifications of gesture and features what impression it has made upon him, he does nothing but smile to the boxes and bow to the company there, with several other such impertinences'.[32] And: 'During the aria of someone acting with him, [the singer] should not move around, stare at the boxes, or interest himself in the orchestra, or in the supernumaries. During the ritornello he shall not go behind the scene to take tobacco, or to complain to his friends that he is hoarse today and has little voice'.[33] Garrick, again, was in the forefront of change. An anonymous theatre-goer recorded his approval of Garrick's stage behaviour while condemning common abuses: 'When three or four are on the stage with him, he is attentive to whatever is spoke and never drops his character when he has finished a speech by either looking contemptibly on an inferior performer, unnecessarily spitting, or suffering his eyes to wander through the whole circle of spectators.'[34]

A limited amount of 'silent acting' is clued into librettos. Metastasio, for example, in his popular opera *Artaserse* (which Guadagni sang in seven different settings), required that 'While Arbace sings the aria ['Fra cento affani'], Artabano, who is not listening to him, goes suspiciously around the stage, looking and listening, so that he can frame his behaviour according to whoever is watching and listening'.[35] But such directions are few and far between. And 'silent acting' was by no means universally

[29] Antonio Planelli, *Dell'opera in music*, (1772), ed. Francesco Degrada, Fiesole: Discanto, 1981, p. 87.

[30] Thomas Wilkes, *A general view of the stage*, London, 1759, p. 155.

[31] 'La quale obbligazione di badare a che parla e di gestire, non è solamente di quello attore a cui è diretta la parola, ma è obbligazione di tutti gli attori che sono in scena.' Planelli loc. cit.

[32] Algarotti, *An essay*, p. 35.

[33] Ernst Christoph Dressler, *Theater-Schule für die Deutschen* (1777), tr. Barnett, *Theatre Research International* 2 (1977): 176.

[34] *Gentleman's Magazine*, 12 (1742): 527.

[35] *Artaserse*, Act I scene 2.

endorsed even by the end of the century. Writing in 1803, Goethe, in his *Rules for Actors*, insisted that actors should direct their performance to the audience, and 'should not, out of misconceived naturalness, play to each other as though no third person were present.'[36] It is hard to imagine the egotistical Guadagni as a committed ensemble player (or even tolerating Artabano's potentially distracting actions while he, as Arbace, delivered the aria), but Burney's evidence of his total absorption in his roles, to the extent of appearing to ignore applause or calls for encores, suggests the probability that he did indeed adopt this innovative stage behaviour.

There was a widely-held opinion that Italian singers could not act. Antoine Le Texier, a French impresario who spent many years in London, and was one of the first to publish serious opera criticism far removed from the adulatory advertising 'puffs' common in the press, deplored the Italian 'national habit of misplaced gestures that say nothing and express nothing.'[37] Algarotti also condemned his countrymen: 'The gait of our actors, their adjustment, their representative deportment and their manner of moving on the stage are as ungraceful as their faulty habit of pronouncing words or expressing sentiments.'[38] Farinelli's poor acting was often targeted. Quantz was brief and brutal: 'Acting was not his forte.'[39] Pickering enjoyed giving a fuller picture:

What a Pipe! What Modulation! What Extasy to the Ear! But, Heavens! What Clumsiness! What Stupidity! What Offence to the Eye! Reader, if of the City, thou mayest probably have seen in the Fields of *Islington* or *Mile-End*, or, if thou art within the Environs of *St James's*, thou must have observed…with what Ease and Agility a Cow, heavy with calf, has rose up at the Command of the Milk-Woman's Foot: thus from the Mossy Bank sprung up the Divine Farinelli. Then with long strides advancing a few paces, his left Hand settled upon his Hip, in a beautiful Bend, like that of the *Handle* of an *old fashion'd Caudle-Cup*, his Right remained immoveable across his manly Breast, till numbness called its Partner to supply the Place; when it relieved itself in the Position of the other *Handle* to the *Caudle-Cup*.[40]

---

[36] 'Sie sollen daher auch nicht aus mißverstanden Natürlichkeit untereinander spielen, als wenn kein Dritter dabei wäre.' Rule 39 in Johann Wolfgang Goethe, 'Regeln für Schauspieler', Weimar, 1803.

[37] 'cette habitude nationale des gestes déplacés…ne disant et n'exprimant rien.' Le Texier, *Journal Étranger*, 1 (June 1777), in Ian Woodfield, *Opera and Drama in Eighteenth-century London*, Appendix 3a, Cambridge: Cambridge University Press, 2001, p. 278.

[38] Algarotti, *An Essay*, p. 34.

[39] Cited in Robert Freeman, 'Farinello and his repertory', *Studies in Renaissance and Baroque Music in Honor of Arthur Mendel*, Kassel: Bärenreiter, 1974, p. 303.

[40] [Pickering], *Reflections upon Theatrical Expression*, pp. 63–64.

Burney quoted La Lande, who 'complains that the fine voices in an Italian opera are not only too few, but are too much occupied by the music and its embellishments to attend to declamation and gesture', but was quick to correct the Frenchman's judgement, placing Guadagni at the apex of his admired Italian performers (his list includes not only Guadagni's first teachers but also his sister Lavinia):

> With regard to this last charge, it is by no means a just one; for whoever remembers Pertici and Laschi, in the burlettas of London, about twenty years ago, or has seen the Buono Figliuola there lately, when *Signora* Guadagni, *Signor* Lovatini, and *Signor* Morigi were in it; or in the serious operas of past times remembers Monticelli, Elisi, Mingotti, Colomba Mattei, Manzoli, or, above all, in the present operas has seen *Signor* Guadagni, must allow that many of the Italians, not only recite well, but are *excellent actors*.[41]

Metastasio did not join in the widespread condemnation of the acting abilities of Italian singers. He expressed admiration for performers who 'act and sing better than usual', who 'act and sing like angels', who 'transport everyone with their figure, their singing and their unbelievable expression of character', and who 'show excellence in voice, taste, and acting.'[42] He was perfectly aware of Farinelli's shortcomings, since he inserted unusually detailed stage directions into the operas whose premières Farinelli was to direct in Madrid.[43] He also had experience of *primi uomini* behaving like *prime donne*, refusing to take direction or even attend rehearsals.[44] Frustratingly, he never mentioned Guadagni's acting. For all his many Metastasian roles, Guadagni would only have been directed by the poet in the couple of operas in which he created a role in a newly-written libretto: in *Il trionfo di Clelia* in 1762, for example, or *Egeria* in 1764. And although we have the librettist's own detailed account of these productions, he is silent on the subject of acting.

Calzabigi is similarly, and curiously, unforthcoming, though we know he interested himself in every aspect of the production of *Orfeo*. There are grounds, though, for believing that Guadagni, working in collaboration with Gluck and Calzabigi, acted with vigour and verisimilitude. The evidence—a mere hint—emerges twelve years later when, reworking the opera for Paris, Gluck trained the French tenor Le Gros in the title role, and a sudden improvement in Le Gros' acting was noted in the

---

[41] Burney, *The Present State of Music in France and Italy*, 2nd ed., London, 1773, p. 350.

[42] See Richard Savage, 'Staging an opera: letters from the Cesarian poet', *Early Music* 26.4 (1998): 583–95.

[43] Ibid., pp. 593–94.

[44] Ibid., p. 586.

press.[45] Gluck may have had Guadagni's interpretation in mind when coaching Le Gros, and it is an attractive possibility that when Gluck exhorted the tenor to perform the cries of 'Eurydice!' in the opening chorus, 'as if someone is cutting off your leg',[46] his insight into the most expressive way of delivering the cries might have been informed by Guadagni's performance of them in Vienna in 1762.

More explicit and better-documented evidence arises in connection with Guadagni's resumption of the role of Orfeo, in the pasticcios of 1770 and 1771, where Burney recorded that 'his attitudes, action, and impassioned and exquisite manner of singing…acquired him very great and just applause.'[47] And for once there is confirmation of Burney's opinion; an anonymous observer of yet another *Orfeo* (Munich, 1773) found that 'there is something grand in the manner of his acting'.[48]

Our knowledge of Guadagni's acting technique is derived from hints and inferences. Although no critic mentions his facial expressions, for example, we can be confident that they were varied and animated since all his mentors valued this above any other skill. And, though the evidence is somewhat involuted, from the description of Gluck rehearsing Le Gros we can infer that Guadagni's acting probably achieved an unusual degree of passion. We know that his gestures were 'full of grace', but not how he linked them together or how he moved on the stage.

His intense relationship with his roles is well documented. Guadagni is one of the first singers to build his career through identification with a single role. His attempts to communicate his total engagement with the character he portrayed did not, however, always find favour with the public: 'His determined spirit of supporting the dignity and propriety of his dramatic character, by not bowing acknowledgement, when applauded, or destroying all theatrical illusion by returning to repeat an air, if encored at the termination of an interesting scene, he so much offended individuals, and the opera audience in general, that, at length, he never appeared without being hissed'.[49] This was a remarkable stand to take at a time when soloists reckoned their success in the number of encores awarded. Guadagni's refusal to give encores might have been a lesson he learned from Laschi, who 'never sought applause at the expense of Nature', but it was also a matter of general debate. Pickering recognised

---

[45] See for example Melchior Grimm, *Correspondance littéraire*, x, 3rd ed., Paris 1877–1882, p. 473; Abbé Arnaud in G M Le Blond, *Mémoires pour servir à l'histoire de la révolution opérée dans la musique par M le Chevalier Gluck*, Paris, 1781, p. 50; *Mémoires secrets pour servir à l'histoire de la république des lettres en France*, vii, pp. 178–79, London, 1779–1789.

[46] 'Criez avec de la douleur, comme si on vous coupoit la jambe', Johann Christian Mannlich, 'Histoire de ma vie', ed. Henriette Weiss von Trostprugg, *La revue musicale*, Nov. 1934, p. 255.

[47] Burney, *General History*, ii, p. 877.

[48] 'Il y a du grand dans son action': a 'Saxon diplomat' describing a performance of *Orfeo* in Munich, cited in Moritz Fürstenau, 'Glucks *Orpheus* in München 1773', *Monatshefte für Musikgeschichte* 4 (1872): 218–24.

[49] Burney, *General History*, ii, p. 877.

the problem and suggested a minimal acknowledgement of applause by 'a modest Inclination of the Head and Body, at an Interval that breaks not into the Prosecution of his Part'.[50] It is almost certainly Guadagni whom Le Texier had in mind when he wrote of 'a much-loved actor (who has not been seen for some time), to whom the audience wishes to express its appreciation by repeated acclamation', whom he advised 'to divest himself of the character he is to represent [before beginning his role], and to appear as himself, acknowledging the applause as respectfully as possible, but at the same time indicating that from the moment his role begins, he will not be able to interrupt his performance without destroying all illusion and dramatic truth'.[51] Le Texier endorsed Guadagni's stand on encores, but urged a more audience-friendly approach to his principled stand. This Guadagni was incapable of doing. Without his notoriously capricious character, and 'high notions of his own importance', he might have had greater influence as an innovative actor. Even with this handicap he was the iconic actor of the reform, working at the forefront of a new style of acting that renewed opera in the later eighteenth century.

---

[50] Pickering, op. cit., p. 67.

[51] 'Un acteur très-aimé du Public, qu'on n'auroit pas vu depuis quelque tems, à qui on témoigneroit des bontés particulières par des applaudissemens multiplés, pouroit, avant de commencer son rôle, se dépouiller pour ainsi dire, du caractère qu'il est chargé de représenter, redevenir lui, et alors témoigner le plus respectueusement qu'il lui sera possible la sensibilité, mais du moment qui son rôle est commencé, il ne peut jamais en suspendre l'éxécution sans détruire toute espece d'illusion et de vraisemblance'. Le Texier, in Woodfield, *Opera and drama*, p. 281.

# 5

## Building a Career on the European Stage (1755–1762)

### SEASON OF 1755–1756

Before relaunching his career in Italy, Guadagni made one, or possibly two, visits to Portugal. Burney records the events with his usual mixture of colourful anecdote and plausible fact:

> In 1754 he was at Lisbon as second serious man under Gizziello, and [in] 1755 very narrowly escaped destruction during the earthquake. After this dreadful calamity, Gizziello, seized with a fit of devotion, retired into a monastery, where he spent the rest of his life. Having a friendship for Guadagni, and being pleased with his voice and quickness of parts, he persuaded the young singer to accompany him in his retreat, where, during a considerable time, he took great pains in directing his studies; and it is from this time that Guadagni's great reputation, as a refined and judicious singer, may be dated.[1]

There is at least a grain of truth in this intriguing account. While there is no surviving record of Guadagni in Lisbon in 1754, and he is not known to have had any contact with Gizziello (the stage name of Gioacchino Conti) before 1755, there is a gap in Guadagni's engagements between his last known concert in Paris on 19 April 1754 and his appearance at Covent Garden on 18 November of that year, and it is possible that during the summer of 1754, he travelled from Paris to the Portuguese capital, where Gizziello had been employed by the royal court since 1752. One name links

---

[1] Burney, *General History*, ii, pp. 875–76.

Guadagni, Paris and Lisbon: Caffarelli, with whom Guadagni had sung in Paris, was on the Lisbon court payroll in 1755 and sang in four operas that season. There is, however, no record of Guadagni ever singing as *secondo uomo* to Gizziello, and the cast list of the only opera in Lisbon in which Guadagni's participation is proved— Antonio Mazzoni's setting of Metastasio's *Antigono*, given in the autumn of 1755—is headed not by Gizziello but by Caffarelli.

Guadagni might have been drawn to Lisbon by hearing of the new court theatre which was being built in 1754, designed for the specific purpose of performing Italian opera. The building project reflected the personal passions of the opera-loving king, José I, who funded it lavishly. A French visitor to the court described both the theatre and, with some national bias, its repertory:

> The decorations and the spectacle are superb. The immense stage, sumptuously decorated, charmed our eyes. Most of us found our ears equally charmed by the Italian music. There were others whom it did not please. Male and female roles are played by castratos. The recitative seemed very boring to me. The Italian music may not be to the taste of those French not used to it. Not that I think their taste should prevail over that of the rest of Europe, merely that I did not care for it much.[2]

The theatre, which opened on 31 March 1755, was devastated in the earthquake of 1 November. The destruction of one of the most gracious of European capitals by earthquake, fire and tsunami left the population nervous and fearful (and provided a far-reaching intellectual challenge to theologians, philosophers and seismologists). After the catastrophe, the royal family took up residence in a tented encampment outside the city, and the palace, with its new theatre, was not rebuilt in the king's lifetime.

The disaster prompted an immediate exodus from Lisbon: Benjamin Keene, the British Ambassador in Madrid, wrote that 'musitians come tumbling in naked upon us every day'.[3] Guadagni, Caffarelli and Gizziello were among those who fled. Whether Gizziello was 'seized with a fit of devotion' and 'retired into a monastery, where he spent the rest of his life' has not been confirmed, though it appears that the singer did not sing in public after the Lisbon disaster. Burney's allegation that Guadagni joined Gizziello in retirement, and profited from singing lessons that transformed him 'from a young and wild singer of the second and third class'

---

[2] Chevalier des Courtils (1755), quoted in translation by Manuel Carlos de Brito, *Opera in Portugal in the Eighteenth Century*, Cambridge: Cambridge University Press, 1989, p. 27.

[3] *The Private Correspondence of Sir Benjamin Keene*, Cambridge: Cambridge University Press, 1933, p. 437.

into 'the first singer of his time',[4] is unconfirmed. Burney's source could only have been Guadagni himself. Certainly there are nine months unaccounted for in the singer's career between November 1755 and August 1756. In the last years of his life, Guadagni petitioned the Portuguese court for a pension as compensation for the abrupt end to his career in Lisbon, pleading that he had abandoned his service to the king only because of the fear that the earthquake had aroused in him. He was granted the sum of 96,000 reals.[5]

Whatever the facts of his Lisbon experience, it proved to be a turning point for Guadagni. When he left England in the spring of 1755, he was ill equipped to work in *opera seria*—a fact which makes his engagement in Lisbon the more surprising and Caffarelli's agency in securing the invitation the more probable. Guadagni's experience in the genre was minimal, and his prolonged residence in London meant that he had few contacts among colleagues and impresarios to ease his way into the continental professional circuit. Nevertheless, after the Lisbon interlude and his recuperation, whether or not it included a period of study with Gizziello, he relaunched his career in Italy, quickly finding success as an itinerant soloist, and graduating rapidly to *primo uomo* roles.

The first engagement of his new career took place at the Teatro delle Grazie in Vicenza. It was a defining moment for Guadagni. Burney's use of the phrase 'Gaetano Guadagni of Vicenza', which misled so many biographers for so many years, suggests that the singer may have, in conversation, talked up the significance of this new beginning in emphatic terms. Vicenza was not his birthplace, but it was in every sense a rebirth when, in August 1756, he sang the role of Arbace in Galuppi's setting of Metastasio's *Artaserse*.[6] It is tempting to think that the engagement was secured at the recommendation of his elder sister, Angiola Guadagni, who took the role of Megabise. The company also included two rising stars of the second half of the eighteenth century who were to cross Guadagni's path frequently in the next decade: the tenor Giuseppe Tibaldi and his wife, the soprano Rosa Tartaglini Tibaldi. Another member of the cast, Marianna Bianchi, was to appear as Euridice to Guadagni's Orfeo in Vienna some six years later.

SEASON OF 1756–1757

Over the next five years, Guadagni was in regular employment in theatres across northern Italy. He could not have returned at a more promising moment. The

---

[4] Burney, *General History*, ii, pp. 800–801.

[5] De Brito, op. cit., p. 31.

[6] Galuppi first set *Artaserse* in 1749 and made a second version in 1751. The Vicenza performance was based on the second version.

mid-century was a time of great activity for noble and civic sponsors of opera houses. There was a rush to build or to improve and expand existing theatres, and a good deal of local pride was involved. Theatre design was widely discussed, and debate raged around the conflicting claims of audibility, which would place the singers at the very front of the stage, under or forward of the proscenium arch, and verisimilitude, which advocated moving the actors further back, so that they stood among the scenery, 'in order to make a part of that pleasing illusion for which all dramatic exhibitions are calculated'.[7] Visitors rarely refrained from measuring one town's theatrical provision against another's. Burney, for instance, compared the Teatro Regio in Turin with theatres in London, Lyons and Paris, while Michael Kelly assessed the Teatro Nuovo in Brescia in comparison with Naples and Padua. A clear hierarchy existed between the most prestigious theatres and the rest. Status was defined not only by the size of the building and the opulence of the decorations, but by the repertory, whether *opera seria* or *buffa*, first performance or revival, by the reputation of the singers employed and by the seasons when opera was presented. The fame of the composer came considerably behind all these factors.

The grandest theatres aspired to present new music, but the difference between a première and a revival was not always clear-cut. So closely was the composition of an opera tailored to the singers who were to perform it, that if it were repeated in a different town, it would inevitably need some rewriting to suit the new cast, and if the re-make was sufficiently substantial, a new work was created, as is the case with Gluck's *Ezio*, recomposed for Guadagni in 1763, or the same composer's *Orfeo*, adapted for Millico in 1769 and Le Gros in 1774. Librettos were recycled constantly, with special pride of place being given to Metastasian dramas. In the course of his career, Guadagni sang in seven separate settings of Metastasio's *Artaserse* and four of his *Olimpiade*. It is this context that the large number of *Orfeo* operas he performed in the 1760s and 1770s, all based more or less on Calzabigi's poem, can be seen to be unexceptional.

The succession of seasons meant that opera performance was almost continuous throughout the year. The most prestigious theatres aimed to operate during Carnival, and some extended this back into the autumn, though then they would often reserve their most important opera for the Christmas period. Less valued were the spring or summer seasons, but it was mutually advantageous if towns avoided competing for the same pool of high-ranking singers for the same few months of the year, so smaller theatres, the Nuovo in Padua, for example, or the Pubblico in Reggio Emilia, delayed the start of their seasons to have a chance of employing the stars.

---

[7] Francesco Algarotti, *An Essay on the Opera*, p. 60.

The majority of opera houses put on two operas during their chosen season, and the average run for each opera was 20 nights, but there were many exceptions. There was no continuity of employment. In order to earn throughout the year, singers circulated around the country, rarely remaining in the same town for more than a few months. At the end of a season, most opera companies, including nearly all *seria* groups, would disband and scatter. Apart from some *buffa* troupes, or the nucleus of a *seria* troupe in the form of a married couple such as the Tibaldis, there was no practice of moving on together as an ensemble.

After his much-needed experience at the comparatively obscure Teatro delle Grazie in Vicenza, Guadagni quickly graduated to sing at the most esteemed opera houses in Italy: the San Benedetto in Venice, the Regio in Turin and (briefly) the San Carlo in Naples, all of which staged predominantly *opera seria*, with a large preponderance of premières. His repertory was now considerably more significant than the minor *opera seria* roles with which he had made his debut in Venice nine years earlier, or the *opera buffa* roles on which he had built his career in London. He sang in operas by the most notable composers of the mid-century, taking part in many premières and creating major roles in, for example, Traetta's *Nitteti*, Piccinni's *Tigrane* and J. C. Bach's *Artaserse*.

From Vicenza, Guadagni made the short journey to Venice for the 1757 Carnival season. His engagement at the most prestigious of Venetian opera houses, the Teatro San Benedetto, is an indication of his rapidly rising status. The theatre had been newly erected in 1755 and Guadagni was engaged to sing in its second season. In keeping with the San Benedetto's artistic policy, both operas were new settings of Metastasian texts. The Carnival season opened on 26 December 1756 with *Catone in Utica* by Vincenzo Ciampi. Guadagni was well known to Ciampi, who had been Crosa's director of music in London, and this connection may have secured him his engagement. The second opera of the season, opening in January 1757, was *Adriano in Siria* by the Venetian composer Francesco Brusa.

In April 1757, Guadagni travelled to Reggio Emilia, where the opera programme was devised to coincide with the spring fair. Here he was reunited with the Tibaldis for an exceptionally lavish production of Traetta's new setting of the Metastasian drama *Nitteti*, composed to mark the reopening of the Teatro dell'Illustrissimo Pubblico (Teatro Pubblico).[8] Apart from Handel, Traetta was at this date the most distinguished composer to have written a role specially for Guadagni. The opera opened on 29 April, and a rare copy of the libretto lists a further 26 performances—in

---

[8] Sergio Romagnoli and Elvira Garbero, *Teatro a Reggio Emilia*, i, Florence: Sansoni, 1980, pp. 126–27. The music of this opera is lost.

other words, it was an outstanding success.[9] The libretto contains a dedication to Francesco III, Duke of Modena, who travelled to Reggio Emilia to see the opera. His visit and the success of the production were noted in the local press: 'Yesterday our court moved to Reggio for the fair and the opera; the latter was greeted with universal applause.'[10]

A visitor to Reggio Emilia gave a description of Teatro Pubblico which touches on an important development in theatre design:

> The auditorium, both in its dimensions and its design, follows the taste of the Comédie Française in Paris; the only point of difference is in the boxes, which are somewhat rounded, rather like bath tubs placed next to each other. What strikes one is that the boxes rise up one above the other by several inches as they recede from the stage. We understand that the architect has sacrificed everything in order to allow the audience to see the performance, though we wish that he could have achieved this without damage to the scheme of decoration. The proscenium arch is thirty feet across, and protrudes some considerable distance over the stalls, which enables the audience to hear the actors clearly, without the latter being obliged to shout.[11]

The concern of theatre architects with the audience's ability to see and hear was a steady trend throughout the eighteenth century, carrying with it the implication that audiences were becoming more attentive. In some theatres, it is probable that the development was driven by an increasing proportion of the paying public among the audience.[12]

---

[9] On 30 April; 1, 3, 4, 7, 8, 9, 11, 12, 14, 15, 16, 18, 19, 21, 22, 25, 26, 29, 30 and 31 May; and 2, 5, 7, 8 and 9 June. The hand-written dates appear in Biblioteca Nazionale Braidense, Milan, Racc. Dram. 4582.

[10] 'Si è trasferita ieri la nostra corte a Reggio per trattenervisi durante la Fiera, e l'Opera in Musica, la quale incontra l'applauso universale.' *Messaggiere di Mantova*, 4 May 1757.

[11] 'La salle, soit pour la grandeur, soit pour le plan, est dans le goût de celle de la Comédie Françoise à Paris; elle en diffère seulement par les loges un peu bombées, qui sont, pour ainsi dire, come des bagnoires, qu'on auroit arrangées les unes à côté des autre; mais ce qui choque le coup d'œil, c'est que ces loges s'élèvent les unes audessus des autres de quelques pouces, à mesure qu'elles s'éloignent du théâtre. On sent bien que l'Architecte a tour sacrifié pour procurer plus facilement à ses spectateurs la vue du spectacle; son intention a été bonne, mais on souhaiteroit qu'il l'eut remplie sans tomber dans cet inconvénient de décoration. Le *proscenium* a trente pieds d'ouverture, et fait une saillie considérable sur le parterre, ce qui fait que l'on entend facilement les Acteurs, sans qu'ils soient obligés de crier.' Joseph Jérôme Le Français de Lalande, *Voyage d'un François en Italie, fait dans le années 1765 et 1766*, i, Paris and Venice, 1769, pp. 514–15.

[12] Giuliana Ricci, *Teatri d'Italia*, Milan: Bramante, 1971, p. 157.

### SEASON OF 1757–1758

The following season found Guadagni travelling throughout northern Italy, a happy and productive period in his career, since he was becoming known and esteemed, and his eccentricities had not yet begun to damage his reputation. His first engagement was in Lucca, where the autumn season at the Teatro Pubblico coincided with the Feast of the Holy Cross (14 September).[13] Guadagni sang in a revival of Galuppi's 1751 version of *Artaserse*. For Carnival, he moved to Parma, where he took part in what Alan Yorke-Long judged to have been 'two undistinguished works'[14]: the pasticcio *Alessandro Severo*, based on Lotti's setting of Zeno's libretto, and the première of Silvani and Ferradini's *Ricimero re di Goti*. The theatre was more distinguished than the repertory. The Teatro Ducale, originally built in 1688 in the Palazzo della Riserva, was remodelled by the theatre architect Pietro Fontana in the 1750s, but unlike most mid-century refurbishments in Italy, the primary aim of the renovation was neither to improve the audience's visual and aural experience, nor to reflect civic pride, but to operate a degree of control over the social environment. The physical structure of the Ducale was designed to reproduce and reinforce rigid social hierarchies. A slight diminution in the size of the royal box enabled the provision of extra boxes to accommodate all the nobility and the majority of the wealthy bourgeoisie; the lower orders were penned into the top gallery, 'to maintain decency'.[15]

Guadagni was to return to Parma two years later in more propitious circumstances. For many singers, the public opera season was over by Easter, but in late spring Guadagni was engaged at the Teatro San Salvatore in Venice. This theatre was for most of the year dedicated to the performance of Goldoni's comedies, but broke its tradition with a short season of some eighteen performances of *opera seria*, beginning on the Feast of the Ascension, which, in 1758, fell on 4 May. The opera was a revival of Giuseppe Scolari's setting of *Artaserse*.

Guadagni hoped for an engagement in Padua at the June Fiera del Santo. He had formed a close friendship, springing from a pupil-teacher relationship, with the young and notoriously temperamental soprano Caterina Gabrielli, who was contracted to sing at the Teatro Nuovo in Galuppi's *Demofoonte*. Nettled at not being offered a part in the opera, Guadagni encouraged the soprano's disaffection with the management with the result that she left the company mid-season. In a letter to Farinelli, Metastasio observed that 'In Vienna, Milan and Lucca, where she has been handled with the necessary skill,

---

[13] See Elisabeth Le Guin, *Boccherini's Body*, Berkeley, Los Angeles and London: University of California Press, 2006, p. 43.

[14] Alan Yorke Long, *Music at Court*, London: Weidenfeld and Nicolson, 1954, p. 26.

[15] Martha Feldman, *Opera and Sovereignty*, Chicago: University of Chicago Press, 2007, p. 107.

she has enchanted everyone; but in Padua, where they have subjected her more to the bit than the spur, they have wasted their money'.[16]

Ironically, Guadagni stayed on, though without an operatic engagement. Padua was occupied that summer with many local celebrations surrounding the elevation of the bishop of Padua, Carlo Rezzonico, to pope (Clement XIII). The enthronement took place on 27 August, and the Paduan celebrations extended throughout the summer. A chronicle of all the festivities held in Padua mentions Guadagni twice: on 11 July he sang a motet during mass in the church of Santa Giustina, and again in the Santo a few days later. It is probable that the same musical items were given on both occasions, as both entries mention a 'beautiful violin concerto' played by Tartini.[17]

Guadagni's busy year ended with a summer engagement in Brescia, where, in August, he rejoined his sister Angiola in a repeat of Galuppi's *Artaserse*. The old Brescian theatre, the Teatro dell'Illustrissima Accademia degli Erranti, had been remodelled in the 1740s, renamed the Nuovo Teatro, and put on a commercial basis, though it appears that the society of noblemen continued to support the enterprise: 'The theatre at Brescia is very large and the auditorium very beautiful…there is an impresario who is responsible for all the expenses, and who takes all the profits, but the academy gives him a certain sum to help with the costs.'[18] Burney visited Brescia in July 1770 and was agreeably surprised by the theatre prices: '20 soldi, about 10d English', a far cry from the half-guinea tickets at the King's Theatre in London, signalling the different social function of opera in the two countries. Burney probably purchased a ticket for the stalls, with their novel tip-up seats.[19] In the course of his travels, he repeatedly remarked that music in Italy was 'cheap and common, whereas in England it is a costly exotic, and more highly prized', attributing to this difference the noisy and distracted audiences in Italy.[20] He also noted that:

> The theatre at Brescia is very splendid, but it is much less than that at Milan, with respect to length; the height is the same. The proportion of boxes round

---

[16] 'In Vienna, in Milano ed in Lucca, dove la giovane è stata maneggiata con la necessaria destrezza, ha incantato tutti i viventi; ma in Padova, dove han voluto usar più la sferza che lo sprone, han gettati i denari.' Metastasio to Carlo Broschi, 23 Sept. 1758.

[17] 'Un mottetto del Signor Gaetano Guadagni…un bellissimo concerto di violino del famoso professore Tartini'. *Funzioni sacre, e feste fatte dalla Città di Padova per l'esaltazione al Sommo Pontificato dell'Eminentissimo Sig. Carlo Rezzonico*, Padua, 1758, pp. v, viii.

[18] 'Le théâtre de Brescia est très grand, et la salle est belle…il y a un *Impresario* ou entrepreneur qui en fait tout les frais, et en retire les profits, mais á qui l'académie donne une somme pour lui aider á en supporter la dépense.' Joseph Jérôme le Français de Lalande, *Voyage d'un François en Italie, fait dans les années 1765 et 1766*, quoted in Vasco Frati, Roberto Mora and Franco Rapuzzi, *Il teatro grande di Brescia*, ii, Brescia: Grafo, 1985, p. 20, note 49.

[19] Charles Burney, *Music, Men and Manners in France and Italy*, London, 1771, p. 64.

[20] *Music, Men and Manners*, 2nd ed,, London, 1773, p. 68.

each theatre is as one hundred to thirty-four: there are five rows in each, so that this house seems much higher than that at Milan. The boxes are more ornamented with glasses, paintings, front-cloths of velvet, or rich silks fringed; and more room is allowed here in the pit, to each auditor, than at Milan; every seat turns up, and is locked till the person comes who has taken it; and here every row, and every box of each row, is numbered, as in our playhouses, when the pit and boxes are laid together.[21]

In 1783 the young Irish tenor Michael Kelly, engaged to sing at the June Fair, made similar comments: '[the theatre] was a very splendid building; the boxes, of which there were five tiers, were ornamented with glasses, like those of San Carlo, at Naples, and the seats in the pit turned up in the same way as in Padua.'[22]

### SEASON OF 1758–1759

The autumn of 1758 found Guadagni in Verona, creating his second role for Traetta, that of Licida in Metastasio's popular drama *Olimpiade*. The event confirmed his status as celebrity singer, employed to ensure the success of a risky enterprise. The Nuovo Teatro dell'Accademia Filarmonica (Teatro Filarmonico) had been inaugurated in 1732, at the beginning of the great period of eighteenth-century theatre-building. The theatre was a gift to the town from Scipione Maffei, historian, dramatist and loyal Veronese (he also gave the town a museum and observatory), who claimed with pride that his building would have few rivals in terms of the perfection of its structure and the dignity of its setting.[23] By the early 1750s, however, a lavish refurbishment and expensive productions had left the theatre in financial difficulties and it sought to recoup its funds by putting on cheap productions of revivals. The 1758–59 season saw an attempt to restore its former fortunes with a prestigious première, and Guadagni and the equally famous soprano-register castrato Manzuoli were brought in to ensure the success of Traetta's opera. There is, unfortunately, no record of its reception, but the theatre survived.

For Carnival, Guadagni was engaged by the Teatro Regio at Turin, where he starred in the premières of Borghi's setting of Metastasio's *Adriano in Siria*, and Mazzoni's setting of Zeno's *Eumene*. The Regio was one of the finest opera houses in

---

[21] Ibid., pp. 117–18.

[22] Kelly, *Reminiscences*, i, p. 83.

[23] 'Un teatro che vien creduto pochi aver che li pareggino per quanto spetta alla perfezione della struttura; come niuno certamente l'uguaglia nella nobiltà degli annessi.' Quoted in Enrico Paganuzzi, *La musica a Verona*, Verona: Banca Popolare di Verona, 1976, p. 240.

Europe, built in 1740 to display the power and wealth of the Savoy monarchy, and renowned for its size, decorations and ingenious machines. Its virtues were praised unreservedly in a publicity pamphlet addressed to foreign visitors:

> This theatre is judged by all to be the grandest and most finely furnished in all Europe; it is deservedly an object of wonder to foreigners on account of its size and spaciousness, the design and comfort of the building, and the beauty of the interior decorations and extensive gilding. The painting of the ceiling is remarkable. Here every Carnival operas are performed with magnificent machinery appropriate to the splendour of the royal court, who attend in the spacious box prepared for them, which is then illuminated. The singers are always the finest in Europe.[24]

The magnificence of the Teatro Regio was admired by many visitors. Burney reckoned it 'one of the finest in Europe'.[25] De Brosses suggested that because the auditorium was restricted to the king, the nobility and their guests, it was judged less rowdy than other Italian opera houses.[26] The Regio was renowned for long and intensive seasons, with performances six nights a week, which often took their toll of the soloists. *Adriano*, opening on 26 December 1758, achieved 19 performances—a shorter run than normal—being interrupted on at least one occasion by Guadagni's illness: the theatre archives reveal that early in January Guadagni collapsed in the theatre and had to be carried home in a sedan chair.[27] *Eumene*, which opened on 27 January 1759, ran its full course of 28 performances.

---

[24] 24 'Questo teatro è giudicato da tutti il più grandioso e compito d'Europa, ed è meritevolmente l'oggetto della meraviglia de' Forestieri per la vastità ed ampiezza sua, e per l'architettura, e comodità dell'edifizio, e per l'interna bellezza degli ornamenti, per lo più dorati. È rimarchevole la pittura della volta. Ivi si recitano ogni Carnevale i Drammi musicali con tale magnificenza di apparato, quale si conviene alla grandezza della Real Corte, che v'interviene sulla Loggia spaziosa a lei destinatta, che poi si suole illuminare. Vi si chiamano sempre i migliori Musici d'Europa.' Giovanni Gaspare Craveri, *Guida de' Forestieri per la Real Città di Torino* (Turin, 1753), quoted in Margaret Ruth Butler, *Operatic Reform at Turin's Teatro Regio*, Turin: Libreria musicale italiana, 2001, pp. 5–6.

[25] Burney, *Music, Men and Manners,* 2nd ed, p. 72.

[26] 'moins tumultueux que ceux des autres villes'. Charles de Brosses to De Neuilly, 3 Apr. 1740, in Charles de Brosses, *Lettres familières écrites d'Italie*, 5th ed., i, Paris: Garnier, 1911, p. 438.

[27] The treasurer paid out 10 soldi to chairmen, 'che hanno portato a casa il Musico sigr. Guadagni per essergli venuto male', in Marie-Thérèse Bouquet, *Storia del Teatro Regio di Torino*, i, Turin: Cassa di Risparmio di Torino, 1976, p. 301.

### SEASON OF 1759–1760

Guadagni's engagements in the 1759–60 season appear to be sparse. It is possible that he returned to Padua, though no specific occasion has been recorded. He was in Lucca for the early autumn season, which opened on the Feast of the Holy Cross, with two revivals of Metastasian texts: Hasse's *Alessandro nell'Indie* and Traetta's *Nitteti*. In the constant whirligig of changing companies, Guadagni found himself again sharing the stage with the Tibaldis and Marianna Bianchi, and in fact *Nitteti* was given with the same cast as in 1757 in Reggio Emilia, a rare but surely welcome saving of rehearsal time.

With no recorded engagement for the Carnival season, we next hear of Guadagni on 10 July 1760, in Naples, singing in a small-scale *festa teatrale*, Gian Francesco de Majo's *I prodigi di Atlanta: prologo da cantarsi a tre voci*, given to celebrate the Queen's name-day. This is the only recorded occasion of Guadagni singing in Naples. One possible reason for this emerges from the archives of the Teatro San Carlo, retold by Benedetto Croce. Croce is a frustrating source. He transcribed anecdotes, apparently accurately, and preserving the eighteenth-century spelling, from both formal and informal archival material, but gave no precise references; the original documents he consulted were largely destroyed in the Second World War. Having reported an earlier favourable assessment of Guadagni's voice, particularly its agility across the registers,[28] he quoted the following description from a list of 'first class castratos' in the theatre archives for 1760: 'Beautiful voice, elegant figure and brilliant singer, but capricious, and rarely gives of his best.'[29] It is one of the first adverse judgements on Guadagni's character that begin to taint the singer's reputation from this point in his career. There was further trouble the following year:

> There were negotiations this season [spring 1761] with the famous Guadagni, who had not wanted to come the previous year, protesting that his voice was too small for the Teatro San Carlo. This time he asked for 1200 zecchini, with the unusual stipulation that Rosa Tartaglini-Tibaldi and Giuseppe Tibaldi should be engaged at the same time. When this was refused, he demanded 1800 zecchini.[30]

---

[28] 'Il detto virtuoso [Guadagni] è dotato di una bellissima voce, fondata con molta chiarezza nelle corde di mezzo, e nelle corde di basso, arbitrandosi con molta pulizia di andare agli acuti di suo piacere e di sua libertà. L'abilità è grande del suo cantare, come il suo personnaggio è molto addato e pulito in teatro, unitamente con una comica aggiustata, naturale, senza affettatura o caricatura.' Source dated 1757 in Croce, *I teatri di Napoli*, p. 751.

[29] 'Buona voce, bella figura, comico e brillante nel cantare, ma capriccioso e che ben di rado adempie il suo dovere.' Croce, op. cit., p. 749.

[30] 'S'erano fatto per questa stagione trattative col famoso Guadagni, che non era voluto venire l'anno prima, confessando che la sua voce era troppo piccola pel teatro S. Carlo. Questa volta chiese 1200 zecchini, con la

His demand for an inflated salary was turned down and Guadagni did not return to Naples. Some confirmation of Croce's anecdote is given by the fact that the two other singers in *I prodigi di Atlanta* were indeed a soprano and tenor. In the event, the work was sung by Clementina Spagnuoli and Anton Raaff. Guadagni presumably preferred the Tibaldis and had tried unsuccessfully to arrange for their engagement.

The reason Guadagni gave for his reluctance to sing at the San Carlo was plausible. His voice was never described as large, and the San Carlo was one of the biggest and noisiest opera houses in Europe. Burney, attending a gala night, praised its magnificent dimensions and opulent decoration, but questioned its efficiency as an auditorium:

> It being the great festival of St Charles and the King of Spain's name-day, the court was in grand gala, and the house was not only doubly illuminated, but amazingly crowded with well dressed company. In the front of each box there is a mirrour, three or four feet long, by two or three wide, before which are two large wax tapers; these, by reflection, being multiplied, and added to the lights of the stage and to those of the boxes, make the splendour too much for the aching sight. The King and Queen were present. Their Majesties have a large box in the front of the house, which contains in height and breadth the space of four other boxes. The stage is of an immense size, and the scenes, dresses, and decorations are extremely magnificent…yet…it must be owned that the magnitude of the building, and noise of the audience, are such, that neither the voices nor the instruments can be heard distinctly.[31]

### SEASON OF 1760–1761

In the autumn of 1760 Guadagni returned to Parma to take part in the celebrations of a marriage of considerable dynastic significance between Princess Isabella Maria of Bourbon-Parma, grand-daughter of Louis XV of France, and Archduke Joseph, later Joseph II of Austria. The wedding was marked with a series of spectacular opera productions in Parma and Vienna. While Vienna saw Hasse's Metastasian *festa teatrale Alcide al bivio* and Gluck's serenata *Tetide*, Parma celebrated with Frugoni and Traetta's *opéra-ballet Le feste d'Imeneo*, given on 3 September.[32] With hindsight,

---

stravagante condizione che con lui dovessero essere scritturati la Tartagli [sic] e il Tibaldi. E non accadendo questo, chiedeva invece 1800 zecchini.' Croce, op. cit., p. 494, note 5.

[31] Burney, *Music, Men and Manners*, 2nd ed., pp. 351–52.

[32] Bruce Alan Brown argues that *Alcide al bivio* is of particular significance: an early reform opera, shaped to a degree by Durazzo's intention of co-ordinating the three wedding entertainments to feature a blend of French

*Imeneo* proved to be something of a milestone in the fusion of French and Italian traditions that was increasingly to enrich Italian *opera seria* towards the end of the century. Frugoni had prepared two earlier librettos for Traetta, both of which were influenced by French models: *Ippolito ed Aricia* based on Pellegrin and Rameau's *Hippolite et Aricie*, and *I Tintaridi* based on Bernard and Rameau's *Castor et Pollux*. But *Imeneo* was even more radically in the French tradition than these, a true *opéra-ballet*. The novelty of the genre in Italy was widely noted.[33]

Despite its landmark status, in dramatic terms *Imeneo* was lightweight. It consisted of an allegorical prologue followed by three independent one-act operas. Visual display was all-important: machines were lavishly employed—the libretto boasted that the stage had been rebuilt to accommodate them[34]—and each act included a self-contained danced divertimento. The occasion was fortunate for all concerned. It brought Traetta to the notice of Archduke Joseph, who immediately commissioned an opera for the following season in Vienna, and it launched Guadagni into his next run of engagements. It is not recorded whether his singing caught the ear of the Archduke, but his performance certainly brought him to the attention of representatives of the Viennese theatre administration, who recommended him to Count Giacomo Durazzo, director of the theatres in Vienna.[35] It is, moreover, highly probable that the soprano Maria Masi Giura, whom the libretto styled as 'currently in the service of the Duke of Württemberg',[36] played a part in his subsequent engagement at Stuttgart. Guadagni was not above putting pressure on his leading ladies to secure him employment, as we saw in the case of Caterina Gabrielli in 1758.

Guadagni was back in Turin for Carnival, where he was due to sing in the première of J. C. Bach's first opera, *Artaserse*. Unfortunately *Artaserse* fell victim to the Teatro Regio's reputation for over-taxing its performers. Following a full month of rehearsals—an exceptional period of preparation—the opera was withdrawn on 6 January 1761, after a mere seven performances, when it was observed that 'since the musico Guadagni had lost his voice and the dancer Saunier was injured to the extent that he could not dance, there was concern whether to give the opera tomorrow or take a recess, because of the risk of greater harm…it was decided to suspend the

---

and Italian characteristics. See '"Mon opéra italien": Giacomo Durazzo and the genesis of *Alcide al bivio*,' in *Pietro Metastasio: uomo universale (1698–1782)*, Festgabe der Österreichischen Akademie der Wissenschaften zum 300. Geburtstag von Pietro Metastasio, ed. Andrea Sommer-Mathis and Elisabeth Theresia Hilscher, Vienna: Verlag der Österreichischen Akademie der Wissenschaften, 2000, pp. 115–42.

[33] 'Ce genre de spectacle est une nouveauté pour l'Italie.' *Journal Étranger*, Nov. 1760, pp. 179–80. A detailed synopsis appears between pp. 179 and 189 but with no evaluation of the music or the singers.

[34] 'Il Palco di questo Teatro nuovamente disegnato, è construtto, e disposto a quante Macchine possono occorrere ne' grandi Spettacoli…', Frugoni, *Imeneo*, Parma, 1760, p. xvi.

[35] Bruce Alan Brown, *Gluck and the French Theatre in Vienna*, Oxford: Clarendon Press 1991, p. 266.

[36] 'In actual servigio si S.A.S. il Duca Regnante di Wirtemberg e Tec'.

following day's performance.'[37] The season's second opera, *Tigrane*, by Piccinni, to a libretto by Goldoni after Francesco Silvani, was premièred on 10 January; it fared better with 22 performances. Guadagni's last known engagement for the season saw him back in Parma for the short Ascensiontide season in another Traetta première, *Enea e Lavinia* to a libretto by Sanvitale after Fontenelle.

### SEASON OF 1761–1762

In a major change of direction for his career, at the end of the 1761 season Guadagni transferred from Parma to Stuttgart. Exactly how he came to be offered this engagement is not clear, but the part played by the wedding opera *Le feste d'Imeneo* in Parma is hard to discount. For the next four seasons he worked in a very different environment from the commercial theatres in which he had largely built his career to this point. The theatres in Stuttgart, Vienna and Innsbruck were either (like the Ópera do Tejo in Lisbon) constructed within court premises or (like the Teatro Regio at Turin) closely associated with the ruling family. Operas were put on not to meet the taste of a paying public but to celebrate events—birthdays, marriages, military victories—in the royal families that commissioned them. Performances that took place in the outlying palaces (Ludwigsburg near Stuttgart, Laxenburg and Schönbrunn near Vienna, the Imperial Palace in Innsbruck) were played exclusively before the court, nobility and visiting dignitaries, and although performances in the larger theatres (the Herzogliches Theater in Stuttgart, the Burgtheater in Vienna) were open to the paying public, there is no evidence that their tastes were consulted in planning the repertory. Thus *L'isola disabitata* was given to mark the name-day of Duke Carl Eugen of Württemberg, and *Semiramide* to honour his birthday; *Il trionfo di Clelia* celebrated the birth of an heir to the Archduchess Isabella, *Egeria* commemorated the coronation of Joseph II, and *Romolo ed Ersilia* the wedding of Archduke Leopold and the Infanta Maria Ludovica. The very opera seasons at Stuttgart were organised around the ruler's personal diary: the autumn season began on his name-day, 4 November, and while Carnival was marked with a second opera on 2 January, a third production was mounted for his birthday on 11 February.

Guadagni's first engagement in Stuttgart was the name-day opera for 1761: Metastasio and Jommelli's *L'isola disabitata*, a pastoral opera of modest dimensions, though the production was probably elaborate and spectacular. It was given

---

[37] 'Essendo osservato che il Musico Guadagni era fuori di voce, e che il Ballerino Saunier è incommodato a segno di non poter Ballare, si è agitato se si dovesse dar l'opera domani, oppure dare un riposo, sul riscio che potesse essere di un maggior Danno il farla Domani…si è stimato di sospenderla per Domani.' Marie-Thérèse Bouquet, *Storia del Teatro Regio di Torino*, i, p. 304.

at Ludwigsburg, the ducal palace some seven miles north of Stuttgart. Burney was critical of the habit among German rulers of building summer palaces, pleasure gardens, and other attractions that displaced the court from its proper capital:

> It is no uncommon thing, in Germany, for a sovereign prince, upon a difference with his subjects, to abandon the ancient capital of his dominions, and to erect another at a small distance from it, which, in process of time, not only ruins the trade, but greatly diminishes the number of its inhabitants, by attracting them to his new residence; among the princes who come under this predicament, are the Elector of Cologne, removed to *Bonn*, the Elector Palatine, removed from Heidelberg to *Mannheim*; and the duke of Württemberg, from Stuttgart to *Ludwigsburg*.[38]

The duke in question was Eberhard Ludwig, who transferred his entire music establishment to Ludwigsburg some five years before his death in 1733.

His heir, Carl Eugen, fostered the musical establishment, building a new opera house in the palace gardens and securing Jommelli to direct it. Jommelli was an innovative composer who aimed to enrich Italian opera by introducing elements from other national traditions. Like Traetta, he was influenced by French opera in making great use of dance, spectacle and chorus, and he also owed much to German taste by enhancing the role of the orchestra; an expressive accompanied recitative is particularly characteristic of his style. Jommelli was joined at Stuttgart within a few years by the choreographer Noverre, the scenic artist Servandoni and the costume designer Boquet, forming one of the most talented operatic teams in Europe. Burney, visiting Ludwigsburg in 1772, after these celebrated artists had left the duchy, looked back to music under Jommelli as 'the best and most splendid in Germany'.[39] Guadagni's next engagement was in the birthday opera *Semiramide*, given on 11 February 1762 and performed in the town theatre in Stuttgart. It was Jommelli's third setting of the Metastasian text. Both casts included Maria Masi Giura, whom we can assume to have been Guadagni's friend, advocate and protectress at this period of his life.

---

[38] Burney, *The Present State of Music in Germany*, 2nd ed., i, London, 1775, p. 99.
[39] Ibid., p. 99.

# 6

## Guadagni in Vienna (1762–1765)

STUTTGART PROVED TO be no more than a stepping stone on the way to Vienna. After working with the most progressive composers in Europe, Traetta and Jommelli, Guadagni was now summoned to Vienna to create a role for Johann Adolf Hasse. Hasse, who spent much of the last decade of his composing life in Vienna producing operas to celebrate court events, is usually regarded as one of the most traditional of composers, but as Bruce Alan Brown has argued, in *Alcide al bivio,* his recent *festa teatrale* for the wedding of Archduke Joseph and Princess Isabella Maria, he had shown himself open to experimenting with the blend of French and Italian influences that were soon to characterise reform operas.[1] On 20 March 1762, the marriage produced a first child, a daughter, and Hasse composed an opera to celebrate the event to a new text by Metastasio, *Il trionfo di Clelia*; the celebratory opera was given in the Burgtheater on 27 April.

Though newly arrived in Vienna, Guadagni found himself in familiar company, since the cast of *Clelia* included Marianna Bianchi and Giuseppe Tibaldi. According to the librettist, the opera was prepared in great haste. Metastasio wrote of his birth pangs equalling those of the Archduchess.[2] Despite the 'orribili confusioni' described by the librettist, the enthusiastic opera-goer and diarist Count Johann Karl Zinzendorf enjoyed the evening, while making one of his customary pedantic reservations:

>...we went to see a performance of the opera called 'Il trionfo di Clelia' that Metastasio has written for the confinement of the Archduchess....There are

---

[1] See above, Chapter 5, note 32.

[2] 'Questa sera anderà in scena la mia *Clelia*, che ho nuovamente partorita per doglia di corpo: onde si sta in orribili confusioni perché, secondo il solito, niente è pronto.' Metastasio to Farinelli, 27 Apr. 1762.

some pretty airs, and everything was well done; the scenery was attractive [especially] the collapse of the bridge over the Tiber; the lighting in the last act was beautiful, although not entirely appropriate to the subject [since] Porsenna would hardly have had chandeliers in his military camp.[3]

Zinzendorf's criticism is typical of the priorities of the audience, who appear to have given more attention to the lighting, scenery, costumes and dance than to the music or singers.

The Burgtheater was the home of Italian opera in Vienna.[4] Administered by a hybrid of private and public funding, the theatre served a mixed audience of nobility and commoners, separated from each other by the structure of the building. It could accommodate well over 1,000 spectators, the majority of whom were members of ancient noble families who rented boxes in the first and second tiers of the auditorium; the wealthy bourgeoisie and newly-ennobled occupied the third gallery, and the stalls held a mixed audience of military officers, theatre personnel and enthusiasts from any category who were more interested in seeing the opera than in socialising. Cheaper seats were available in the top gallery (the 'Paradis') and at the back of the stalls, available to anyone who could afford them. On special celebratory occasions, for example the Viennese celebrations for the coronation in Frankfurt of the future Joseph II as King of the Romans, a number of performances were given without charge. The theatre also hosted spoken plays in French and *opéra-comique*, and was a focus for the infusion of French culture into the Imperial capital contrived by a collaboration between the empress's chancellor of state and minister for foreign affairs, Prince Wenzel Anton Kaunitz, and the director of theatres, Count Giacomo Durazzo. Their taste was evident in the performance of operas by Traetta and Gluck (and now Hasse), which deliberately introduced elements of French opera into the Italian genre.

---

[3] '…nous allâmes voir représenter l'Opéra intitulé Le Triomphe de Clélie que Metastasio a fait pour l'accouchement de l'archiduchesse.… Il y a de jolis airs et tout fut bien exécuté, les decorations sont belles, la rupture du pont sur le Tibre, l'illumination au dernier acte est belle, quoiqu'elle ne paroit pas tres bien convenir au sujet, Porsenna n'aura guères eu de lustres dans son camp.' Karl Zinzendorf, 'Journal du Comte Charles de Zinzendorf et Pottendorf', ms, in Haus-Hof-und Staatsarchiv, Vienna, 'Journal', 27 Apr. 1762. The Journal is excerpted in *Aus der Jugendtagebüchern 1747, 1752 bis 1763*, ed. Maria Breunlich and Marieluise Mader, Vienna: Böhlau Verlag, 1997. Entries taken from Breunlich and Mader's edition, which contain minor textual corrections, are identified as such.

[4] See 'The old Burgtheater: a structural history 1741–1888', Konrad Zobel and Frederick Warner, *Theatre Studies* 19 (1972–73): 19–53; Otto Schindler, 'Das Publikum des Burgtheaters in der Josephinischen Ära', in *Das Burgtheater und sein Publikum*, ed. Margret Dietrich, i, 1976, pp. 11–95; Daniel Heartz, 'Nicolas Jadot and the building of the Burgtheater', *Musical Quarterly*, 68.1 (1982): 1–31.

Although the Burgtheater was often referred to (by Burney, for example), as the 'court theatre' or, more accurately, as 'the theatre next to the court', other theatres within the local Imperial palaces also provided a venue for Italian opera; the most important of these were at Schönbrunn and Laxenburg. The second town theatre, the Kärntnertortheater, was known as the German theatre; its brief was to feature plays in the German language. In Guadagni's first season in Vienna, the Kärntnertortheater was undergoing reconstruction after one of the many fires that plagued eighteenth-century theatres. As in Stuttgart, the opera seasons in Vienna were closely tied to the interests and activities of the court. The summer operas were planned around celebrations of Maria Theresia's birthday on 13 May and the autumn season opened on or near the Emperor's name-day on 4 October; the third most important date was the conventional opera season of Carnival from 26 December to the beginning of Lent.

A major source of information about Guadagni's first two seasons in Vienna is the *Répertoire* of Philipp Gumpenhuber, a manuscript schedule of rehearsals and performances given at the Burgtheater and Kärntnertortheater between 1758 and 1763.[5] Gumpenhuber's list enables us to reconstruct much of Guadagni's professional activities in Vienna. We learn, for instance, that rehearsals for *Il trionfo di Clelia* were expected to begin on 17 April, but were postponed till the 20th on account of Guadagni's illness. The opera proved popular, receiving 22 performances in all, and launched Guadagni very effectively on the Viennese stage.

He soon became a regular contributor to the concerts (*Accademie*) which were held in the Burgtheater throughout the year, mostly on Fridays but with increased frequency during the Lenten season. Guadagni's first academy, however, was at the summer palace of Laxenburg on Monday 10 May, where he sang together with Tibaldi and the castrato Carlo Nicolini, who had also been among the cast of *Clelia*. Unless a complete cantata or oratorio was being performed, Gumpenhuber rarely gave details of the vocal items, but it seems likely that these singers would have repeated their arias from *Clelia*. The academies always included instrumental items, usually concertos, where, in the absence of other evidence, the performer is presumed to be the composer: on this occasion there was a violin concerto by Pugnani and an oboe concerto by Johann Schmid. At the next academy on 14 May, a regular Friday Burgtheater concert, the singers were unnamed but identified as 'almost all those who had had the honour to appear in the recent opera'; they sang 'several

---

[5] See Gerhard Croll, 'Neue Quellen zu Musik und Theater in Wien 1758–1763: ein erster Bericht', *Festchrift Walter Senn*, Munich and Salzburg: Katzbichler, 1975, pp. 8–12; also Brown, *Gluck and the French Theatre in Vienna,* especially pp. 61–62. I am grateful to Gerhard Croll and Irene Brandenburg, University of Salzburg, for allowing me to see a photocopy of Gumpenhuber's *Répertoire*.

new arias,'[6] and there was a horn concerto by Ignaz Leutgeb, the soloist for whom Haydn and Mozart were to write concertos. Guadagni sang in a total of seventeen academies in the summer to early autumn of 1762, between *Clelia* and *Orfeo*. In addition he sang on two occasions at the festive dinners, the somewhat feudally-named *Service à table*, with which imperial birthdays were marked.

His next opera in Vienna was a more modest affair than *Clelia*. *Arianna* was a *festa teatrale*, prepared, according to the preface to the libretto, in a hurry, with pre-existing arias arranged by Gluck to fit a new libretto by Migliavacca. *Arianna* was first performed at Laxenburg on 27 May 1762. There was minimal rehearsal; if Gumpenhuber is to be believed, the little opera was rehearsed in the morning, given a *répétition générale* in the afternoon and premièred in the evening. This was Guadagni's first collaboration with Gluck, the composer who was to change the course of his career. In *Arianna*, however, he had little enough opportunity to make his mark, since his contribution amounted to one aria, one duet and a quartet.[7]

<h2 style="text-align:center">SEASON OF 1762–1763</h2>

Nevertheless, Guadagni had been noticed. He had already attracted the attention of Durazzo's agents through his performance in Traetta's innovative *Le feste d'Imeneo* in Parma in 1760. Further recommendations could well have come from Jommelli or his patron Carl Eugen in Stuttgart. Identified as a singer with unusual vocal and acting abilities, and—an important bonus—willing to experiment beyond the rigid conventions of *opera seria*, Guadagni had been brought to Vienna to play a part in the emerging reform of opera. So far he had had little opportunity to demonstrate his abilities, but Calzabigi and Gluck's *Orfeo ed Euridice*, the first major landmark of the reform, was devised to exploit his qualities to the full. This opera (or *festa teatrale*—however revolutionary its dramatic principles, the work was intimately linked with the imperial calendar of family feasts) was given at the Burgtheater on 5 October 1762. It transformed the career and reputation of more than one of the artists involved in its composition.

There are remarkably few sources that tell us how *Orfeo* came to be written. Of the three principal creative minds involved, Durazzo, Gluck and Calzabigi, only the librettist Calzabigi has left an account of the collaboration, and it needs to be read with the caution that it was written more than 20 years after the event, when *Orfeo* had become an acknowledged success, and Calzabigi, aware that he had

---

[6] 'Presque tous les Sujets qui ont eu l'honneur de paroitre dans la dernière Opera ont chanté plusieurs airs nouveau.' Gumpenhuber, *Répertoire*, 14 May 1762.

[7] Klaus Hortschansky, '*Arianna*—ein Pasticcio von Gluck', *Die Musikforschung* 24 (1971): 407–11.

written nothing of comparable stature since the end of his collaboration with Gluck, intended to claim his share of the success. He had the advantage of preaching to the converted. Many among his French readers did not need convincing of the fundamental importance of declamation, and the undesirability of such Italian traits as lengthy stretches of passage work, intrusive cadenzas and orchestral episodes:

> I am no musician, but I have made a great study of declamation....It is twenty-five years since I first became persuaded that the only music suitable for dramatic poetry...was the lively and energetic music that conformed most closely to natural declamation....I arrived in Vienna in 1761, full of these ideas. The following year, his excellency Count Durazzo...to whom I had recited my *Orfeo*, commissioned me to have it performed in the theatre. I agreed on condition that the music should be written in accordance with my wishes. He sent me M. Gluck, who, he assured me, would fall in with all my ideas....I read him my *Orfeo*, showing him...the nuances that I put into my declamation and that I wanted him to make use of in his composition: the pauses, the slowing down, the speeding up, the sound of the voice, now stronger, now weaker as in an aside. I also begged him to forgo passage-work, cadenzas and ritornellos....M. Gluck agreed with my suggestions.[8]

It is striking that no mention is made of Guadagni here. Yet as Calzabigi elsewhere revealed, the role was 'tailor-made' for him.[9] Everything we know about his style of singing fitted him for the leading role in an opera devised in accordance with reform principles. Qualities nurtured during Guadagni's seven-year period in England suddenly became relevant. The same reason that prompted Handel to write some of his greatest roles for actresses-turned-singers—Susanna Cibber and Kitty Clive—made Guadagni's particular abilities a useful starting point for Calzabigi and Gluck. Here for the first time the training in expression and in the projection of

---

[8] 'Je ne suis pas Musicien, mais j'ai beaucoup étudié la declamation...j'ai pensé, il y a 25 ans, que la seule musique convenable à la poésie dramatique...étoit celle qui approcheroit davantage de la declamation naturelle, animée, énergique....J'arrivai à Vienne en 1761, rempli de ces idées. Un an après, S.E.M. le Comte Durazzo...à qui j'avois récité mon Orphée, m'engagea à le donner au Théâtre. J'y consentis, à condition que la musique en seroit faite à ma fantaisie. Il m'envoya M. Gluck, qui, me dit-il, se prêteroit à tout....Je lui fis la lecteure de mon Orphée...lui indiquant les nuances que je mettois dans ma déclamation, les suspensions, la lenteur, la rapidité, les sons de la voix tantôt chargés, tantôt affoiblis & negligés dont je desirois qu'il fît usage pour sa composition. Je le priai en même-temps d'en bannir *i passaggi, le cadenze, i ritornelli*....Gluck entra dans mes vûes.' Calzabigi to *Mercure de France*. 15 June 1784 (pub. 21 Aug. 1784).

[9] 'fatto a posta', Calzabigi to Prince Wenzel Anton Kaunitz, 6 Mar. 1767, in Vladimir Helfert, 'Dosud Neznámý Dopis Ran. Calsabigiho z r. 1767', *Musikologie*, 1 (1938): 114–22. For a more detailed consideration of how the role of Orfeo was constructed to match Guadagni's strengths and weaknesses, see Chapter 12.

words that Guadagni had absorbed from Handel came to fruition in an operatic context. Moreover Guadagni was perfectly aware of Gluck's debt to Handel, and its manifestation in the music of *Orfeo*. In his preface to the first London production of the opera in 1770, he remarked that 'The original Composer [Gluck] made himself a perfect master of his author's meaning; and infused the genius of the poetry into his music; in which he followed the example of my great master Handel, the phoenix of our age; who in all modes of musical expression, where sense was to be conveyed, excelled beyond our praise'.[10]

The opera also exploited Guadagni's celebrated acting skills learned from Pertici and Garrick. The opening scene cries out for eloquent gestures sustained throughout the choruses; Act II provides the opportunity for varied facial expression, as Orfeo reacts to the furies with terror and to the Elysian scene with ecstasy; Act III requires agitated movement across the stage during his struggle to lead Euridice from the Underworld. Guadagni must have heard and perhaps participated in a good deal of discussion of the artistic aims of the reform. His performances in London, and the controversy they attracted, suggest that he had fully absorbed the innovative concept of the integrity of the dramatic role—the necessity for a singer to put the interpretation of a character before the promotion of his own skills, even when such integrity came into conflict with conventional soloist-audience relations.[11]

Although Guadagni was, by this stage in his career, accustomed to expect 'first man' status, no other opera in which he had yet participated, or would in the future participate, was built so relentlessly around one singer. Orfeo is literally never off stage, and he sings almost continuously. (The supporting cast of two, Amore, sung by Lucile Clavereau, and Euridice, Marianna Bianchi, have, besides ensembles, just one aria each.) We can be sure that among those who collaborated to bring *Orfeo* to the stage, Gluck, Durazzo and Calzabigi, Guadagni's vocal and dramatic skills were fully discussed. The role was written to display the power of a supremely eloquent singer; there is an abundance of passionate declamation, and the vocal lines show a simplified lyricism closer to folk song than the instrumentally-conceived vocal style of *opera seria*. There is no hint of the passage-work and cadenzas that Calzabigi later argued against, and the longest ritornellos in the opera are the six-bar introductions to Orfeo's 'Che farò' and Amore's 'Gli sguardi trattieni'.

Nothing about the opera, its composition and its production was run-of-the-mill. Ten years after the première, Gluck told Burney about the unusually rigorous rehearsals he had insisted on: 'He on no account suffered them to leave any part of

---

[10] *Orfeo ed Euridice*, London: Griffin, 1770.
[11] See Chapter 8.

their business, till it was well done, and frequently obliged them to repeat some of his manœuvres twenty or thirty times'.[12] His perfectionism confirmed by a member of the orchestra, Joseph Kämpfer: 'Twenty or thirty repetitions were not enough for him [to drill] the highly-skilled members of the orchestra, which included a number of virtuosos'.[13] Preparations in the Burgtheater commenced at the beginning of September, and Gumpenhuber's schedule confirms that there were twelve rehearsals—more than usual—for the various groups of performers, and a separate technical rehearsal for the stage management.[14]

The composition process was protracted. Much of Guadagni's role must have been completed months before the first night. We owe to the diarist Zinzendorf the information that Gluck and Calzabigi gave a foretaste of the remarkable underworld scene at a dinner on 8 July: 'We dined at Calzabigi's in the Kohlmarkt, with the Duke of Braganza, M. Durazzo, Count Philipp who sat between us, Chevalier Gluck and Guadagni. Everything was well prepared, the wine excellent. After the meal Guadagni sang some airs from an opera that Calzabigi has written, called *Orfeo ed Euridice*. Gluck acted out the furies'.[15] Again on 6 August, 'Count Philipp took me…to the Duke of Braganza's where we dined with Calzabigi, Laugier, Guadagni and Lion, also Chevalier Gluck who played some airs from the opera of *Orfeo*; Guadagni sang'.[16]

To preview an opera in this way was unusual, though Gluck made it a regular event when introducing his operas in Paris in the 1770s. Nor was it common outside Italy for singers to take their place as equals in aristocratic society.[17] Their ambiguous social status must often have caused quandaries like that addressed in England half a century earlier by the Countess of Sunderland, who wanted to invite to her country house a visiting Italian soprano and her husband, stipulating 'provided they would not be above dining with the servants, or by themselves…I don't think any singing

[12] Burney, *The Present State of Music in Germany*, i, p. 344.

[13] 'Zwanzig, dreyssigmal reicht nicht, daß er die geübtesten Spieler der Capelle, unter denen gewiß Virtuosen sind, die Passagen wiederholen läßt.' Joseph Kämpfer, in Carl Friedrich Cramer (ed.) *Magazin der Musik*, Hamburg, 1783, pp. 561–62. The correspondence between the two accounts suggests that the 'twenty or thirty' repetitions had passed into oral history.

[14] Bruce Alan Brown, *Gluck and the French Theatre in Vienna*, p. 373.

[15] 'Nous dînâmes chez Monsieur de Calzapigi sur le *Kohlmarkt* avec le duc de Brangance, Monsieur de Durazzo, le comte Philippe qui était assis entre nous deux, le chevalier Gluck et Guadagni. Tout était bien apprêté, le vin excellent. Après table Guadagni chanta des airs d'un opéra que Calzapigi a composé sous le nom "d'Orphée et d'Euridice". Gluck contrefit les furies.' Zinzendorf, 'Journal', Vienna, 8 July 1762, in Breunlich and Mader, p. 291.

[16] 'Le comte Philippe me mena…chez le duc de Brangance où nous dînâmes avec Calzapigi, Laugier, Guadagni et Lion, et le chevalier Gluk qui joua des airs de l'opéra d'Orphée, et Guadagni chanta.' Zinzendorf, 'Journal', 6 Aug. 1762, in Breunlich and Mader, p. 297.

[17] Private communication from John Rosselli to the author.

will make amends to me for dining and supping with 'em every day'.[18] Later in the century, and especially in England, the situation relaxed, but in mid-century Vienna it was by no means common for singers to sit down to dinner with the aristocracy and be entertained as equals.

One explanation has been proposed by Gerardo Tocchini, who noted that the circle described by Zinzendorf contained at least seven Freemasons, including the Zinzendorf brothers Karl and Ludwig, the Duke of Braganza, Gluck, Calzabigi, Guadagni and Alexandre-Louis Laugier. Tocchini also asserted that the evenings took the usual form of masonic meetings—a meal followed by music—and that in performing the opening scene of Act II, Gluck had deliberately selected what Tocchini argues was 'the most masonic scene in the whole opera'.[19] Freemasonry was the basis of many socially-diverse gatherings, and music an indispensable factor in all masonic meetings; the Freemason Guadagni was to pass much of the last phase of his career in the intimate company of the Freemason nobleman Giuseppe Ximenes.

Despite his centrality to the opera, it is difficult to gain any idea of the impact of Guadagni's performance on the Viennese audience. He is not mentioned in any formal review of the opera. An unusually lengthy notice in the *Wienerisches Diarium* on 13 October was probably contributed by Calzabigi, and unsurprisingly devoted the lion's share of critical discussion to the librettist's interpretation of the myth, though Gluck, the choreographer Angiolini, and the designer Giovanni Maria Quaglio are given credit for their contributions. We owe to a long assessment of the libretto in the *Journal encyclopédique* the information that 'the Viennese court could not leave off applauding the music and the words of this drama, which was given some thirty performances at which their majesties have been regularly present.'[20] The number of performances mentioned in the review is about right: there were nineteen scheduled performances in the autumn of 1762, one of which was cancelled owing to the illness of the young Archduchess Johanna Gabriella, and a further thirteen performances in the spring and summer of 1763.

Imperial approval was confirmed by Zinzendorf, who reported that at the sixth performance of the opera, the Empress gave Guadagni a ring worth 300 ducats, while Gluck received a snuffbox worth 100. There is nothing surprising about the disparity between the rewards. At any time during the eighteenth century, and in any country in Europe, a leading singer could expect to be paid considerably more

---

[18] John Rosselli, *Singers of Italian Opera*, p. 12.

[19] Gerardo Tocchini, *I fratelli d'Orfeo*, Florence: Olschki, 1998, pp. 66–67.

[20] 'La Cour de Vienne ne pouvoit se lasser d'applaudir au chant et aux paroles de ce drame qui a eu environ trente représentations auxquelles LL MM II on constamment assisté.' *Journal encyclopédique*, 15 Feb. 1763, p. 134. This periodical was often published several months after the printed date.

than a composer. The accounts of the French troupe in the Burgtheater show that for his performances in 1763–64, Guadagni was paid 6,000 florins, whereas for the composition of *Orfeo* Gluck received a mere 825.[21]

Testimonies to Guadagni's singing appear briefly in the diaries and reminiscences of amateurs. Without giving details, Zinzendorf contrasted Guadagni's excellent singing with the poor performances of Clavereau and Bianchi.[22] More informatively, the poet and diarist Nicolay considered that Guadagni 'had feeling and understanding and was receptive to direction, three gifts rarely found in Italian virtuosos.... This modest singer allowed himself no added ornamentation or cadenzas, but performed everything most faithfully as the composer had intended'.[23] It is surprising to find the sometimes prickly and arrogant Guadagni described as *bescheidne* (modest). The quantity of ornamentation he added to his role is also something of a puzzle. There is no way of knowing exactly what decoration Guadagni employed in his London performances, nor to what extent this relates to how he sang the role in Vienna. The ornamentation Corri attributed to his performances at the King's Theatre is modest enough, but even so, it may indicate that in London he allowed himself greater freedoms.[24]

The momentum instigated by the dramatic innovations in *Orfeo* was halted by the remaining works that season. The second opera was a revival of Giuseppe Scarlatti's setting of Metastasio's ever-popular *Artaserse*; Scarlatti's setting had first been heard in Lucca in 1747. The opera was designed to open on 26 December but was postponed owing to the death from smallpox of the Archduchess Johanna Gabriella. Then the *répétition générale* scheduled for 31 December was cancelled due to Guadagni's illness. The première finally took place on 4 January 1763. Zinzendorf attended the first night:

---

[21] Daniel Heartz, '*Orfeo ed Euridice*: Some criticisms, revisions, and stage-realizations during Gluck's lifetime', *Chigiana* 9–10 (1975), p. 386; Franz Hadamowsky puts Guadagni's salary at 6,600 florins, see 'Leitung, Verwaltung und ausübende Künstler des Deutschen und Französichen Schauspiels', in *Jahrbuch der Gesellschaft für Wiener Theaterforschung* 12 (1960): 113–33.

[22] 'A 6 heures au théâtre...où Guadagni chanta supérieurement bien autant que l'Amour et Eurydice chantait mal.' Zinzendorf, 'Journal', 10 Oct. 1762, in Breunlich and Mader, p. 305.

[23] 'Guadagni, der erste Sänger, hatte Gefühl, Sinn, und Lenksamkeit, drey seltene Gaben bey Italiänischen Virtuosen....Der bescheidne Sänger hatte sich keinen Zusatz, keine Ferma erlaubt, alles nur in den Sinne des Meisters auf das getreueste vorgetragen.' Edmund Heier, *L H Nicolay (1737–1820) and His Contemporaries*, The Hague: Martinus Nijhoff, 1965, pp. 115–16.

[24] Domenico Corri, *A Select Collection of the Most Admired Songs, Duetts etc from Operas in the Highest Esteem*, Edinburgh, 1779, i, pp. 38–43. On the doubtful authenticity of Corri's ornamentation, see the discussion in Chapter 9.

…to the theatre, where I saw the first performance of Metastasio's opera called 'Artaserse', cut and set to music by Scarlatti. The music was not beautiful, and the airs were not very pleasing. The second actress, Torre, sang well in the air from Act I scene 7, 'Bramar di perdere'; Guadagni did well in 'Per quel paterno amplesso' in Act II scene 10, and Bianchi in the following scene, 'Va tra le selve Ircane'.[25]

The Carnival season ended with a brief revival of *Orfeo* (13 and 14 February) after which the Burgtheater was closed to prepare it for the Lent concerts.[26]

The nature of the preparation is not made clear, though it appears that the stage was built up in a series of tiers to accommodate the chorus and orchestra, and the illumination of the theatre became a talking point.[27] The Lent concerts, held on Sundays, Tuesdays and Thursdays, had been initiated by Durazzo in 1755. The content was similar to that of the regular Friday concerts: a mixture of arias and instrumental items, predominantly concertos. In the early years of the Lent series a number of choral items were regularly included. According to Metastasio, the programmes included 'sacred or moral arias or cantatas, oratorios, psalms translated into German, choruses, madrigals, symphonies, caprices, and every elegant thing that the holy fathers of harmony have been able to conceive'.[28] There seem to have been fewer choral works in 1763, though the series included two full-length dramatic works. The first of these was given on Sunday 27 February when Guadagni took the role of Ozia in Holzbauer's *La Betulia liberata*, Metastasio's *azione sacra* based on the apocryphal Book of Judith, popular in Vienna for many years in a setting by Andrea Bernasconi.

Following a repeat performance of *Betulia*, on Tuesday 1 March, a curious incident took place—an early instance of Guadagni's recalcitrance towards authority. The evidence is of the slenderest. Describing the academy he had attended on 3 March,

---

[25] '…au théâtre où je vis la première représentation de l'opéra de Metastasio intitulé "Artaserse", abrégé et mis en musique par Scarlatti. La musique n'est pas belle, les airs peu agréables. La seconde actrice Torre chant bien cet air dans la VII^e^ scène du 1^er^ acte, *"Bramar di perdere"*, Guadagni celui-ci *"Per quel paterno amplesso"* etc scène X du 2^e^ acte, la Bianchi dans la scène suivante, *"Va tra le selve Ircane"*'. Zinzendorf, 'Journal', 4 Jan. 1763, in Breunlich and Mader, p. 309.

[26] On Ash Wednesday, 16 Feb. 1763, Gumpenhuber recorded: 'On a commencé à racomoder le Theatre pour les Academies'.

[27] 'La numerosa orchestra ed i molti cantori che servono ne' cori sono elevati sul palco in ben disposte scalinate, e circondate da una scena d'ottima architettura: le logge all'intorno sono tutte esteriormente illuminate: pendono dal soffitto sui popoli spettatori quantità di lampadari di cristallo, tutti ricchissimi di candele', Metastasio to Antonio Tolemo Trivulizio, 17 Feb. 1755.

[28] '…Arie e Cantate sacre o morali, Oratorii, Salmi volgarizzati, Cori, Madrigali, Sinfonie, Caprici, e quanto di elegante han saputo imaginar i santi padri dell'armonia.' Metastasio to Trivulizio, 17 Feb. 1755.

and after praising Nicolini's performance, Zinzendorf revealed that Guadagni had 'refused absolutely to sing that day'.[29] Whether his refusal was prior to the concert, or on the evening itself, perhaps in a fit of pique at Nicolini's success, is not clear. The two castratos had been working in close quarters for several months, and Guadagni had shared the stage with Nicolini without incident in both *Artaserse* and *Betulia*, besides the first three Lent concerts of the season. Guadagni was absent from the next concert on 6 March, and when he reappeared at the concert on 8 March the episode was still news: the same day, at dinner with Kaunitz, Durazzo had an argument with Count Wenzel von Paar over 'the Guadagni affair'.[30] Shortly after the event, Guadagni received a 'sweetener', or extraordinary payment, and he appears to have given no further trouble that season. Tales of Guadagni's rebellious behaviour become more common in following years.

The second dramatic offering in the Lenten concerts of 1763 was given on Sunday 13 March, Giuseppe Bonno's setting of Metastasio's allegorical drama *Il sogno di Scipione*. Guadagni continued to sing in the concerts, with one exception, until the end of Lent. At the last academy, Gumpenhuber gave a rare indication of programme content: 'Guadagni sang an aria accompanied by a solo on the violoncello played by [Antonio] Vallotti'.[31] The description fits the aria 'Ah, per pietà placatevi' from Traetta's *Ifigenia in Tauride*, which was to be premièred the following season.[32] If this is the case, it suggests that the academies sometimes gave previews of forthcoming music rather than always repeating popular numbers.

Guadagni's next opera engagement was a revival of Bonno's setting of Metastasio's *L'isola disabitata*, first performed in Vienna in 1754, and given at the Burgtheater on 12 May as part of the empress's birthday celebrations.[33] Bonno's little *azione teatrale* proved popular summer fare. It was repeated at Laxenburg on 15 and 16 May, at Schönbrunn on 10 July, with a further four performances at the Burgtheater. Meanwhile rehearsals for *Orfeo* started up, and Gluck's opera was taken back into

---

[29] 'Nicolini…fut universellement applaudi. Guadagni a refusé tout net de chanter ce jour.' Zinzendorf, 'Journal', 27 Apr. 1762; 3 Mar. 1763.

[30] 'M. de Paar disputa beaucoup avec Durazzo sur le chapitre de Guadagni.' Zinzendorf, 'Journal', 8 Mar. 1763.

[31] 'Le Sʳ Guadagni a chanté…un [air] accompagné d'un seul sur le violoncel joué par le sieur Val[l]otti', Gumpenhuber, 22 Mar. 1763.

[32] See below, Example 12.9.

[33] Earlier sources, for example Haas, Kunz and Zechmeister, wrongly attribute the score to Giuseppe Scarlatti. Scarlatti's *L'isola disabitata*, given in Venice and Vienna in 1757, is a setting of a libretto by Goldoni. See Robert Haas, *Gluck und Durazzo im Burgtheater*, Vienna: Amalthea, 1925, p. 71; Harald Kunz, 'Höfisches Theater in Wien zur Zeit der Maria Theresia', *Jahrbuch des Gesellschaft für Wiener Theaterforschung*, Vienna, 1953–54, p. 107; Gustav Zechmeister, *Die Wiener Theater nächst der Burg und nächst dem Kärntnerthor von 1747 bis 1776*, Vienna: Böhlau, 1972, p. 485.

the repertory, with eleven performances between 24 July and 18 September, when rehearsals began for the new opera by Traetta.

### SEASON OF 1763–1764

The Emperor's name-day opera was Traetta's setting of Coltellini's *Ifigenia in Tauride*.[34] Traetta had already composed *Armida* to a libretto devised by Durazzo and Migliavacca from Quinault's text for Lully, retaining much of its French structure. His reformist credentials were now firmly established in Vienna, and he was a natural choice to follow Gluck with a work in the same vein as *Orfeo*. In fact *Armida*, *Orfeo* and *Ifigenia in Tauride* can be viewed as companion works, connected not only by their innovative integration of chorus and dance into the aria-based discourse of *opera seria*, but, more specifically, by their inclusion of scenes portraying furies: Zinzendorf attended *Ifigenia* and commented on 'the furies which…are strongly in fashion at the French Theatre in Vienna'.[35] The two innovations worked together; the portrayal of the furies called for the full resources of spectacle and a wide range of choral and orchestral timbres, and the taste for such fantastic scenes did much to support the necessity for a substantial dance and chorus component in new operas and ballets. Guadagni, as Oreste, found himself once more singing alongside the Tibaldis, who took the roles of Ifigenia and Toante. *Ifigenia* was premièred on 4 October before the imperial court at Schönbrunn; an entry in the *Wienerisches Diarium* mentions the magnificent lighting in the palace theatre.[36] After the first three performances, it transferred to the Burgtheater. This powerful opera contains one of Guadagni's finest and least-known roles as Oreste.[37] *Ifigenia* received sixteen performances that autumn; the number would had been higher had the theatres not closed to mourn two royal deaths. Towards the end of November, the Archduchess Isabella Maria, the birth of whose first child had been celebrated with Hasse's *Trionfo di Clelia*, gave birth to a second daughter. This time there was no celebratory opera: the child, Marie Christine, died at birth and the mother died a few days later of smallpox. The theatres were closed between 21 November and 4 December.

---

[34] See Daniel Heartz, 'Traetta in Vienna: *Armida* (1761) and *Ifigenia in Tauride* (1763)', *Studies in Music*, Ontario: University of Western Ontario Press, 1982, p. 81; Lucio Tufano, 'Vienna 1763: Calzabigi, Coltellini e *Ifigenia* in una lettera di Pietro Metastasio', in *I viaggi di Orfeo: Musiche e musicisti intorno a Ranieri Calzabigi*, Rome: Edicampus Edizioni, 2012, pp. 19–42.

[35] '…les furies, qui…sont fort arrivés au Théatre françois de Vienne.' Zinzendorf, 'Journal', 8 Dec. 1762. See Brown, *Gluck and the French Theatre*, p. 289.

[36] *Wienerisches Diarium*, 5 Oct. 1763.

[37] See Chapter 12.

The Carnival opera, opening on 26 December 1763, was a revised version of Gluck's *Ezio*, first given in Prague in 1749.[38] It is surprising that after the conspicuous success of *Orfeo*, 'tailor-made' for Guadagni, Gluck did not take more trouble to adapt the title role to exploit the singer's strengths. His most controversial change was to assign him a highly dramatic da capo aria, 'Se il fulmine', which not only has a more vigorous melodic line than he had hitherto given Guadagni, but includes passages of energetic detached singing that could not be further from Guadagni's preferred style. The aria was a self-borrowing from Gluck's own setting of *Il trionfo di Clelia*, given in Bologna just seven months earlier. There is no obvious reason why Gluck should have burdened Guadagni with such uncongenial material unless he wanted to repeat the success of the number at Bologna, regardless of suiting his singer (though this argument is weakened by the fact that *Clelia* had met with no great success). He appears to have paid for his misjudgement. Guadagni's performance was in some way inadequate. According to the *Wienerisches Diarium*, 'The public were justifiably outraged by Ezio when he did badly in the first performance and tried to hinder the universal success which the music deserved. However, he has been instructed in his task, and we can now watch the work with unalloyed pleasure.'[39] This is one of several unexplained criticisms Guadagni attracted in Vienna; equally enigmatic is, from the following season, '*Telemaco* went very badly because…Guadagni was a rogue'.[40] The most likely explanation is that Guadagni did not conceal his distaste for, or inability to perform, 'Se il fulmine'. Zinzendorf did not even mention Guadagni, but enthused over the Tibaldis' singing.[41]

The last operas of the season were part of the lengthy and geographically-spread celebrations for the coronation of Archduke Joseph as King of the Romans. This esoteric title was conferred by the reigning Emperor of the Holy Roman Empire (in this case, Francis I) on his heir (the future Joseph II). The ceremonies took place in Frankfurt, with the formal election on 27 March and the coronation 3 April. One observer of the processions and ceremonies was the young Goethe, who included a colourful description of the festivities in his autobiographical *Dichtung und Wahrheit*.[42] A large party of musicians travelled from Vienna for the occasion;

---

[38] For a summary of the differences between the two versions, see Gabriele Buschmeier, '*Ezio* in Prag und Wien', in *Gluck in Wien*, ed. Gerhard Croll and Monika Woitas, Kassel: Bärenreiter, 1989, pp. 85–88.

[39] 'Das Publikum hat sich mit gerechtem Eifer wider den Aetius empöret, daß er in der ersten Vorstellung seine Sache schlecht gemacht, und den allgemeinen Beyfall, den die Musik verdienet, zu verhindern gesucht hat. Allein er ist zu seiner Schuldigkeit angewiesen: und sehen nun das Stück mit vollkommenen Vergnügen.' *Wienerisches Diarium*, 7 Jan. 1764.

[40] Calzabigi to Kaunitz, 6 Mar. 1767.

[41] 'Il y a quelques airs de Tibaldi et un de sa femme qui sont beaux.' Zinzendorf, 'Journal', 26 Dec. 1763, in Breunlich and Mader, p. 384.

[42] Johann Wolfgang Goethe, *Aus meinem Leben: Dichtung und Wahrheit* (Tübingen and Stuttgart, 1811), tr. John Oxenford as *Truth and Fiction*, bk. 5, London, 1848.

according to Ditters' eyewitness account, this included Durazzo, Gluck, Guadagni and twenty musicians of the Hofkapelle.[43] We know little about the music performed. A short opera by Gluck and Coltellini, *Enea e Ascanio*, now lost, was sung by Tibaldi and Toschi. Ditters played a violin concerto, and bemoaned the fact that he spent more on equipping himself with suitable clothes for the occasion than he received in payment. Guadagni's contribution is not known; whatever it was, he was paid 300 ducats for his services.

Back in Vienna, the celebrations continued with three days of dramatic performances for which the public was granted free entrance to the theatres. The entertainment included Piccinni's *La buona figliuola* and Galuppi's *Le nozze di Dorina* in which Guadagni's sister Lavinia sang.[44] Guadagni's turn came when he created the role of Mercurio in Metastasio and Hasse's *Egeria*, given in the Burgtheater on 24 April. The production was lavish, and the librettist gave a glowing account of the occasion:

> I have never heard music more harmonious, masterly and attractive than that which [Hasse] has written on this occasion…the singers vied with each other to show off their superior abilities; the costumes, including those of the many choruses, were splendid, appropriate to the characters, and of a sumptuousness worthy of the Imperial court, moreover, because a high standard was aimed at in every department, the scenery and the machines achieved elegance, charm and the power to please, exceeding rational hopes and expectations. All in all…it was the most engaging and agreeable spectacle that has been seen in this court for a long time.[45]

Metastasio's commendation was the warmest tribute he ever paid to Guadagni, whom he never, in all his voluminous correspondence, mentioned by name. Perhaps he hesitated to praise one who was in some sense a rival singer when writing to his correspondent and intimate friend Farinelli. Also among the cast were the Tibaldis, Toschi, and Maria Theresa Sartori. The costumes praised by Metastasio had been

---

[43] Carl Ditters von Dittersdorf, *Lebensbeschreibung* (Leipzig, 1801), repr. Munich, 1967, pp. 129–30.

[44] Zechmeister, *Die Wiener Theater nächst der Burg und nächst dem Kärntnerthor*, p. 263.

[45] '…non ho mai sentita musica più armoniosa, magistrale e popolare insieme di quella che ha scritta il Sassone in questa occasione…I cantori hanno fatto pompa a gara della loro abilità veramente non ordinaria: gli abiti, non meno de' personaggi che dei numerosi cori, sono stati splendidi, caraterizzati eccellentemente, e di una ricchezza digna della Corte Imperiale: e perché quando le cose son destinate ad andar bene tutto vi concorre, la decorazione e le macchine sono riuscite eleganti, ridenti e felici più di quello che si poteva ragionevolmente aspettare e desiderare. In somma…il più ridente e più gradito spettacolo che da lunga tempo in qua si sia veduto in questa Corte.' Metastasio to Farinelli, 26 Apr. 1764.

brought to Vienna from Paris by Durazzo at great expense.[46] Guadagni's final contribution to the celebrations was De Majo and Coltellini's *Alcide negli orti Esperidi*, given in the Burgtheater on 7 June.

Shortly before the end of the season Durazzo resigned his direction of the imperial theatres. The reasons, not entirely clear, are scrutinised by Bruce Alan Brown in *Gluck and the French Theatre in Vienna*.[47] By way of compensation, Durazzo was sent to Venice as imperial ambassador, where, within a year or two, he was to supply a crucial missing link in our knowledge of Guadagni's career.

### SEASON OF 1764–1765

Meanwhile in Vienna the autumn season opened with an opera by Gaßmann, who had newly arrived in the capital in the spring of 1763 to compose operas and ballets for the Burgtheater. Unmoved by the innovations of Gluck and Traetta, he selected a popular old Metastasian text for his first opera for Vienna, *Olimpiade*, given on 18 October. His second opera was composed to mark Joseph's second marriage, to Maria Josepha of Bavaria, which took place on 23 January 1765 (a marriage as ill-fated as his first, since Maria Josepha died two years later, also of smallpox). The wedding was celebrated at Schönbrunn by a pair of festive works, both to Metastasian texts: on 24 January Gluck's *Il parnaso confuso* was performed by members of the royal family, with six of the empress's children appearing on stage and Archduke Leopold directing the orchestra. The following day the professionals took over, and Guadagni shared the stage with the Tibaldis, Elisabeth Teuber and Luca Fabris in Gaßmann's *Il trionfo d'amore*. The court official Count Johann Joseph Khevenhüller-Metsch noted that Metastasio had been compelled, through pressure of time, to adapt an old libretto for the present occasion.[48]

When the court moved back to town, the festivities continued with the première of Coltellini and Gluck's *Telemaco* at the Burgtheater (to which the public was again granted free admission to enable them to share in the celebrations).[49] Either because of its occasional nature, or because of unspecified problems, only two performances

[46] See Brown, *Gluck and the French Theatre in Vienna*, pp. 432–33.

[47] Ibid., especially chapter 11, 'After Durazzo'.

[48] 'Dise Pièce ist eine alte pour l'époque du jour etwas aufgebuzte Composition des Abbate Metastasio, als welchem die Zeit zu kurtz geworden, zwei neue Dramme zu verfertigen.' Diary entry for 25 Jan. 1765, in Elisabeth Großegger, *Theater, Feste und Feiern zur Zeit Maria Theresias, 1742–1776, nach den Tagebucheintragungen des Fürsten Johann Joseph Khevenhüller-Metsch*, Vienna: Österreichische Akademie der Wissenschaften, 1987, pp. 224–25.

[49] *Wienerisches Diarium*, 30 Jan. 1765.

were given, on 30 January and 2 February. Rumours of difficulties with the production emerge from a letter written two years later by Calzabigi:

> *Orfeo* went well because we discovered Guadagni, for whom it seemed tailor-made; it would have fared disastrously in other hands. But *Telemaco*, with the finest poetry and exceptionally sublime music, went very badly indeed, because Rosa Tibaldi was no actress, Guadagni was a rogue, and the celebrated Elisabeth Teuber was unsuited to play the part of Circe, having too small a voice for a sorceress, or to do justice to music worthy of an enchantress and an enchantment.[50]

The exact nature of Guadagni's roguery is, again, unexplained. It cannot be the case, as we surmised in connection with *Ezio*, that the music was uncongenial to Guadagni. The arias feature all his favourite styles, with sustained cantabile singing, long notes with opportunities for *messa di voce* and syllabic numbers appropriate to his preferred *parlante* delivery. A notable example, that displays all these characteristics, is the delightful 'Ah! Non turbi il mio riposo'.[51] Some flare-up of his intermittent 'arrogance' or 'laziness' seems the likeliest cause. On 13 May, Gaßmann's *Olimpiade* was repeated, with some changes of cast, as part of the empress's birthday celebrations.[52]

The summer season ended with another royal marriage. To celebrate the wedding of Archduke Leopold to the Princess Maria Luisa of Bourbon, the court translocated to the imperial palace at Innsbruck, where Metastasio and Hasse's *Romolo ed Ersilia* was performed in the Schloßtheater on 6 August 1765, the day after the wedding. There were contradictory accounts of its reception. The *Innsbrucker Mittwochige Ordinarii Zeitung* reported that amidst general admiration, it won the applause of both the court and the cognoscenti,[53] while Khevenhüller alleged that it received no great applause, that the libretto was judged to contain no new ideas, the music

---

[50] 'L'Orfeo andò bene, perche s'incontrò quel Guadagni, per cui pareva fatto a posta, e sarebbe riuscito malissimo in altra mano. Ma il Telemaco, poesia ottima e musica singolarmente divina, andò malissimo perche la Tipaldi non era attrice, il Guadagni un birbante, e la famosa Taiberin inetta al rolo di Circe e senza voce sufficiente per far da Maga, e render bene una musica degna d'una incantatrice e d'un incantesimo.' Calzabigi to Kaunitz, 6 Mar. 1767.

[51] This aria can be heard on 'Arias for Guadagni'.

[52] *Wienerisches Diarium*, 15 May 1765.

[53] 'Dieses…hat den Beyfall des Hofes und aller Kenner, nebst einer allgemeinen Bewunderung sich erworben.' Ursula Simek, *Das Berufstheater in Innsbruck im 18. Jahrhundert*, Vienna: Verlag der Österreichischen Akademie der Wissenschaften, 1992, p. 137. The enthusiastic report in the *Innsbrucker Mittwochige Ordinarii Zeitung* was repeated verbatim in the *Wienerisches Diarium*, 14 Aug. 1765.

somewhat gloomy and old-fashioned and the ballet-pantomimes stiff and formal.[54] The opera was repeated on 11 and 17 August. The occasion was beset with misfortune; shortly before the wedding the bride's uncle died, and the mournful occasion turned into a double tragedy with the sudden death of the emperor on 18 August. All theatrical activity was immediately suspended, and the Viennese theatres were closed for a year of mourning. Guadagni may have thought it a judicious moment to withdraw to Italy.

---

[54] 'Das Spectacle hatte aber keinen sondbahren Applauso, obschon der Libretto vom Abbate Metastasio, die Musique vom Hasse und die Ballets vom Hilverding componiret waren; dem ersteren stellte man aus, daß keine neue Gedancken darinnen befindlich, der zweiten, daß sie etwas traurig und alt-vätterisch ausgefallen, und in denen letzteren zu ville und zu gezwungene Pantomimes angebracht worden wären.' 6 Aug. 1765, in Großegger, *Theater, Feste und Feiern zur Zeit Maria Theresias*, p. 241.

# 7

## Return to the Veneto (1765–1769)

෨

THERE IS NO trace of Guadagni in librettos or theatre archives during the next season. However, a colourful episode, related in convincing detail in a letter from Durazzo to Kaunitz, locates him in Venice at the end of 1765. (Durazzo's account to some extent corroborates an anecdote circulated by Cramer.[1]) According to Durazzo, on his return to Italy Guadagni was sought out by several theatres, but declared that he would perform only in churches or at court. (If true, it would be good to know the reason for this preference.) He eventually accepted a post at San Marco, with an additional duty to sing at the Doge's table, for an annual salary of 200 ducats; the 'service de table' amounted to no more than three engagements a year, and Guadagni would be free during Carnival to undertake other work wherever he could find it. He was to be installed on Christmas Eve, and had gone so far as to stipulate that the orchestra be enlarged and improved by the appointment of some ten or twelve new players. By custom, the musicians of San Marco dressed in clerical garb, donning a surplice over their black gowns to distinguish them from the secular musicians brought in from the Venetian theatres. But Guadagni turned up in a golden robe and was persuaded to adopt the sacred vestment only on hearing that without it he could not take up his engagement. He sang his appointed motet and left before the end of the service. The following day was Christmas Day, but nothing was heard of the new recruit. Consequently, on St Stephen's Day, an armed escort was despatched to force him from his house and accompany him through the

---

[1] See note 37 of Introduction, on Carl Friedrich Cramer.

streets, across the square crowded with masked merrymakers, up the great staircase and into the hall where the Doge's dinner was being held. After insisting that he sing, the Doge informed him that as punishment he was to be taken to the castle on the Lido, incarcerated there for a fortnight, after which he would be expelled from Venice. Appalled at the idea of expulsion, Guadagni fell to his knees at the foot of the throne, weeping uncontrollably, and begged for pardon, declaring that he had not absented himself through malice but because he was ill. All the nobility laughed and were moved to urge the Doge to pardon him.[2]

It appears that this absurd narrative, so typical of many less well-attested anecdotes about Guadagni, is likely to be authentic. As imperial ambassador to the Venetian republic, Durazzo was almost certainly present at the dinner, and his account has the additional virtue of immediacy, being written within days of the event. Some twenty years later the story was still being told. Cramer's version differs in that he describes it as the custom that the first singer at San Benedetto should sing at the Christmas services in San Marco and at the Doge's banquet, and adds the further detail that Guadagni initially refused to sing because he 'was not accustomed to sing at dinner'. According to Cramer, he used the Venetian dialect word 'disnar', which would imply that he did not sing while eating, or at table—rather different from performing in a

---

[2] Durazzo's account, in his typically imperfect French, runs as follows: 'Hier nôtre ami Guadagni à donné au public une scene trop comique pour que vous n'en aiez pas le recit pour rire un moment. A son retour en Italie il à été cherché par plusieurs Theatres, et à toujours déclaré qu'il ne vouloit plus chanter qu'aux Eglises, ou pour des Cours. Le Procurateur Morosini qui est un homme de gout et qui cherche a se distinguer aiant l'inspection de la Musique de S. Marc a engagé le Sr. Guadagni avec des appointemens de 200 Ducats ou de 800 fl par an sa vie durante pour la Chapelle, et les services de Table du Doge qui sont trois dans toute l'année, laissant au même Guadagni la permission d'aller pendent le Carneval ou il seroit apellé. La nuit de la veille de Noel à été le moment de l'installation puisque pour repondre au Choix du nouveau musicien on avoit refait la moitié de l'orchestre et engagé dix ou douze nouveaux sujets. L'usage est que tous les Musiciens de la Chapelle s'abillent en Prêtres, ou peu s'en faut puisque sur un abit noir, ils mettent un surplus ou Rochet qui les distingue des autres Musiciens prophanes qui sont invités de tous les Theatres de Venise. Nôtre homme est arrivé a la sacristie avec un abit tout d'or, et n'à consenti qu'avec beaucoup de peine a endosser l'harnoi sacré sans le quel on lui à déclaré qu'il ne pouvoit prendre possession de sa charge. Il à chanté son motet ordinaire, et s'est retiré sans attendre la fin de matines. Le lendemain jour de Noel point de nouvelles du nouveau champion, ny le matin ny le soir; Enfin hier jour de St Etienne n'aiant point paru a l'Eglise on l'à envoié chercher à sa maison par une Garde d'Esclavons ou Capelletti les quelles le sabre a la main l'ont accompagné a travers plusieurs rues, et au milieu de la Place qui pour lors etoit remplie de Masques de toutes especes, et par le Grand escalier jusques a la salle ou etoit la Table Publique. Apres l'avoir contraint de chanter on lui à dit qu'on alloit le mener au Chateau del Lido ou il seroit 15 jours en prison la chaine au pied, et qu'ensuite il seroit chassé de Venise. L'idée dello sfratto à épouvanté notre homme qui est allé se mettre a genoux sur la marche du Throne, et à déclaré qu'il n'avoit pas manqué par malice mais parcequ'il étoit malade, et à demandé pardon en pleurant a toutes forçes. Toutes les grosses Peruques ont ri, et se sont attendries, et on permis au Doge de lui accorder sa graçe.' Durazzo to Kaunitz, Venice, 29 Dec. 1765, in Gerhard Croll, 'Musiker und Musik in der Privatkorrespondenz von Wenzel Anton Fürst von Kaunitz', *Staatskanzler Wenzel Anton von Kaunitz-Rieberg,* ed. Grete Klingenstein and Franz Szabo, Graz: Schneider, 1996, pp. 352–53.

servant's capacity. Cramer turns the joke back on Guadagni, who was, on account of this scruple, compelled to sing from a kneeling position before the Doge.

The escapade did Guadagni no lasting harm: some six years later, the same Doge, Alvise Mocenigo, ennobled him with the order of Cavaliere di San Marco. We must presume that he maintained his employment at San Marco for the remainder of the year, and possibly for many years subsequently: early in 1776 he was excused a fine for not singing in the Santo in Padua because his Christmas duties at San Marco were held to take precedence.[3]

SEASON OF 1766–1767

The following season he remained in Venice and resumed his theatrical career at San Benedetto. The first opera of Carnival was a new version of the ever-popular *Olimpiade*, with Guglielmi, Pampani, and Brusa setting an act each. During its rehearsal period, it was poorly previewed by the Venetian writer and philosopher Giammaria Ortes:

> The music will be of the most commonplace, and ill-matched, comprising the first act by Pampani, the second by Sarti, and the third by Brusa. [*recte*: Guglielmi, Pampani, Brusa]. The audience will be displeased to find nothing new in what cannot but be old, and to find [Anna Maria] Picinelli, Guadagni and [Luca] Fabris no better than what they were in previous years.[4]

When the opera opened on 26 December 1766, Ortes changed his opinion: 'The opera here in San Benedetto was a great success, for if truth be told the two singers Guadagni and Fabris sang and declaimed very well; and since they are for the moment great friends with each other, each one strove to better the other's performance'.[5] The second opera of the season, Bertoni's *Ezio*, was given to celebrate a visit

---

[3] See Boscolo and Pietribiasi. *La cappella musicale antoniana*, p. 285.

[4] 'La musica sarà delle più comuni, e mal assortita ancora, steso il primo atto dal Pampani, il secondo dal Sarti, e il terzo da Brusa. L'uditorio resterà mal contento di non trovar nuovo quel che non può esser che vecchio, e di non trovar la Picinelli, Guadagni e Fabbri migliori di quel che fossero negli anni avanti.' Ortes to Hasse, 20 Dec. 1766. Ortes' voluminous correspondence is in the Cicogna collection in the Museo Correr in Venice (Cod. Cicogna 2658). A selection of the letters to Hasse and his family is published in Livia Pancino, *Johann Adolf Hasse e Giammaria Ortes: lettere (1760–1783)*, Turnhout: Brepols, 1998.

[5] 'L'Opera qui in S. Benedetto ebbe molto incontro per li due musici Guadagni e [Luca Fabris], che veramente recitano e cantano assai bene, ed essendo per ora fra essi molto amici, ciascuno prova a far meglio comparire l'altro.' Ortes to Hasse, 10 Jan. 1767.

to Venice from Guadagni's former employer Carl Eugen of Württemberg. Ortes found the music 'unremarkable'.[6]

It is of some interest that Guadagni's sister Angiola sang in both *Olimpiade* (as Argene) and *Ezio* (Onoria), and it is fascinating to speculate whether she played a part in smoothing down Guadagni's ruffled feathers and relaunching him on his operatic career, just as she appears to have done in 1756 after the trauma of the Lisbon earthquake. There was something of a family reunion in Venice that season. Romance was in the air: the comic opera running at the San Moisè was *Il matrimonio per concorso* by Felice Alessandri, soon to become the husband of Guadagni's youngest sister, Lavinia; they married early in 1767, between Carnival and the opening of the spring season in Florence. Furthermore, the cast of *Il matrimonio* included not only Lavinia but the tenor Antonio Nasolini, future husband of Angiola; this couple married in 1768. Guadagni was to spend the rest of his life in close contact with these family members.

Carl Eugen's visit was commemorated with a further musical celebration on 11 February, when the four principal singers at San Benedetto, Picinelli, Guadagni, Fabris, and Giuseppe Alferi, sang a 'Cantata for four voices on the occasion of the spectacle performed before his Serene Highness the Duke of Württemberg and Teck'. Although in the following account the music is attributed to Bertoni, who probably directed it, the libretto informs us that it was by the young composer Andrea Lucchesi; the libretto was by Gozzi. The occasion was particularly magnificent:

> The theatre was decorated from top to bottom in the most elegant manner; the front of the boxes were painted silver and supported a framework into which flowers and other ornamentation were miraculously intertwined, a display both varied and harmonious and infinitely pleasing to the eyes. The ceiling was adorned with scrolls and painted designs on a silver background.
>
> Twenty-five crystal chandeliers were suspended from the ceiling, arranged symmetrically to illuminate the theatre, the central one being of gigantic dimensions; moreover, in between the boxes, there were crystal brackets supporting huge candles which added to the brilliance. The parterre was covered with carpets, and against the front of the boxes in the first tier were placed seats for the ladies and gentlemen attending the celebration. A staircase furnished with silvered balustrades rose from the stage; the orchestra, numbering some 80 players, dressed in uniforms of blue decorated with silver lace and frogging,

---

[6] Ortes to Hasse, 21 Feb. 1767.

was disposed on either side of it. Over the stage a magnificent triumphal arch had been erected, which reached to the ceiling. From within this arch hung a large red curtain which hid the rest of the stage.

His Serene Highness arrived [towards sunset].[7] He was greeted by the ladies and gentlemen, who were dressed in their finest clothes, radiant with gold and jewels. After a sinfonia there followed a most beautiful Serenata, which made allusion to the Duke's birthday. The poetry was by Signor Conte Gasparo Gozzi, and music by Signor Bertoni, director of the girls' choir at the celebrated Ospedale dei Mendicanti. The singers were Signor Guadagni and Signor Lucca Fabris, both of them singers of the first rank, together with Signora Picinelli and the tenor Aferi. When the Serenata was concluded, the curtain of the triumphal arch, which had hidden the stage behind it, was raised to reveal a dining table in the form of a horse-shoe; it was so richly furnished that everyone who saw it was amazed. The magnificence of the table was further augmented by the splendour of the adornments on stage, where a pair of large looking glasses, plaques, sideboards, and other valuable furnishings were bathed in light, giving the appearance of an enchanted space.

His Serene Highness ascended the stage, together with the ladies and gentlemen, and took his place in the middle of the table, with on one side the wife of the imperial ambassador, and on the other the Princess Savorgnan Rezzonico, whose husband was a nephew of His Holiness.[8] The other women followed, taking their places to one side or the other. The gentlemen stood behind their chairs, waiting on the ladies while being themselves served by waiters in splendid liveries. Three courses were served; the food was exquisite, prepared by the cooks with the most fastidious care; there were drinks of every description, and elaborate desserts, decorated with sweetmeats and exotic flowers, so that it seemed that nature had been persuaded to bring forth the fruits of springtime even in this harsh and bitter season. His Serene Highness not only made frequent toasts to the ladies, but from time to time left his place to pay his respects to this one or that, serving them himself, and showing that courtesy

---

[7] 'verso le ore una della notte', Italian time. From the fourteenth century until the middle of the eighteenth century Italy had its own system of the 24-hour clock. The first hour began with the Angelus, usually coinciding with sunset, and thus varying with the seasons. In February, this would place the Duke's arrival in the late afternoon. The system persisted in some regions into the nineteenth century, and all references to the hour in Italian sources should be treated with caution.

[8] In 1758 the Paduan Carlo Rezzonico became Pope Clement XIII; in the same year his nephew Ludovico Rezzonico married Faustina Savorgnan, an event commemorated in a ceiling painting by Tiepolo in the Ca' Rezzonico in Venice.

and liberality which, together with all his gifts, adorn his princely and generous spirit.

After supper, everyone descended to the parterre and devoted themselves to the ball, which lasted till [the following morning.] It is impossible to describe the profusion of refreshments in their freshness and flavour, the abundance of which were offered not only to the nobility in the parterre but also to those who remained in the boxes to observe this illustrious, magnificent, and well-managed entertainment.[9]

Guadagni appears to have had no further operatic engagements that season. Perhaps he had reason to compare conditions in Venice unfavourably with those he had left in Vienna. The following month, he wrote to Kaunitz asking to be considered for a part in the forthcoming celebrations in Vienna for the wedding of Archduchess Maria Carolina and Ferdinand IV of Naples and Sicily. The letter, a routine plea, is significant in that it is the only surviving letter in Guadagni's own handwriting:

Your Highness, News has reached me that on the occasion of the imminent marriage of the Royal Archduchess with the illustrious King of the Two Sicilies an opera is to be prepared and that Your Highness will direct it so that it will be performed with the most luxurious magnificence. Trusting in the gracious attention which Your Highness was pleased to pay me in Innsbruck, I venture to ask that I might be engaged, being moved not by greed for the advantage which it is in your gift to bestow, but declaring myself from this time forth wholly content with whatever you might deign to dispose. By granting this, Your Highness would confer on me that favour which would uniquely enable me to confound my enemies, who have put it about that I was dismissed by express order of Her Majesty, rumours that have wounded me to the heart. I assure Your Highness of my eternal gratitude, and would employ all the little talent given to me by the Almighty to bring honour to Your Highness and to merit your patronage.[10]

---

[9] *Dei magnifici spettacoli, altre feste, e spezialmente della sontuosa regatta del 3 giugno 1767 istituita ad ornorare il soggiorno in Venezia di Sua Altezza Sereniss. Carlo Eugenio Duca di Vittemberga, Teck ecc.*, Venice, 1767, pp. 5–8.

[10] 'Altezza, La voce sparsa che in occasione del prossimo sposalizio della Real Archiduchessa con S. ill. il Re delle due Sicilie debbasi far opera e che V. A. debba dirigela affiné venga eseguita con la più grandiosa Magnificenza. Confidato io nelle graziose esibizioni che V. A. con piaque farmi in Insbruck, audisco supplicarla d'essere preferito, Mosso non per avidità d'Interesse quale ripongo nelle Mani di V. A. dichiarandomi da quest'ora contentissimo di tutto ciò della degnerosi dispare. Degnandosi V. A. conferirmi codesta grazia che per me sarebbe singolarissima per confonder i miei malevoli, quali sanno divigato da per tutto esser io stato scacciato per ordine espresso di S. M. I., ciò che mi causa un'afflizione che [?] mi resta nel cuore; assicura V. A. che

In the event there was no wedding opera. The ceremony was conducted by proxy on 12 May 1768 without celebrations.[11]

### SEASON OF 1767–1768

The following season took Guadagni to Rome; it was, as far as we know, the only occasion he ever sang there. The reigning composer was Piccinni, who had enjoyed an immense following in Rome ever since his successful setting of Goldoni's adaptation of Richardson's novel, *Pamela*, as *La Cecchina, ossia la buona figliuola* in 1760. The opera circulated throughout Europe in a remarkably short time. The Carnival operas were Piccinni's new *opera seria*, *Olimpiade* (his second setting of this Metastasian text), and Sacchini's *Artaserse*. They were given in the large and magnificently-decorated Teatro Argentina. An English traveller's description of audience behaviour suggests a marked improvement in attention and appreciation from accounts dating from earlier in the century:

> I could perceive that the people of fashion, who came every night, began, after the opera had been repeated several nights, to abate in their attention, to receive visitors in their boxes, and to listen only when some favourite airs were singing: whereas the audience in the pit uniformly preserve the most perfect silence, which is only interrupted by gentle murmurs of pleasure from a few individuals, or a universal burst of applause from the whole assembly.... At certain airs, silent enjoyment was expressed in every countenance; at others, the hands were clasped together, the eyes half shut, and the breath drawn in with a prolonged sigh, as if the soul was expiring in a torrent of delight.[12]

For reasons that remain obscure, Guadagni returned to Padua in the spring of 1768 and petitioned the Arca to renew his appointment. There may have been family circumstances that encouraged him to re-establish himself in the city, bearing in mind how the close-knit family supported each other at various points in their careers. While Lavinia and Alessandri set off for a couple of seasons in London, Angiola settled in Padua, marrying the tenor Antonio Nasolini, who was on the payroll at

---

gliene conserverò eterna obligazioni, ed impiegavo tutto il poco di talenta donatomi dall'Altissimo per far onore all' A. V. e meritarmi il suo Patrocinio. Mentre in attenzione de veneratissimi comandi di V. A. a cui con profondissimo inchino mi dò l'onore di dichiarami, Dell' Altezza Vostra, umilissimo ed ossequiosissimo serva, Gaetano Guadagni. 18 Mar. 1767.' In the Moravský zemský archive in Brno, G436.

[11] See Andrea Sommer-Mathis, *Tu felix Austria nube. Hochzeitsfeste der Habsburger im 18. Jahrhundert*, Vienna: Musikwissenschaftlicher Verlag, 1994.

[12] John Moore, *A View of Society and Manners in Italy*, ii, London, 1787, pp. 85–86.

the Santo from 1758 to 1799. Also present in the city was Gaetano's elder brother Giuseppe, who had served in the Cappella continuously since 1751. Giuseppe's family included two sons, who contributed in various ways to Gaetano's comfort in the latter years of his life: Antonio, who owned a draper's shop, predeceased the singer and left him a handsome annuity, while Vincenzo appears to have become Gaetano's companion and was later his principal heir. The influx of Guadagnis may have been prompted by Giuseppe's ill health: he retired from the Santo in 1769 and died the following year.[13]

Guadagni's application to the Santo and its reception were very different from his original engagement. The minutes of his appointment describe him as 'the celebrated contralto Gaetano Guadagni'. In a remarkably bold demand, he applied to receive the exceptional salary of 400 ducats a year, using as precedent the salary of a recently deceased singer, Mariano Nicolini. This was double his salary at San Marco, and made him by far the best-paid musician in the Cappella, where the musical director Vallotti received only 240 ducats. His new contract committed him to singing at the five principal feasts, specified as the Santa Lingua (mid-February), Easter, Pentecost, the Sunday during the Octave of St Anthony (mid-June), and Christmas; he was also required to sing at any further services where the orchestra was employed. He was obliged to seek permission from the authorities before accepting invitations to sing at foreign courts. The salary was closely tied to Guadagni's attendance at the five feasts: initially it was to be paid in five instalments of 80 ducats; payment was to be made after each of the five feasts, and absence from one of the feasts would lose him the entire instalment. The payments were, however, awkwardly spaced, leaving him with no money coming in between midsummer and Christmas. The arrangement, which seems to have been framed with the suspicion that Guadagni might not fulfil his statutory obligations, was subsequently modified so that he was to be paid 80 ducats every three months 'like the other salaried musicians', with 160 ducats paid in the final trimester. The governors, 'mindful of his fame and qualities,' which judgement Vallotti endorsed, elected him unanimously.[14] He took up his position on 16 May.

The mutual esteem between Vallotti and Guadagni is evidenced in tributes on both sides. Within months of Guadagni's readmission, Vallotti had confirmed his estimation of the singer by writing a new setting of the antiphon 'O lingua benedicta', an integral part of the liturgical celebrations of St Anthony. This setting, for alto solo and strings, was performed by Guadagni for nearly 20 years both in regular

[13] Giuseppe Gennari, *Notizie giornaliere* i, pp. 363, 404, 477.
[14] See entries for 30 Apr., 16 May, and 6 Aug. 1768 in Boscolo and Pietribiasi, op. cit., pp. 247–49.

services and whenever distinguished visitors came to the Santo.[15] Guadagni for his part commissioned from the engraver Ignatio Colombo a portrait of Vallotti, with this dedication:

> This picture portrays the face of Vallotti, and depicts his character on his face. Music, you who boast Phoebus and the Muses as your leaders here acknowledge that this is your leader, your judge and your father. I, Ignatio Columbo, fashioned this portrait at the request of that most outstanding musician Cavalier Gaetano Guadagni.

Two years later Burney described the musical establishment at the Santo:

> There are on common days forty performers in the service of this church; eight violins, four violetti or tenors [violas], four violoncellos, four double basses, and four wind instruments, with sixteen voices. There are eight *castrati* in salary, among whom is Signor Gaetano Guadagni, who, for taste, expression, figure, and action, is at the head of his profession. His appointment is four hundred ducats a year, for which he is required to attend only at the four [*recte*: five] principal festivals. The first violin [Giulio Meneghini, who had recently replaced the aging Tartini] has the same salary. The second *soprano*, Signor Casati, has a feeble voice, but is reckoned to sing with infinite taste and expression. The famous Antonio Vandini is the principal violoncello, and Matteo Bissioli Bresciano the first hautbois in this select band.[16]

Employment at the Santo occupied only part of Guadagni's year. He played a conspicuous role in many musical events in the city. One of the most important sources for his Paduan activities is the diary of Giuseppe Gennari, tireless archivist of the city of Padua. The first event he records after Guadagni's return to the Santo is a sumptuous feast given on 30 August in honour of the newly-elected Provedittore (governor) of Padua, Marino Cavalli, sponsored by the Accademia Delia, of which Cavalli was patron. The academy commissioned a cantata for the occasion, with words by a local nobleman, Count Nicolò Mussato, and music (now lost) by Josef Mysliveček. The singers were Guadagni and Antonio Casati. Unfortunately, like many of his

---

[15] See Example 12.10 discussed below, ms in Biblioteca Antoniana A–VI–518, dated February 1769. This was the sixth and last setting of the antiphon by Vallotti, the first for alto solo.

[16] Burney, *The Present State of Music in France and Italy*, p. 136. Burney was mistaken over Meneghini's salary, which was a mere 100 ducats. Even Tartini received only 170.

contemporaries, Gennari was more concerned to describe the lighting and special ornamental effects than to give any details of the music:

> 30 August 1768: this evening a ball was given at the Accademia Delia in honour of His Excellency Governor Marino Cavalli, elected as patron of the academy. The hall of the academy was gracefully decorated for the occasion with small lamps that reflected the light to delightful effect; three huge, well-lit mirrors were placed against three of the walls; the fourth side was occupied by the singers. Each of the mirrors was flanked by two gilded statues on decorated plinths; on the fourth side, above the musicians, were displayed the arms of the academy, and on the opposite wall those of His Excellency the Governor....The feast began [in the early evening], with a chorus of excellent music to words by Count Antonmaria Borromeo; then a cantata for two voices was performed, with words by Count Nicolò Mussati, sung by two skilful singers, Casati and Gaetano Guadagni. After the music the ball began, which lasted late into the following morning.[17]

Two days later, on 1 September, a second work by Mysliveček was given: the serenata *Narciso al fonte*, with words by Zangarini. Gennari again noted the occasion:

> This morning, the noble ministers, accompanied by more than a hundred gentlemen in court dress, presented the oration on behalf of the city to the most excellent governor, who, with fourteen of our most noble women, welcomed them very graciously...to the lodgings of Count Abate Vigodarzere. The house, surrounded by fine verdure, was illuminated, and there, until [late in the evening] was given a serenata in which Casati and Guadagni sang, each rivalling the other in skill.[18]

These two performances are typical of Guadagni's activities in the sphere of private music making. Although Padua contained two fine opera houses, the Obizzi and the Nuovo, Guadagni sang only once at each of them. The majority of his performances were in private houses, which, besides the Accademia Delia and the Casa Vigodarzere, included the Palazzo Pretorio, the Palazzo Dondo Orologio, and the Casa Memmo. For regular employment in the public theatre, he had to seek opportunities outside the city.

[17] Gennari, *Notizie giornaliere*, i, p. 33.
[18] Gennari, op. cit., i, pp. 34–35.

SEASON OF 1768–1769

Perhaps for this reason, Guadagni showed no intention of retiring permanently to Padua. During the following season he exercised his right to apply for leave to take operatic work, and was engaged at San Benedetto for an extended autumn and winter programme. The first opera, Borghi's *Alessandro in Armenia*, to a libretto by Doriano, opened on 26 November 1768 and was the occasion of an interesting in-company incident which, if true, reflects well on Guadagni's altruism and generosity. The troupe for this season included the notoriously temperamental prima donna Anna de Amicis. Ortes, our principal eyewitness in Venice at this period, described how De Amicis wanted to include an aria with obbligato violin, in the latest fashion. Nazari, the leader of the orchestra, asked for an extra 100 zecchini for performing the solo. The impresario was unwilling to meet his demands, but the tenor, Zanetti, who took the role of Tigrane, offered to play the violin solo for a fee of 50 zecchini, 20 of which were contributed by Guadagni who was allegedly eager for the aria to go ahead for the greater success of the opera.[19] The incident also illustrates the versatility of some eighteenth-century singers (though there is no record of how Zanetti's cut-price performance was received).

The second opera, opening on 26 December, was a revival of Galuppi's *Arianna e Teseo*, with a libretto by Pariati. The two operas prompted an important observation by Ortes, who gave a rare opinion on Guadagni's lack of, or reluctance to exploit, virtuosity:

> As for our opera here [in Venice], it can be said that music of the second opera at San Benedetto, which was by Buranello, was better than the first—in which, by the way, the only outstanding numbers were an aria sung by Guadagni, a duet and the sinfonia. The libretto is *Arianna e Teseo*, and the scene with the Minotaur isn't at all bad....De Amicis, the prima donna, had great success in the first opera, *Alessandro in Armenia*...something which comes easily to those who sing in the bravura style as she does, but which rarely happens to those who sing with expression, such as Guadagni, who always gives pleasure but rarely astonishes.[20]

[19] Livia Pancino, *Johann Adolf Hasse e Giammaria Ortes*, pp. 169–70.

[20] 'Quanto all'opere qui nostre, si può dire che questa seconda in San Benedetto sia miglior della prima per la musica, che è appunto di Buranello, nella quale per altro di eccellente non v'è che un aria cantata da Guadagni, un duetto, e la sinfonia. Il libretto è l'Arianna e Teseo, e la scena del Minatauro non è cattiva....Nell'opera passata, ch'era Alessandro in Armenia...la Amicis ch'è prima parte di donna incontrava molto di più; ciò che avvien facilmente a chi canta di bravura come essa, a avvien ben di rado a chi canta d'espressione come Guadagni che piacerà sempre senza sorprender mai.' Ortes to Hasse, 31 Dec. 1768.

The third opera of the season, given in January 1769, was Mysliveček's setting of
Metastasio's *Demofoonte*. According to Ortes, its popularity was due to a child
dancer, Olinto, the son of the ballerina Dessales, who stole the show by exploit-
ing 'a thousand comic gestures' taught him by Guadagni.[21] For the summer season
Guadagni was engaged with a different company at San Salvatore to sing in Guglielmi
and Mazzolà's *Ruggiero*, premièred on 3 May; by way of colleagues he exchanged De
Amicis for the more amenable Cecilia Grassi. Ortes judged that its popular success eclipsed the opera (Sacchini's *Nicoraste*) at San Benedetto.[22] A few weeks later,
Guadagni returned, with the company from San Salvatore, to San Benedetto for a
short run of Galuppi's *Il re pastore*.

At some point during this season Guadagni was recruited by George Hobart,
newly appointed manager of the King's Theatre, to boost the precarious fortunes
of Italian opera in London.[23] Rumours of Guadagni's engagement were rife as early
as April. Elizabeth Harris, writing to her son, noted that 'they talk of having the
Guadagni and the Amici, but I have liv'd long enough to know that spring talk and
winter performances are not always the same'.[24] In the event, Hobart failed to engage
De Amicis.

Guadagni's next move was a return to Padua, where he succeeded in obtaining
an engagement at the Teatro Nuovo in Bertoni's *Il trionfo di Clelia*, which opened
on 10 June. Gennari found the music unimpressive but the ballets, danced by a pair
of French dancers, Le Picq and Binett, appearing for the first time in Italy, 'stupen-
dous', drawing in a great number of spectators, as did Guadagni and Grassi, who
brought their reputations with them from Venice.[25] The opera, which Gennari

---

[21] 'La terza opera in S Benedetto che è il Demofoonte è più tosta piacuta.... E per cosa particolare, chi crede
ella fra gli altri si porti meglio? Questi è il bambino Olinto, ch'è un bamboccio figlio della ballerina
Annina de Scales [Dessales], e che, istruito da Guadagni in mille scimmiottagini, insegnategli nell'aria del
terzo atto rappresentare il suo carattere e la sua situazione a meraviglia bene.' Ortes to Cristina Hasse, 4
Feb. 1769.

[22] 'Le opere per altro, sebbene si sian studiati di renderle delle migliori, non son riuscite che mediocri: la
Macarini e Aprile in un teatro non fan migliore comparsa della Grassi e di Guadagni nell'altro. La musica
di tutti e due è però buona, e fatta l'una da Sacchini [= *Nicoraste* at San Benedetto] e l'altra da Guglielmi
con qualche gara di superarsi l'un l'altro, pare che il pubblico giudichi più a favore questo secondo.' Ortes to
Hasse, 6 May 1769.

[23] Ian Woodfield, *Opera and Drama in Eighteenth-Century London*, Cambridge: Cambridge University Press,
2001, pp. 20–22.

[24] Elizabeth Harris to James Harris Jr, 21 Apr. 1769, in Burrows and Dunhill, *Music and Theatre*, p. 545.

[25] 'La musica non è granché ma i balli sono stupendi, i due divi si sentivano un po' dappertutto....L'eccellenza
di monsieur Picq e di mademoiselle Binec, ballerini francesi, non più veduta in Italia, vi attirò cotal numero
di spettatori perché quanto ai musici, così Gaetano Guadagni come Cecilia Grassi, furono sentiti più volte a
Venezia ed altrove'. Gennari, op. cit., i, pp. 43–44.

noted as a great financial success, ran till the end of the short summer season on 4 July. Guadagni's last engagement that summer was on 22 July, to sing at a lavish evening concert ('richly illuminated, and with exquisite refreshments') at the Palazzo Pretorio for the visiting emperor, Joseph II.[26] A month later, he sought permission for a prolonged visit to London.[27]

[26] 'Addì 22, giorno di sabato, alle 17 ore giunse in Padova Giuseppe II imperatore…La sera nel palazzo pretorio ci fu bella ricrezione di numerose dame e di cavalieri con ricca illuminazione e squisiti rinfreschi, e vi furono cantate molte arie musicali da virtuosi e virtuose a bella posta invitati colla speranza che sua maestà cesarea potessa trattenersi in Padova.' Gennari, op. cit., i, pp. 45–46.

[27] 19 Aug. 1769: 'Fu accolta all'unanimità la supplica con cui Gaetano Guadagni contralto chiede do poter recarsi a Londra, ove è stato richiesto per cantare per un anno', see Boscolo and Pietribiasi, op. cit., p. 253.

# 8

## Success and Scandal in London (1769–1771)

⌒

### SEASON OF 1769–1770

GUADAGNI ARRIVED IN London in the autumn of 1769. For once, we have reliable information about his lodgings: a notice in the *Public Advertiser* of 13 January 1770 mentions 'his house in Market Lane, near the [King's] Theatre'—a small street parallel with the Haymarket and fronting the west side of the theatre. Guadagni may have noted with wry amusement that *opera buffa*, which, as a member of Crosa's troupe, he had helped to introduce to the capital in 1748, was now far more popular than *opera seria*, to the extent that in the previous season only comic operas had been performed, the repertory being dominated by Piccinni's *La buona figliuola*. But Hobart, the new manager at the King's Theatre, now planned to offer a mixed season, and announced his double team of serious and comic singers in the *Public Advertiser* of 5 September 1769 with Guadagni at the head of the company. His salary was rumoured to be £1,150, the usual figure for a leading *primo uomo*.[1]

Among the comic team was his sister Lavinia, who was to become the unwitting cause of friction between Guadagni and the management. Deploying his cast of *buffa* singers for the first opera of the season, Piccinni's *Le contadine bizzarre*, Hobart demoted Lavinia, making his mistress, Anna Zamperini, first woman in her place. Riots broke out between the supporters of both singers, and Hobart appears to have taken unnecessarily officious steps to control the disruption:

> The talk of the Town today has been on a supposed riot to happen to night at the opera occasioned by the passionate indiscretion of Mr Hobart, the manager who the last opera night was so enraged at hearing some hissing at his

[1] *London Magazine*, 40 (1771), pp. 93–97.

favourite Zamparini from the upper gallery [that he] went up himself & posted a centinel in it, directing him to take notice of any person who hiss'd there. The captain of the guard took off the soldier soon, but tis said Mr Hobart got another placed there, & having threatened to continue this practice, great indignation has arisen & a riot threatened.[2]

There is no record of Guadagni's reaction to what Burney diplomatically refers to as 'an imagined affront',[3] but the situation cannot have made for easy relations with Hobart. The first serious opera of the season, a pasticcio based on Piccinni's *Olimpiade*, which Guadagni had premièred in Rome two years previously, caused no such affray. It seems to have had a successful run, with a total of sixteen performances in the course of the season. The second serious opera was Guglielmi's setting of an old Metastasian favourite, *Ezio*, which opened on 13 January 1770 (discussed in Chapter 9).

Among Guadagni's more surprising activities in the autumn of 1769 is his membership of the Noblemen and Gentlemen's Catch Club, an essentially aristocratic and very English institution, which met weekly for dinner and music making, particularly for the performance of catches and glees, whose composition the club encouraged with competitions and prizes. Professional musicians, such as Arne, Vento and Barthélémon, were recruited as 'priveleg'd members', who could attend the dinners and put on occasional public concerts, advertised as 'by permission of the Catch Club'. According to the minutes of the society, Guadagni attended just one meeting.[4] Another 'priveleg'd member' was the soprano-register castrato Tenducci, who attended two meetings and performed in one of the public concerts. Tenducci arrived in London in the early months of 1770. Although he was not engaged at the King's Theatre, by his very presence and availability in the capital he constituted a potential rival for Guadagni, taking over his roles on a number of occasions. The first such instance was the Decayed Musicians' concert on 2 February: although Guadagni's participation was widely advertised, at the last minute, whether through indisposition or pique, he was replaced by Tenducci—an indication of future problems for Guadagni, since the following season Tenducci supplanted him entirely at the King's Theatre.[5]

[2] Edward Hooper to James Harris, 28 Nov. 1769, in Burrows and Dunhill, *Music and Theatre in Handel's World*, p. 570.

[3] Burney, *General History*, ii, p. 877.

[4] Brian Robins, *Catch and Glee Culture in Eighteenth-Century England*, Woodbridge: Boydell Press, 2006, p. 46. I am grateful to Brian Robins for further information on Guadagni and the society.

[5] Burrows and Dunhill, op. cit., p. 580.

The oratorio season had developed considerably since Guadagni's earlier London visit. In Lent 1770 there were three oratorio series, working in rivalry with each other: J. C. Bach put on Italian oratorios at the King's Theatre, and two series of Handel's oratorios were given by J. C. Smith and John Stanley at Drury Lane, and by Samuel Arnold and Edward Toms at Covent Garden. The Drury Lane and Covent Garden series ran in direct competition with each other, performing on the same nights and competing for the same soloists. Guadagni was engaged by two of the three companies. On 1 March he sang in Jommelli's *La passione* at the King's Theatre, and when this was repeated for three further performances, a favourite item in his repertory, Pergolesi's *Stabat mater*, was added, to general praise: 'Guadagni sings and charms all ears: the *Stabat Mater* is performed at the Haymarket better than ever it was in England.'[6] He sang again at the King's Theatre on 22 March in J. C. Bach's oratorio *Gioas re di Giuda*, with a libretto based on Metastasio's text, first performed in Vienna in 1735. When the work was repeated on 29 March and 5 April, Guadagni was indisposed and was again replaced by Tenducci. Despite Poore's appreciative comment, Bach's season at the King's Theatre was not well supported—'neither flattering nor profitable', according to Burney, though the king and queen attended regularly.[7] The sparse houses were a talking point: 'General Fitzpatrick meeting Mr Hare, a Member of Parliament famed for his ready wit, said to him, "Do you go to the oratorio in the Hay-Market this evening?"—"Oh no," replied Mr Hare, "I have no wish to intrude on His Majesty's privacy".'[8] Guadagni played a larger part in the oratorios at Drury Lane. Although his participation can only be confirmed in *Alexander's Feast* on 14 and 28 March, and *Acis and Galatea* on 16 March, it seems likely that he also sang in *Samson* (2 and 30 March), *Judas Maccabaeus* (7 and 21 March) and *Messiah* (23 March and 4 and 6 April).

As these titles suggest, oratorios did not, at this period, need to be sacred texts to qualify as Lenten fare. Nor did there appear to be any embargo on operas which advertised 'magnificent scenery, costumes and dancing'. On 7 April, the last day before the theatres closed for Holy Week, Guadagni introduced the London audience to Gluck's *Orfeo*, though not in a form that Gluck would easily have recognised. To accommodate the work to the London taste, it had been turned into a pasticcio.

London at this period might well be described as the pasticcio capital of Europe.[9] The popularity of pasticcios, where fresh arias might be inserted into an old score or

---

[6] Edward Poore to James Harris Jr, 23 Mar. 1770, in Burrows and Dunhill, op. cit., p. 585.

[7] Burney, *General History*, ii, p. 877.

[8] William Thomas Parke, *Musical Memoirs*, i, London: Colburn and Bentley, 1830, p. 55.

[9] See Michael Burden, 'Metastasio's "London Pasties": Curate's egg or pudding's proof?' in *Pietro Metastasio uomo universale (1698–1782), Festgabe der Österreichischen Akademie der Wissenschaften zum 300. Geburtstag von Pietro Metastasio*, ed. Andrea Sommer-Mathis and Elisabeth Theresia Hilscher, Vienna: Verlag der Österreichischen Akademie der Wissenschaften, 2000, pp. 293–309.

additional scenes and characters into an old libretto, marks a point in opera history when the constant production of new operas, given for a season and then discarded, was about to give way to the growth of repertory opera, where an entire text, words and music, would be repeated from season to season and transferred from city to city with minimal changes to suit a change of cast or conditions. The *Orfeo* given in 1770 took Gluck's complete score as its basis, but added to it, in an attempt to accommodate local taste. Extra scenes and characters, including roles for Orfeo's father Eagro, Euridice's sister Egina, Pluto and a Blessed Spirit were introduced to solve the recurrent problem of expanding Gluck's concise score into a full evening's entertainment. Responsibility for textual additions devolved upon the house poet at the King's Theatre, Giovanni Bottarelli. The additional music was composed by J. C. Bach and Guglielmi, and Guadagni himself contributed a new setting of 'Men tiranne'.[10] The pasticcio proved popular. An unusually extensive *Favourite Songs in the Opera Orfeo* included, besides Guadagni's new aria, an equal number of items by Gluck and J. C. Bach.[11] Burney later expressed his disapproval of the additions (even though he had never seen a production of the 1762 original):

> The unity, simplicity, and dramatic excellence of this opera, which had gained the composer so much credit on the Continent, were greatly diminished here by the heterogeneous mixture of Music of other composers, in a quite different style; whose long symphonies, long divisions, and repetitions of words, occasioned delay and languor in the incidents and action. A drama, which at Vienna was rendered so interesting as almost to make the audience think more of the poet than musician, in England had the fate of all other Italian dramas, which are pronounced good or bad in proportion to the talents and favour of the singers.[12]

Despite Burney's reservations, J. C. Bach's version of *Orfeo* was entirely successful. It proved to be a springboard for a series of further pasticcio adaptations of *Orfeo*, at least two of them compiled by Guadagni himself, that came to dominate his repertory for the remainder of his career.

The initiative to produce the opera in London seems to have been Guadagni's, spurred on, perhaps, by his pique at being passed over for a production of *Orfeo* in Parma in 1769. For his contribution to the wedding of the Habsburg Archduchess

---

[10] Guadagni's 'Men tiranne' is discussed in Chapter 9. The score is available on the Companion Website, where the aria can also be heard, sung by James Laing.

[11] *Favourite Songs in the Opera Orfeo*, London: Bremner, 1770.

[12] Burney, *General History*, ii, p. 877, note (s).

Maria Amalia and Prince Ferdinand of Parma, Gluck had contrived a composite work in three acts called *Le feste d'Apollo*, itself a pasticcio, though the fact that it was assembled by a single composer gave it, perhaps, a greater degree of integrity than a multi-authored hotchpotch. Gluck expended little energy in its composition: the libretto comprised a prologue and three acts, all by different authors, which was furnished with music recycled from Gluck's earlier works. *Orfeo* was given as the third act, with some revisions simplifying the orchestral score and with the title role adapted for the soprano-register castrato Giuseppe Millico. Guadagni must have felt slighted, and his promotion of the opera in London, just nine months later, may have been an attempt to reclaim the role for himself.

Guadagni provided a preface to the London pasticcio—the somewhat laboured English suggests that he may have written it himself—in which he argued the case for the work, praising in particular Calzabigi's text, which remained almost intact, though its impact was diluted by the added scenes and extra characters:

To the NOBILITY and GENTRY.

ILLUSTRIOUS PATRONS,

The taste which the English Nation has always shown, (in a superior degree to almost any other) for true harmony, engaged me to propose the performance of this Opera, to the Gentlemen Managers of the King's-Theatre, not doubting but its excellent composition, added to the classical merit of the drama, would afford something beyond what is usually seen, to gratify real judges; to whom in your Persons it is particularly dedicated.

The original Composer made himself a perfect master of his author's meaning; and infused the genius of the poetry into his music; in which he followed the example of my great master Handel, the phoenix of our age; who in all modes of musical expression, where sense was to be conveyed, excelled beyond our praise.

In order to the more immediate observation of this beauty, resulting from a happy coalition between the writer and composer of an Opera, I most earnestly wish that such Ladies and Gentlemen, as propose to honour the exhibition of this drama with their presence, would read the piece, before they see it performed; I believe they will not find their attention ill repaid: and as a small, but zealous instance of humble gratitude, for long enjoyed countenance, and repeated favours; I flatter myself, the supporters of the Italian drama in England, will condescend to accept this dedication of the Opera of Orpheus, and his warmest endeavours to contribute to their entertainment, from their most obliged, and most obedient humble servant,

GAETANO GUADAGNI.

It is worth noting that despite the long and successful run that *Orfeo* had enjoyed in Vienna, this is the first occasion on which we learn Guadagni's own opinion of the work. Beyond the carefully placed compliments to his audience, and his claim to share in the reflected glory of his 'great master', there is here a serious plea on behalf of the opera, and for the integrity of the union of words and music that Gluck strove for. It is hard to resist the conclusion that this issue had been discussed among Gluck, Calzabigi and Guadagni, and that the singer was taking up cudgels on behalf of the reform of opera, in perhaps one of the most hostile environments for reform ideals in Europe. His explicit request to the audience to read the libretto before visiting the theatre is unprecedented. Audiences could, and probably would, have taken this step without Guadagni's recommendation (librettos were usually on sale some days in advance of a production), but Guadagni's request underlines his commitment to the importance of the words, a major aspect of the reform of opera.

The production received a run of twelve performances and won considerable applause. James Harris was particularly enthusiastic:

Went in the evening to the opera of Orfeo[,] the King and Queen there— house remarkably crowded—opera very pleasing—so far French, as to admit into it dancing & chorus—the rest, pure Italian—Grassi shone & Guadagni— twas over by nine. The scenery of Hell magnificent—so also that of the Temple of Love—I have never seen such a spectacle.[13]

Guadagni's performance drew from Burney one of his most explicit descriptions of the singer on stage:

…his attitudes, action, and impassioned and exquisite manner of singing the simple and ballad-like air: *Che farò*, acquired him very great and just applause; but…his determined spirit of supporting the dignity and propriety of his dramatic character, by not bowing acknowledgement, when applauded, or destroying all theatrical illusion by returning to repeat an air, if encored at the termination of an interesting scene, he so much offended individuals, and the opera audience in general, that, at length, he never appeared without being hissed.[14]

Corroborative evidence of the catcalls emerged the following year when Guadagni was on trial for taking part in an illegal opera performance. During cross-examination,

[13] Burrows and Dunhill, op. cit., p. 587.
[14] Burney, *General History*, ii, p. 877.

Hobart was asked whether he had taken part in provoking Guadagni, whereupon 'Mr Hobart replied, that one night when Guadagni made an insolent speech to the audience, he (being in the gallery) joined with the whole house in hissing him, because he had hired him to sing and not to speak'.[15] Guadagni's 'insolent speech' was presumably a declaration of his determination not to give encores.

The granting of encores was a well-debated issue in the 1770s. It is not clear whether Guadagni's behaviour was motivated more by a desire to irritate the management or by his high principles inspired by his work with Garrick and Gluck, both of whom valued the continuity of a performance uninterrupted by gratuitous applause. His stand was endorsed by his more progressive contemporaries. Ian Woodfield has identified him as the 'much-loved actor' for whom the diplomatic Le Texier devised a compromise to accepting applause:

> Would it not be possible for a much-loved actor (who has not been seen for some time), to whom the audience wishes to express its appreciation by repeated acclamation, before beginning his role, to divest himself of the character he is to represent, and to appear as himself, acknowledging the applause as respectfully as possible, but at the same time indicating that from the moment his role begins, he will not be able to interrupt his performance without destroying all illusion and dramatic truth?[16]

The season ended for Guadagni with two more oratorios: Giardini's *Ruth*, in the chapel of Lock Hospital on 24 April, and a performance of *Judas Maccabaeus* given at the King's Theatre on 4 May as a benefit for Frasi.

We next hear of Guadagni at the country home of the wealthy landowner and passionate amateur musician Sir Watkin Williams Wynn, at Wynnstay in Denbighshire. Guadagni spent eight weeks there during August and September. The focus of his visit was the celebrations surrounding the installation of a new Snetzler organ in the parish church of St Mary Ruabon, the gift of Sir Watkin:

> Our jubilee week at Wynnstay is at last over. We had a grand oratorio at the opening [of] the new organ at Ruabon Church, on the Tuesday, where several solos were performed by Mr Paxton, the first violoncello, and Signor

---

[15] *General Evening Post*, 12–14 Feb. 1771.

[16] See Chapter 4, note 52. Le Texier, *Journal Etranger* no. 1 (1777) is reproduced in Ian Woodfield, *Opera and Drama in Eighteenth-century London*, pp. 276–82.

Giardagni [sic], the first singer in the kingdom. The company were all invited to Wynnstay to dinner, and a grand entertainment we had.[17]

For his musical activities at Wynnstay, Guadagni was paid £100.[18] It is not clear exactly when and where he had met Sir Watkin. It could have been in Venice in the early months of 1769 when Sir Watkin was undertaking the Grand Tour. Another possible occasion was at the Catch Club, which Sir Watkin joined in 1768, two years before Guadagni's brief membership. He was to become an important figure in Guadagni's life in the following season.

### SEASON OF 1770–1771

Guadagni remained absent from the London scene for the autumn of 1770, and when Hobart reassembled his company at the King's Theatre, he was not among the cast, possibly as the result of a dispute over his salary. It was reported that he had demanded £1,600 (a substantial rise on the previous season's figure of £1,150), with a lump sum of £1,000 to be paid before the season opened.[19] Hobart offered the larger sum but in weekly payments, which Guadagni apparently declined. Predictably, he was supplanted by Tenducci, and reacted by making life as difficult for Hobart as he could contrive. In January 1771 he took part in a disastrous enterprise that directly challenged Hobart's opera at the King's Theatre.

To understand the nature of his offence, it is necessary to recall the terms of the Licensing Act of 1737, a notorious act which had several aims. In this most satirical of ages, numerous laws were enacted to protect the king and government from ridicule. The measures also aimed to impose public order in the vicinity of theatres, and to prevent financial instability resulting from the endemic risks involved in putting on Italian opera in London. One consequence of the act was to ensure that only the King's Theatre was licensed to produce Italian opera.[20] Performances for profit in other locations were illegal, and the ban was strictly enforced. Among a number of ingenious attempts to circumvent the law, a particularly bold move was made by the enterprising Teresa Cornelys. Cornelys, who as Teresa Imer had appeared on the London stage as a soprano in the 1740s, returned to London in

[17] Roger Kenyon, 7 Sept. 1770, in *Historical Manuscripts Commission, 14th Report, appendix, Part IV.* The cellist was Stephen Paxton; Sir Watkin was his pupil.
[18] See note by Graydon Beeks in *Early Music*, 27 (1999), p. 510.
[19] *London Magazine*, Feb. 1771, pp. 93–97. Opera salaries for the seasons 1769–70 and 1770–71 are missing from the accounts preserved in the Drummonds Bank, which record only the number of subscribers and subscription income for these seasons.
[20] V. J. Liesenfeld, *The Licensing Act of 1737*, Madison: University of Wisconsin Press, 1984.

1759, took a substantial house in Soho Square, enlarged it, redecorated it, and put on musical evenings with the additional enticements of cards, dancing and masked balls. These attracted the patronage of some of the most elevated members of London society.

Cornelys had a scandalous past to live down. Both before and after her one legal marriage she conducted a series of liaisons, including a long-standing relationship with Casanova by whom she had a daughter. Her relentless pursuit of the aristocracy was as much a search for respectability as for fame and fortune. She spared no expense in her quest to dazzle London society: Walpole wrote of Carlisle House as a 'fairy palace'[21] and Fanny Burney recorded her admiration of 'the splendour of the illuminations & embillishments, & the brilliant appearance of the Company'.[22]

While balls and concerts were within the law, Cornelys's ambitions ran to nothing less than founding an opera company to rival the King's Theatre, which she attempted to achieve in the early months of 1771, thinly disguising her enterprise as a private society convening for the purpose of 'Harmonical Meetings'. She enticed the violinist Giardini, the composer Vento, and Guadagni to manage the project, and Vento's opera *Artaserse* was chosen for the attempt. There appears to have been considerable interest among the public. On 5 January, Elizabeth Harris wrote that 'I hear the opposition opera at Carlisle House is in great forwardness & that they have six hundred subscribers'.[23] This was surely a wild exaggeration, since the King's Theatre had only 18 subscribers for the same season.[24] Nevertheless, even if the number of subscribers had been 60 rather than 600, Cornelys was doing considerably better than the King's Theatre. After an open rehearsal on 12 January, Elizabeth Harris observed that 'Giardini's opera at Mrs Cornelley's [sic] really fills, and undoubtedly will greatly injure that of Mr Hobart's in the Haymarket'.[25] Walpole reported that, 'Mr Hobart began to starve and the managers of the [other] theatres were alarmed'.[26]

Alarm spread to the magistrates. The public rehearsals for Mrs Cornelys's opera were brought to the attention of Sir John Fielding, chief magistrate for the County

---

[21] Walpole to Mann, 22 Feb. 1771 in *Correspondence*, xxiii, p. 271.

[22] 28 Mar. 1770, *The Early Journals and Letters of Fanny Burney*, ed. L. E. Troide, Oxford: Oxford University Press, 1988, i, p. 120.

[23] Elizabeth Harris to James Harris Jr, 5 Jan. 1771, Burrows and Dunhill, op. cit., p. 616.

[24] Elizabeth Gibson, 'Italian opera in London 1750–1775: Management and finances', *Early Music*, 18 (1990), Table 1, p. 51.

[25] Elizabeth Harris to James Harris Jr, 12 Jan. 1771, Burrows and Dunhill, op. cit., p. 618.

[26] Walpole to Mann, *Correspondence*, xxiii, 22 Feb. 1771, p. 271.

of Middlesex, in whose purlieu the illegal enterprise was taking place, and the following curious scene took place:

> Tis a sad thing that the Harmonic Society should cause disturbance[.] Lady North[umberland] got one day this week sixty subscribers on her book[;] meanwhile Fielding menaced Guadagni. That brave and generous countryman of Caesar & Pompey set him and his law at defiance[,] asserting that he sung without any reward or hire. The Justice ask'd if he would so answer on oath. [Guadagni replied that] he was as ready to put his hand to the bible as his betters.[27]

He was eventually called upon to make good his boast. After just two public performances, the opera was closed down and Cornelys and Guadagni were brought before the Bow Street magistrates' court, charged with putting on an opera 'for hire, gain, or reward, without a licence…in direct defiance of two acts of parliament which expressly declare all persons concerned in acting or causing to be acted any theatrical or operatical entertainment, without a patent, or permission of the lord chamberlain, to be common vagrants, liable to a penalty of 50*l* for every such offence.'[28]

The trial took place on 13 February. Witnesses for the prosecution included Guadagni's colleagues J. C. Bach and Carl Friedrich Abel, who gave evidence that Guadagni had said to them that 'he must sing where he was asked, and that he must get his bread'.[29] The strongest evidence against Guadagni came from Hobart, who had sent a servant anonymously to obtain a ticket for the second performance of *Artaserse*, which took place on 31 January. Hobart's testimony was sufficient to convict Guadagni of having taken part in an unlicensed opera, but the singer escaped the charge of singing for 'hire, gain or reward' on a technicality. Although Hobart had paid the full twelve guineas for a complete series of Harmonic Meetings, he did not apply for a subscription until after the first performance, so he was given tickets numbered two to twelve; the charge of singing for reward, however, was so worded that it referred only to the first performance on 24 January, and since Hobart could

[27] Richard Owen Cambridge to James Harris, 12 Jan. 1771, Burrows and Dunhill, op. cit., p. 617. Cambridge's letter perhaps reveals how 60 subscribers turned into 600. Sir John Fielding was half-brother to the novelist and playwright Henry Fielding; in 1773, he was lampooned in *The Bow Street Opera*, a remake of *The Beggar's Opera*, which charged Fielding with making arbitrary judgements and being open to bribery.

[28] *London Magazine*, Feb. 1771, p. 94.

[29] The trial is recorded in full, with verbatim witness statements, in the Sessions Rolls of the Middlesex Justices in the Metropolitan London Archives, MLA MJ//SR/ 3240.

not produce a ticket for that performance, the charge was dismissed.[30] Guadagni, therefore, was convicted of vagrancy and fined £50. The trial, illustrated in Figure 0.1, shows Guadagni pleading his case in very imperfect English. One report of the trial revealed that Guadagni had asked Fielding if he could give his evidence in French and 'that able magistrate replied to him in the same language'.[31]

The case was reported with relish in the press and revisited in many letters and diaries of the period. It made a wretched start to Guadagni's last months in England. The oratorio season opened shortly after the trial. Guadagni transferred his allegiance to Covent Garden, under the management of Samuel Arnold and Edward Toms. It is doubtful whether he sang in the first two oratorios which took place in the same week as his trial. *Judas Maccabaeus* was performed on 15 February, and on 20 February *Messiah* was given as a stop-gap to replace the advertised performance of Arnold's *The Cure of Saul*, which had been intended to feature Guadagni as its star attraction, and whose participation was advertised up to the day before the planned performance: 'For the greater advantage of the Oratorio of the Cure of Saul, which is to be performed Tomorrow Evening at the Theatre Royal Covent Garden, Mr Arnold has recomposed all the Songs in the Part of Signor Guadagni.'[32]

Guadagni's absence was noted with alarm. The *Morning Chronicle* of 26 February rumoured that he had fled the country, a fiction corrected in the *Gazeteer*:

> The paragraph that appeared in yesterday's Morning Chronicle, *That our first serious man of the Opera-house was gone for a foreign kingdom*, is utterly void of truth, and thrown out by his enemies, to injure him in the opinion of the public, as he being extremely ill with a violent cold, did go to visit a friend in the country, where he staid from Saturday to Monday, for the benefit of the country air, in order to recover himself to do justice to the parts of singing he is to perform at the Oratorio's, Opera house etc.[33]

Guadagni resumed his career with a performance of *Samson* on 1 March (with 'a favourite Italian Song by Signor Guadagni'). On 6 March, Arnold attempted to profit from Piccinni's popularity in the capital with *The Death of Abel*, adapted from Piccinni's *La morte di Abele*. Elizabeth Harris attended the oratorio but noted that 'I heard Guadagni sing which was all I wanted but he is so lazy that he will not do his

---

[30] For further details of the trial, see Patricia Howard, 'Guadagni in the dock: A crisis in the career of a castrato', *Early Music*, 27 (1999): 87–95, and ' "Mr Justice Blindman" and the "Priestess of fashion" ', *Il saggiatore musicale*, 7.1 (2000): 47–59.

[31] *General Evening Post*, 14–16 Feb. 1771.

[32] *Gazeteer*, 19 Feb. 1771.

[33] *Gazeteer*, 27 Feb. 1771. I am grateful to Eva Zöllner for information on the oratorio seasons in 1770 and 1771.

best'.[34] He was, however, still an attraction, and subsequent performances of *Messiah* were announced in the *Public Advertiser* as including 'a favourite Italian Song by Signor Guadagni' (8 March) and 'by particular Desire, Sig. Guadagni will sing a new English song by Mr Arnold' (13 March). Guadagni's oratorio engagements at Covent Garden ended with two performances of Arnold's *The Resurrection* on 15 and 22 March. He also sang in two private concerts at Wynn's house in Grosvenor Square on 3 and 25 March.[35] Arnold and Wynn were friends who had stood by him in a difficult period.

The post-Lenten period was the favourite time for benefit concerts. Provocatively, Guadagni returned to Soho Square to sing in concerts for Giardini (18 March), Vento (10 April) and the cellist Jean-Pierre Duport (15 May). His participation in a benefit concert for the violinist Maddalena Sirmen at Almack's, a popular concert room in King's Street St James's, suggests the intriguing possibility that he might have come to know Sirmen in Padua through her teacher Tartini. Further benefit concerts included a performance of Giardini's *Ruth* at the Lock Hospital on 27 April. A return to the King's Theatre was particularly significant, marking his re-entry into the mainstream of London music; he sang there in benefit concerts for the oboist Johann Christian Fischer (15 May) and for his old colleague Frasi (*Judas Maccabaeus*, 4 May). Quite remarkably, on 17 April he was given his own benefit performance of Vento's *Artaserse*, apparently with the original cast which had flouted Hobart so dramatically three months earlier.

The season ended with a revival of *Orfeo*, opening on 30 April. Guadagni wrote a new preface for the libretto, rather different in tone from the previous year's:

TO Sir WATKIN WILLIAMS WYNN, Bart.

SIR,

It is observed, by a famous French writer, that notwithstanding the general complaint to the contrary, gratitude is of all the virtues, that which is most congenial to human nature; and there is scarcely one in the world, who being conscious of a real benefit, would not rejoice to repay it, if he had it in his power.

Thus, when some time ago I received marks of your kindness, I sigh'd to think, it was so great, that I could never hope to shew my gratitude. What, said I to myself, can I do in return? My benefactor is too exalted, to have any of

---

[34] Elizabeth Harris to James Harris Jr, 8 Mar. 1771, in Burrows and Dunhill, op. cit., p. 626.

[35] When he received £20 and five guineas respectively: Graydon Beeks, *Early Music*, 27 (1999), p. 510.

my little services necessary or useful to him: but you who delight in the happiness of the meanest, soon relieved my anxiety, by letting me know, that tho' I could not serve, I might endeavour to please you, and you would condescend to accept those endeavours, as a handful of gems, in lieu of a hecatomb.

You think proper to say, I can sing and act, you command me to do so; and permit me to boast, with all due respect to the publick, that in performing the part of Orpheus, I require no other bribe, or reward, than the pleasure of shewing you a ready obedience. I have the honour to be, with the greatest respects,

SIR

Your most obliged, most grateful, and most devoted humble servant,

GAETANO GUADAGNI

The suggestion that he would sing six performances without fee is improbable, though Guadagni harked back to it when he met Burney in Munich the following year. His language in the preface and in his conversation with Burney echoes the charge on which he was tried: that of singing 'for hire, gain, and reward' in an unlicensed opera. Burney's report of their conversation reveals Guadagni still sore from his unhappy last season in England: 'Guadagni complains of illiberal treatment from the public, who, when he sung in the opera of Orfeo, merely to oblige them, and Sir W. W. without fee or reward, hissed him for going off the stage when he was encored, with no other design than *to return in character*'.[36]

Guadagni left England in the summer of 1771 never to return. He had had mixed fortunes. Despite the trial, he had received some of the highest fees awarded to any first man in London. He had enjoyed distinguished and congenial patronage, and had reinforced his claim upon the role of Orfeo to the extent that all subsequent interpreters of the role in London had to stand comparison with him. The aria 'Che farò' quickly became a firm favourite with London audiences.

Parody is a sure measure of popularity. The iconic status of 'Che farò' was exploited when it was used to comic effect in Guglielmi's satirical opera *Le pazzie d'Orlando*, to a libretto by Badini, premièred at the King's Theatre on 23 February 1771, in the immediate aftermath of the trial. In Act II of *Le pazzie*, Orlando, driven mad with jealousy over Medoro's seduction of Angelica, is turned to stone by the sorceress Alcina, who tells the lovers that only music can restore him to life. Medoro, portrayed as a Parisian fop, sings an air by Rameau, which fails to revive his rival; Angelica then attempts the most tender, the most moving arietta she knows, namely 'Che

---

[36] Burney, *The Present State of Music in Germany*, i, p. 126.

farò' ('un'arietta/Tutta tutta tenerina,/Che per muovere gli affetti/La miglio non si può dar'). This successfully reanimates Orlando. In a footnote to the libretto, Badini explains 'As here a rock is to be animated, I hope the introduction of Orpheus's song will not be thought improper'.[37]

As a curious postscript to his celebrity, we note Guadagni's inclusion in a book of manners, as an example of one whose fame and fashion made his appearances an unmissable event. The following model letter appears in *The Lady's Polite Secretary*, instructing how to refuse a highly-desirable invitation:

> Madam, I have the favour of your obliging letter, and think myself unhappy that I cannot accompany you to the concert on Friday as you mention. I know the value of the tickets, and therefore return them immediately, that some other Lady, less unfortunately circumstanced than I happen to be on that day, may have the pleasure of using them. . . . I shall be happy to attend you, Madam, any other time, for I long to hear this *Guadagni*, who has not sung this whole week that I have been in London.[38]

[37] *Le pazzie d'Orlando*, London, 1771, p. 54. The idea of 'Che farò' as the epitome of expressivity continued to resonate in the nineteenth century, especially in the writings of George Eliot, e.g. *Scenes of Clerical Life*, and *Armgart*.

[38] Lady Dorothea Du Bois, *The Lady's Polite Secretary OR The New Female Letter Writer*, London, 1771, pp. 19–20.

# 9

## Guadagni the Composer

GUADAGNI'S LONDON VISIT of 1769–1771 saw what may have been his first attempts at composition. His portfolio is small—only three arias are currently known, though a curious error briefly credited him with a larger and more significant achievement than he can in fact lay claim to: a rumour, originating in Paris during the 1770s, spread the idea that Guadagni, not Gluck, had written most of the music of the role of Orfeo. The allegation appears to have begun with the Comte d'Escherny.[1] It was repeated by La Borde[2] and was included in the earliest dictionary entries.[3] However, only two of Guadagni's surviving arias are contributions to *Orfeo*, and they were composed well after 1762, designed to be inserted in pasticcio versions of the opera. The third aria was intended to be inserted in a setting of *Ezio*. All three arias exist in full score; one was published, the others remain in manuscript.[4] The scores of the arias are included on the website as Example Web.1 ('Men tiranne'), Example Web.2 ('Che puro ciel'), and Example Web. 3 ('Pensa a serbarmi, o cara') ⬤.

---

[1] 'Les plus beau chants de Gluck ne lui appartenoient pas...c'est Guadagni lui-même qui fournit à Gluck la meilleure partie des chants de son rôle d'Orphée', cited in Gustave Desnoiresterres, *Gluck et Piccinni: la musique française au XVIIIᵉ siècle*, 2nd ed., Paris: Didier, 1872, p. 272, n. 1.

[2] 'Guadagni avait déjà composé lui-même tout le chante de son rôle'. Jean-Benjamin de La Borde, *Essais sur la musique ancienne et moderne*, iii, Paris, 1780, p. 317.

[3] 'Er ist überdies auch Komponist, indem er sich seine Rolle zum Orfeo selbst in Musik gesetzt haben soll'. Ernst Ludwig Gerber, *Historisch-biographisches Lexicon der Tonkünstler*, Leipzig, 1790.

[4] 'Men tiranne' in *The Favourite Songs in the Opera Orfeo*, London: Bremner [1770]; 'Che puro ciel' in Biblioteca Antoniana, Padua, Arch. Mus. D.IV.1624, pp. 251–67; 'Pensa a serbarmi, o cara', in Conservatorio di Musica F. E. dall'Abaco, Verona, VRO131 Murari Bra MS 123 and Civico Museo Bibliografico Musicale, Bologna, FF182.

In addition, we can count among Guadagni's compositions the 'extemporaneous effusions' that Burney regarded as the high point of his performances in London.[5] Being 'extemporaneous', these are of course no longer available for scrutiny. In Guadagni's own arias there is only one brief written cadenza, occurring at the conclusion of 'Men tiranne'.[6] There are, however, pauses (in 'Men tiranne', bars 24, 27 and 37; in 'Pensa a serbarmi', bars 35, 71 and 74); conventionally these would invite an improvised cadenza. Beyond these there is the tantalizing possibility that the ornamentation which Domenico Corri associated with Guadagni's role in the pasticcio *Orfeo* in 1770 and 1771 bears some relation to how he performed this music.

Corri's *Select Collection of the Most Admired Songs, Duetts, etc from Operas in the Highest Esteem* purports to transcribe music from the last quarter of the eighteenth century with additional markings indicating how it was performed by named artists, including crescendos and diminuendos, rubato and portamento, suggestions for breathing, and a variety of ornaments.[7] Corri included three numbers from *Orfeo*, one from each act: 'Chiamo il mio ben così', 'Deh placatevi' and 'Che farò' with its preceding recitative. He inserted short florid cadenzas at the end of each stanza of 'Chiamo il mio ben così' and also at the conclusion of 'Deh placatevi'. 'Che farò' is more continuously ornamented (see Example 9.1).

Richard Maunder states baldly that 'all of the ornamentation is Corri's own'.[8] We need not necessarily be so dismissive. The ornamentation that Corri adds to his *Select Collection* is sufficiently varied from one item to another to suggest that it was thoughtfully devised to fit his notion of what was appropriate for each aria. The elegant appoggiaturas and shapely cadential insertions included in the three arias 'Composed by M. Gluck / Sung by Sig.ʳ Guadagni' are notably more restrained that the vigorous trills and turns with which he embellished, for example, Sacchini's 'Deh t'invola dal mio seno gelosia' ('Composed by Sig.ʳ Sacchini / Sung by Sig.ʳᵃ Todi'), or the flamboyant decoration in Giordani's 'Già che morir degg'io' ('Composed by Sig.ʳ Giordani / Sung by Sig.ʳ Millico'). The ornamentation Corri ascribed to (or prescribed for) Gluck's arias is more akin to the lyrical cadential expansions he added to Handel's 'Dove sei, amato bene' ('Composed by Mʳ Handel / Sung by Sig.ʳ Senesino'), or 'Verdi prati' ('Composed by Mʳ Handel / Sung by Sig.ʳ Carestini').

[5] Burney, *General History*, ii, p. 876.

[6] See Web Example 1, bars 41–44.

[7] Domenico Corri, *A Select Collection of the Most Admired Songs, Duetts, etc from Operas in the Highest Esteem*, Edinburgh: J. Corri, 1779. Richard Maunder (see note 8) suggests that the date of publication is probably 1782 or 1783.

[8] *Domenico Corri's Treatises on Singing: a four-volume anthology*, ed. Richard Maunder, i, Introduction, New York: Garland, 1993, p. ix.

EXAMPLE 9.1 *Corri's ornamentation for 'Che farò', from Gluck, Orfeo ed Euridice (1762)*

But while it is evident that Corri matched his expressive interpretation and his embellishments to the style of the music, it remains impossible to guess to what extent he derived them from any individual singer's performance. Our only certain knowledge of Guadagni's ornamentation is confined to what he wrote into his own small portfolio of compositions, and here the evidence conflicts with Burney's encomium. 'Effusions' are thin on the ground. Rather, Guadagni's intentions can be seen as responding to Gluck's well-known strictures against 'the abuses introduced by the ignorant vanity of singers', and especially against 'useless and unwanted ornaments'.[9] On the evidence of the very modest decoration written into his own compositions, Guadagni's concept of ornamentation precisely coincided with Gluck's.

The preface to the 1770 *Orfeo* informed its readers that J. C. Bach had 'very kindly condescended to add of his own new composition all such choruses, airs, and recitatives…except those which are sung by Signora Guglielmi, and they are likewise an entire new production of Signor Guglielmi, her husband'.[10] What neither the preface nor the text of the libretto indicates is that one of Calzabigi's arias, 'Men tiranne', Orfeo's final and successful plea to the furies, was recomposed by Guadagni. We owe the attribution to the inclusion of the aria in the *Favourite Songs*, where it is identified as Guadagni's own.

---

[9] 'quegli abusi, che introdotti…dalla mal intesa vanità dei cantanti'; 'degl'inutili superflui ornamenti'. Gluck, Preface to *Alceste*, Vienna: Trattner, 1767.

[10] *Orfeo*, London: Griffin, 1770.

This little aria has had a bad press. Daniel Heartz has written particularly scathingly:

Guadagni replaced…Gluck's dark-hued setting in F minor, with its wonderful echoes in the violas and lower strings…with a pretty little tune in F major, somewhat reminiscent of 'Cerco il mio ben' in style, a style he must have felt was more favorable to his talents.…Aside from any question of suitability to the dramatic situation, we should have to give his little piece poor marks for its compositional skill. Note, for example, how awkward is the connection between the first and second phrase. The rinforzando indicated in measure 2 gives us no choice but to hear this as a strong measure, setting in motion a metric pattern of alternating weak and strong measures. The cadence arrives, appropriately, as a strong (m 7); but then there is another accented measure (8) as all the band land on the tonic F; to which another is added by beginning the second phrase squarely on the same tonic (m 9). The result is ungainly.…What Guadagni's little insert Air does to the musical drama is horrible to contemplate. Gluck saved F major by avoiding it throughout the underworld scene, so it would be fresh to our ears in accompanying and translating into music the radiant vision of Elysium in Scene 2, the Dance of the Blessed Spirits. This most carefully calculated use of light and shade, this chiaroscuro, is the single most impressive effect in the whole opera.[11]

Bracing ourselves for horrors, we can now contemplate Guadagni's aria. A performance of the aria is included on the website and the score appears as Web Example 1 🔊.

Heartz's criticism seems to me to be wrong-footed. Guadagni's phrase structure plays elegantly with six-bar phrases, a common metrical unit of the galant style (for an example it is necessary to look no further than the British national anthem). The first half of the vocal melody runs: 6 + 6 + 3 + 4 (+ 4 repeated). After a three-bar link, the second half is less regular, though based on the same units: the phrase lengths consist of 6 + 3 + 4, with the four-bar phrase extended to seven bars by means of a short cadenza. The only ungainly element is the intrusive violin flourish in bars 6–7, unwanted both metrically and expressively, and nothing but a distraction from Guadagni's soothing and seductive melody.

Heartz is on surer ground when he castigates Guadagni for ruining Gluck's key scheme. The tonal structure of the original score is remarkable for its cohesion. The furies, initially in C minor, move to the darker key of F minor for their confrontation with Orfeo, and Orfeo himself makes the parallel journey from E flat major to

TABLE 9.1

The key structure of *Orfeo* Act II scene 1 in the scores of 1762, 1769 and 1770

| Item | Vienna 1762 | Parma 1769 | London 1770 |
|---|---|---|---|
| Ballet | E flat major | E flat major | ? |
| Harp prelude | C minor | C minor | ? |
| Chorus, 'Chi mai dell'Erebo' | C minor | C minor | C minor |
| Ballet | C minor | C minor | C minor |
| Chorus, 'Chi mai dell'Erebo' | C minor | C minor | C minor |
| Ballet | E flat major | [cut] | ? |
| Aria, 'Deh placatevi' | E flat major | F major | E flat major |
| Chorus, 'Misero giovane' | E flat minor–F minor | F minor–G minor | E flat minor–F minor |
| Aria, 'Mille pene' | F minor–C minor | G minor–D minor | [cut] |
| Chorus, 'Ah, quale incognito' | F minor | G minor | [cut] |
| Aria, 'Men tiranne' | F minor | G minor | F major |
| Chorus, 'Ah, quale incognito' | F minor | G minor | F major |

F minor. In the London score the balance of the dialogue is different. Not only are the numbers 'Mille pene' and 'Ah quale incognito' cut, but Guadagni's Orfeo never plumbs the depths of F minor, remaining serene and persuasive in E flat and F major. It is difficult, however, to justify labelling this as an act of vandalism when we contemplate the transpositions Gluck had already made in Parma to accommodate the title role to Millico's soprano register. The different tonal trajectories are be shown in Table 9.1. (As no complete score exists for the London version, it is not clear from the libretto whether all the ballet movements marked *?* were performed.)

'Men tiranne' falls at a pivotal moment between the chorus in which Orfeo is denied entrance to the Underworld and the one which grants him passage. It would, perhaps, be fanciful to account for the key by relating it to the F major ballet that opens the next scene, and to claim that by singing in this key, Orfeo is showing that he is worthy to enter the Elysian Fields since he already speaks the language of the Blessed Spirits. However in the changed context of the pasticcio score, Orfeo's F major air has its own logic, defining the contrast between the minor-key furies and his own major-key world.

Another virtue of Guadagni's aria, grudgingly conceded by Heartz, is its consistency with the characterisation of Orfeo throughout the opera. It is rational that Orfeo, who expresses his grief lyrically and in major keys, notably the F major of 'Chiamo il mio ben' in Act I, and the C major of 'Che farò' in Act III, should adopt this tonal world for his final plea to the furies. Guadagni's poised, shapely melodic line can take its place beside these numbers with honour. The justification for his interpretation of the dramatic situation lies in the words themselves:

| | |
|---|---|
| Men tiranne, ah, voi sareste | Alas! You would be less cruel |
| Al mio pianto, al mio lamento | to my mournful cries and lamentations, |
| Se provaste un sol momento | if you felt, but for an instant |
| Cosa sia languir d'amor. | the pangs of one lingering with love.[12] |

Gluck's short, urgent, agitated *aria parlante* is driven by the second couplet, and portrays the pangs of love (see Example 12.6). Guadagni's lyrical *aria cantabile* springs from the opening words of the aria; it represents the furies' relenting, and expresses the compassion he hopes to evoke in them.

Guadagni was very much attached to his composition and, as far as we know, always replaced Gluck's air with his own on every occasion that he sang Gluck's opera after April 1770. It is significant that when Tozzi and Bertoni made their own settings of Calzabigi's text, Tozzi in 1775 and Bertoni in 1776, both took the mood and style of Guadagni's aria for their settings of 'Men tiranne', including the six-bar phrase lengths, though Bertoni's elegant vocal line also owes something to Gluck's 'Deh placatevi'. (See Examples 9.2 and 9.3.)

There is less to be said for Guadagni's remake of 'Che puro ciel'. This does not date from the London visit. It was written for a private performance in Padua, sometime between 1775 and 1785. And it must be admitted at the outset that Guadagni's authorship is presumed rather than proven. A manuscript score in the Biblioteca Antoniana in Padua (Archivio musicale D.IV.1624) comprises a new pasticcio version of the opera. The title page identifies the composer as Cristoforo Gluck. There is no indication of when or where the score was performed. Although it is clearly based on the original Viennese version of 1762, there are numerous deviations, ranging from radical differences in the scoring ('Ah, se intorno', for example, is scored for three violins, two violas, two bassoons and bass) to the inclusion of material from the London pasticcios. The Paduan score lacks some of the text introduced by Bottarelli: the scenes for Eagro, Egina and Tiresia are absent, though the roles of

---

[12] Translation as in the libretto, London, 1770.

EXAMPLE 9.2  Tozzi, 'Men tiranne', from *Orfeo ed Euridice* (1775)

EXAMPLE 9.3  Bertoni, 'Men tiranne', from *Orfeo ed Euridice* (1776)

Plutone and the Ombra (Blessed Spirit) are retained. The libretto is similar in content to the pasticcio version Guadagni put on in Munich in 1773.

There are a number of inconsistencies in the score and parts. The role of Orfeo employs three different clefs. For 'Men tiranne', Guadagni's 1770 version is used, strongly suggesting his participation in this production—no other castrato is known ever to have performed this setting—and the vocal line is written in the G clef, as if copied directly from the *Favourite Songs*. However the new version of 'Che puro ciel' assigns Orfeo a soprano clef even though the music remains within Guadagni's preferred mezzo range of e flat' to e flat". The remainder of the role of Orfeo is written in the alto clef, following Gluck's original score. A further crumb of evidence in support of Guadagni's participation lies in the part-books. Those prepared for the soloists Euridice, Amore, Plutone and the Ombra contain all their solo numbers. For Orfeo there exists a part-book, marked 'Parte d'Orfeo Soprano', containing just one item, the re-composed 'Che puro ciel'. The implication is that this soloist did not need a copy of the rest of his role. Who else could this be but Guadagni?

At this period of his life Guadagni sang regularly in private concerts, and his repertory was dominated by performances of *Orfeo* in one version or another. Librettos for the semi-private *accademie* were only occasionally published. The three *Orfeo* librettos printed in Padua between 1776 and 1784 were probably designed to accompany performances of Bertoni's *Orfeo*, since the dates of publication match known performances of that opera on 2 May 1776, 5 July 1778, and 17 May 1784. But although none of these librettos corresponds exactly with the contents of D.IV.1624, there is much overlapping material, and Cattelan has suggested that one of them might have been used to accompany the performance of the Paduan pasticcio.[13] The contents of Act II of the Paduan score are shown in Table 9.2 (see page 146).

In Gluck's score, 'Che puro ciel' is the centrepiece of the second act. The expansive sound picture, the intricate orchestral texture and poised declamation make this one of the most elaborate numbers Gluck ever wrote. Inevitably, Guadagni's resetting of 'Che puro ciel' matches neither the expressive scope nor the orchestral brilliance of the original. The score appears as Web Example 2 ⬤.

Guadagni's setting rejects the unity of Gluck's movement, dividing the text into three sections:

*Recitativo accompagnato*

| | |
|---|---|
| Che puro ciel, che chiaro sol, | How clear the sky, how bright the sun |
| Che nuova serena luce è questa mai! | How new and serene this light is! |
| Che dolce lusinghiera armonia | What sweet, enchanting harmony |
| formano insieme | is made by the fusion of |
| il cantar degli augelli, | birdsong |
| il correr de' ruscelli, | babbling streams |
| dell'aure il sussurar! | and murmuring breezes! |
| Questo è il soggiorno | This is the abode |
| de' fortunati Eroi! | of the blessed heroes. |
| Qui tutto spira | Here everything breathes |
| un tranquillo contento, | a happy tranquility |
| ma non per me. | but not for me. |
| Se l'idol mio non trovo, | If I cannot find my love, |
| sperar non posso! | there is no hope for me! |

---

13 Paolo Cattelan, 'Altri Orfei di Gaetano Guadagni', in preface to Ferdinando Bertoni, *Orfeo*, Milan: Ricordi, 1989, pp. lxxi–lxxii.

*Arioso*

| I suoi soave accenti, | Her sweet voice, |
|---|---|
| gli amorosi suoi sguardi, | her loving glances, |
| il suo bel riso, | her lovely smile |
| sono il mio solo, il mio diletto Eliso! | are my only Elysium! |

*Recitativo accompagnato*

| Ma in qual parte [l]ei sarà? | But where will she be? |
|---|---|
| Chiedasi a questo | Let me ask |
| Che mi viene a incontrar | those who come to meet me, |
| stuolo felice. | this happy crowd. |
| Euridice dov'è? | Where is Eurydice? |

The division into three sections alters the impact of the words. Whereas Gluck's unified, continuous sound picture portrays the singer marvelling at the enchantments of Elysium, and represents those enchantments so luminously that the listener, too, falls under their spell, Guadagni's Orfeo is more introspective, more self-aware, and more decisive in the final moments. In the opening passage, he experiences the seductions of the scene, and notes somewhat cursorily (for all the world, as if he is ticking them off on a clipboard) the charms of the birds (bars 34–36), streams (bars 39–40) and breezes (bars 42–43). Whereas in Gluck's score birds twitter, streams purl and breezes whisper throughout the movement, Guadagni supplies the appropriate sound effects in a few perfunctory bars.

The change of style and tempo at bar 61 turns the focus from the external world to the charms of Euridice. Where Gluck's setting at this point continues to urge the attractions of Elysium, Guadagni's turns from external nature to a lyrical portrayal of Euridice's beauty, in which Orfeo claims, in an arioso that is almost a curtailed *aria cantabile*, that Euridice's beauty is superior to the attractions of paradise. In the closing recitative, where Gluck continues to portray the delights of nature, Guadagni's Orfeo rejects those delights, and takes the initiative to resume the search for his wife. Cattelan has suggested that Guadagni's setting shows Orfeo less enslaved by the visual and aural beauty of the scene, pursuing his quest to rejoin his wife undistracted by the seductive pleasures of Elysium.[14] It cannot be denied that Guadagni's setting is routine. He shows himself perfectly acquainted with all the appropriate vocal tags and orchestral clichés, but the movement lacks overall cohesion and offers no serious alternative to Gluck's masterpiece.

---

[14] Ibid., p. lxxiii.

TABLE 9.2

Content of Act II in the Paduan pasticcio

| Item | Composer |
| --- | --- |
| Scene 1 | |
| Ballet, E flat major | Gluck |
| Recitative, Plutone, 'Implacabili Dei' | J. C. Bach |
| Aria, Plutone, 'Per onor dell'offeso', G minor | J. C. Bach |
| Chorus, 'Chi mai dell'Erebo', C minor | Gluck |
| Ballet, C minor | Gluck |
| Chorus, 'Chi mai dell'Erebo', C minor | Gluck |
| Aria, Orfeo, 'Deh placatevi', E flat major | Gluck |
| Chorus, 'Misero giovane', E flat minor | Gluck |
| Aria, Orfeo, 'Men tiranne', F major | Guadagni |
| Chorus, 'Ah, quale incognito', F minor | Gluck |
| Scene 2 | |
| Recitative, Euridice, 'Questo è dunque Eliso' | J. C. Bach |
| Aria, Euridice, 'Chiari fonti', B flat major | J. C. Bach |
| Recitative, Ombra, 'Del bel regno' | Guglielmi |
| Aria, Ombra, 'Qui costante amor', G major | ?Guglielmi, marked in score as 'Aria di Bach' |
| Recitative, Euridice, 'Deh lasciatemi in pace' | J. C. Bach |
| Aria, Euridice, 'D'obbliar sospiro', E flat major | J. C. Bach |
| Ballet, F major | Gluck |
| Recitative and Arioso, Orfeo, 'Che puro ciel', B flat major | Guadagni |
| Chorus, 'Vieni a regni', F major | Gluck |
| Ballet, B flat major | Gluck |
| Recitative, Orfeo, 'Anime avventurose' | Gluck |
| Chorus, 'Torna, o bella', F major | Gluck |

The third piece we have from Guadagni's pen is a setting of the aria 'Pensa a serbarmi, o cara'. The circumstances surrounding the composition are obscure. The text comes from Metastasio's *Ezio*, a libretto that Guadagni sang in three different settings in the course of his career. It is a matter of speculation as to which of these accommodated Guadagni's alternative aria. Metastasio's *Ezio* was a popular text in the mid-century, first set by Porpora in 1728 and followed within months by a setting by

Pietro Auletta. New settings, in which the libretto was constantly revised, followed at the rate of almost one a year for the next half-century. It is a strong dramatic text, full of intense emotions, in which conflicting obligations towards lover, family and state are cunningly balanced: the Roman general Ezio returns victorious to Rome to find that the emperor has, in his absence, chosen to woo Fulvia, Ezio's promised bride. After a tangle of villainy and counter-villainy, during which Ezio is framed for a plot against the emperor, a revolt by the people of Rome gives him the opportunity of saving the emperor's life. Grateful at last, the emperor reunites him with Fulvia.

'Pensa a serbarmi' is not one of the dramatic highlights. Located in the first act, at a point where Ezio has just learned of the Emperor's designs on Fulvia, it gives Ezio the opportunity to reassure Fulvia of his love in a classic *aria cantabile*.

| | |
|---|---|
| Pensa a serbarmi, o cara, | Cherish, oh dearest, |
| I dolci affetti tuoi, | your tender feelings for me, |
| Amami e lascia poi | Love me, then leave aside |
| Ogn'altra cura a me. | all other cares to me. |
| Tu mi vuoi dir col pianto | Your tears tell me |
| Che resti in abbandono. | that you fear being abandoned. |
| No, così vil non sono, | No, I am not so vile, |
| Ne[15] meco ingrato tanto, | nor would Cesar be |
| No, Cesare non è. | so ungrateful to me. |

The score appears as Web Example 3 ◧.[16]

The aria exists in two manuscript copies. There is no extant autograph score. (Although we have no known sample of Guadagni's handwritten musical nota-tion, several documents from his hand survive—a letter, his will, some signatures—which differ in a number of respects from the text entered into these scores.) The earlier copy is housed in the Verona Conservatory[17] (see Figure 9.1). A later copy of the aria was acquired in the second half of the nineteenth century by the Bologna Conservatory[18] (see Figure 9.2). It appears to have been copied directly from the Verona score, transposing the aria into G major. The vocal line of the Verona score is written in the alto clef; it spans the range a flat–e flat" and lies comfortably within Guadagni's alto register. In the Bologna score the vocal part is written in the soprano clef with the compass c"–g"; this version of the aria has been used to support the

---

[15] 'E meco' in Metastasio's original.

[16] The aria can be heard on 'Arias for Guadagni'.

[17] Conservatorio di Musica F. E. dall'Abaco, Verona, VRO131 Murari Bra MS 123. I am grateful to Luca de Paolis for making a copy of this ms available to me.

[18] Museo Internazionale e Biblioteca di Musica di Bologna, FF 182.

FIGURE 9.1 Guadagni, 'Pensa a serbarmi', Verona score, p. 1, Conservatorio di Musica
F. E. dall'Abaco, Verona.

FIGURE 9.2 Guadagni, 'Pensa a serbarmi', Bologna score, p. 1, Civico Museo Bibliografico Musicale,
Bologna.

FIGURE 9.3 Verona score, bars 36–39.

hypothesis that Guadagni's voice type changed from alto to soprano towards the end of his career.[19]

The aria (in both versions) is scored for the standard combination of strings and continuo with pairs of flutes and horns. Guadagni's orchestration is not adventurous: the violins play mostly in thirds or sixths where they are not in octaves or unison; the flutes usually double them at the octave; the violas are only rarely independent of the bass line. Each of the scores provides its own puzzle. A particular point of interest in the Verona score is the addition of a supplementary figured bass line (written in another hand, which might be Guadagni's), beginning where the voice enters in bar 15 and continuing till the singer's last note in bar 84 (see Figure 9.3). This addition constitutes yet another version of the aria, transposed into F major. The implications are intriguing. Clearly, having written the aria in E flat major, Guadagni decided on a subsequent occasion to sing it in F. But when and where, and who was the keyboard player? Who would be unable to transpose the aria up a tone yet at the same time be able to realise the figured bass? And were the opening and closing ritornellos, for

---

[19] See especially Cattelan, 'Altri Orfei', p. xlviii. I have discussed this hypothesis in 'Did Burney Blunder?' *Musical Times* 139 (1998): 29–32.

EXAMPLE 9.4　Guadagni, 'Pensa a serbarmi, o cara' (?1770), bars 79–84

which no figured bass line was supplied, omitted on this occasion? If so, the F major version could only have been used at a very informal private performance, perhaps with Guadagni accompanying himself at the keyboard. Another oddity, of greater potential significance, is that the Verona score labels the flute parts 'Flute', rather than the expected 'Flauti', which raises the possibility that this score was copied from one originating in England—more on this below.

The Bologna score is written in a more fluent, professional hand. The most substantial textual deviation from the Verona score occurs at bars 82–83, where there is additional ornamentation in the vocal line, which the copyist has failed to render accurately, adding a quaver to bar 83 (see Example 9.4). The Bologna copy includes a number of other errors, the most drastic being that the copyist misread the horn parts in his source score. In the Verona score, the horns enter on the tonic, E flat (see Figure 9.1, bar 5). The parts are written as if for horns in C, that is, the notes are written at actual pitch, though notated an octave lower than sounding, in accordance with a widespread eighteenth-century practice. It appears that the Bologna copyist misread the parts, ignoring both the clef and key signature. His copy, therefore, has the horns entering on E (in a chord of G major), and are consequently a third too low throughout. This, together with the added ornamentation mentioned above, is persuasive evidence that the Bologna copy is later than, and derives from, the Verona score.

We must assume that Guadagni devised the aria to fit his voice, catering for its strengths and avoiding exposing its weaknesses. It is a classic *aria cantabile,* defined by the eighteenth-century philosopher John Brown as perfectly adapted to express 'sentiments of tenderness'.[20] There can be no better example of Guadagni's preferred style of singing. The aria exploits the expressive legato that was

---

[20] John Brown, *Letters upon the Poetry and Music of Italian Opera,* Edinburgh, 1789, p. 36. This book is accessible on several online sites, including http://ota.ahds.ac.uk/text/5289.html. Also from Eighteenth Century Collections Online at http://name.umdl.umich.edu/004895823.0001.000.

EXAMPLE 9.5  Guadagni, 'Pensa a serbarmi, o cara' (?1770), bars 36–39

his trademark—'delicate, polished and refined', according to Burney.[21] The vocal line is a tender, lyrical expression of reassurance; the phrases rise and fall with a satisfying balance. The rhythms are shaped by the text in a style of declamation of which Gluck would have approved. (In the words of his librettist, 'I consider that a note should never have the value of more than one syllable: it is ridiculous to extend the pronunciation of 'amore' to a hundred notes when nature has limited it to just three.'[22]) Guadagni not only found an accurate musical equivalent for the spoken words, but played with alternative rhythms in his setting of the caressing injunction 'Amami', giving a degree of impetuosity to the passage. (See Example 9.5.)

In a short dramatic climax at 'No, così vil non sono', the dark modulation to the supertonic minor, reinforced with dynamic accents, briefly gives scope for some impassioned singing. We know little about this aspect of Guadagni's performance. His ability to project big dramatic statements is rarely mentioned by his contemporaries. Although Pepoli described him as 'a passionate singer',[23] as a committed adherent of the reform, he had a vested interest in talking up Guadagni's dramatic gifts, and his observation of the singer's passion is not confirmed by any other writer, unless George Bussy Villiers's description of a performance of *Orfeo* given 'passionately and hastily' can be definitively related to Guadagni.[24]

The expected *da capo* is shortened. Eliminating any trace of the conventional structural landmark, Guadagni reprised only lines 3–4, 'Amami e lascia poi / Ogn'altra cura a me', resulting in a through-composed aria with binary elements. The shortened *da capo* is characteristic of the *aria cantabile*, contriving an air of intimacy and spontaneity in what is famously an all-too-predictable form. It is significant that one of the few alterations that Gluck made to this aria when revising his *Ezio* score of 1750 for performance in 1763 was to drop the *da capo* form. He replaced it with a *dal segno* structure, jettisoning the opening twelve-bar ritornello when repeating the first section.

[21] Burney, *General History*, ii, p. 876.

[22] Calzabigi, letter to Kaunitz, 6 Mar. 1767.

[23] Alessandro Pepoli, 'Lettera ad un uomo ragionevole sul melodramma detto serio', published as a preface to *Meleagro*, Venice, 1790, p. 4.

[24] See Chapter 12, note 19.

Gluck's changes to the aria form may have been motivated by his reform principles. The *da capo* procedure loses its *raison d'être* when the composer's intention is to
suppress the conventional ornamentation in the return of the first section. Guadagni
had no greater relish for technical display than had Gluck. Despite the technical
demands of some of his roles, not a single critic ever commended his virtuosity. Only
one brief passage in the whole aria (bars 80–82) could be described as mildly ath-
letic, and elsewhere the ornamentation is restricted to conventional appoggiaturas
and cadential trills (though whether the notation fairly represents Guadagni's actual
performance is of course another matter).

The range of dynamics is striking. The violins are marked *con sordini* throughout,
but Guadagni used emphatic *forte piano* shifts (for example, bars 78–80) and, as in
'Men tiranne', constantly employed *rinforzando* to indicate a short, pulsating crescendo (a notational usage coined by the Mannheim symphonists). The markings
may give some clue to the dynamic range Guadagni was capable of producing in
performance. Burney implies that this was limited. He describes Guadagni attacking a note 'with all the force he could *safely* exert' (my emphasis), before reducing
the volume 'to a thread'.[25] On the evidence of this setting, if Guadagni attempted to
match the orchestral accompaniment he must have constantly varied his dynamics
to produce 'well-chosen contrasts of light and shade'.[26]

Guadagni's composition prompts some intriguing questions as to when and where
it was first performed. He sang three settings of Metastasio's libretto in the course
of his career. His first *Ezio* was given at the Burgtheater in Vienna in 1763, when
he sang the title role in Gluck's revised score.[27] His next *Ezio* was Bertoni's setting,
premièred at the Teatro San Benedetto in Venice in 1767 and reprised at the Teatro
Filarmonico in Verona in 1772.[28] The third *Ezio* in which he sang was by Guglielmi,
first produced at the King's Theatre in London in 1770.[29] We can discount Gluck's
*Ezio* as the context for Guadagni's aria. Gluck was hardly the composer to tolerate an
insertion aria, and in any case his relations with his leading singer were at a low ebb
during the short run of the opera, when Guadagni had 'outraged' the audience for
unspecified shortcomings at the first performance.[30] It would in any case be unusual

[25] Burney, *General History*, ii, p. 876.
[26] Gluck, Preface to *Alceste*, Vienna, 1769.
[27] Gluck ed Gabriele Buschmeier, *Sämtliche Werke* iii/24, Kassel: Bärenreiter, 1992.
[28] Two copies of the ms score of Bertoni's opera are in the Ajuda Library, Lisbon, 44-II-50 a.51 and 54-I-57 a.58.
I am grateful to Cristina Pinto Basto for making the score available to me. A copy of the libretto is in the
Biblioteca Nazionale Braidense, Milan, RACC. DRAM. 4629.
[29] All that survives of this work is a libretto and the usual collection of *Favourite Songs*. The libretto was published by Griffin and the *Favourite Songs* by Bremner, both London, 1770.
[30] *Wienerisches Diarium* 7 Jan. 1764. See Chapter 6.

for an insertion aria to be introduced into the first season of a new opera, and for this reason Guadagni's aria is also unlikely to have been introduced into Bertoni's *Ezio* in 1767. It could well, however, have appeared in the revival of Bertoni's opera in Verona in 1772. Supporting, though far from conclusive, evidence for this lies in the existence of the copy of the aria in the Verona conservatory, the possession of a contemporary. The signature 'Co. Campagna' in the top left of Figure 9.1 is probably that of the owner of the manuscript, Count Francesco Campagna, a member of the Accademia Filarmonica from 1778.[31] The third and most likely possibility, however, is that the aria was incorporated into Guglielmi's setting, first produced in London in 1770.

There are several points in favour of Guglielmi's *Ezio*. The opera opened in London on 13 January 1770. It was given on six further occasions. The libretto reveals that Guglielmi chose not to set the aria 'Pensa a serbarmi', substituting instead an aria text from an unknown author, 'Nel suo dolor ristretto'. Tonally speaking, either Bertoni's or Guglielmi's opera would provide a possible context for Guadagni's insertion aria. 'Nel suo dolor' is in F major, as is Bertoni's setting of 'Pensa'; to replace either with an aria in E flat major would not outrage the tonal schemes though it would it not be the obvious choice. In this context, the F major transposition clued into the Verona score acquires a new relevance, though unfortunately it does nothing to solve the puzzle of which opera Guadagni's aria was intended for.

Guglielmi's 'Nel suo dolor', published in the *Favourite Songs*, seems particularly ill-suited to Guadagni's voice (see Example 12.3). Its heroic tone is expressed in striding arpeggio passage-work and large leaps, the greatest of which spans an octave and a sixth; it dwells extensively on the register below middle C, descending to low G (c' to g). Guglielmi's aria displays neither Guadagni's preferred style nor his customary register, and it is not improbable that the unsympathetic nature of the setting might have prompted Guadagni to produce an alternative, based on Metastasio's original text for that point in the drama. This could perhaps have been intended for his benefit performance scheduled for 25 January, a popular occasion for the introduction of new material. In the event the benefit was cancelled at the last minute owing to the singer's illness,[32] but there were five further performances that season, in one or more of which Guadagni could have performed his aria. An additional argument in favour of Guglielmi's opera as the context for Guadagni's insertion aria lies in the manuscript copy in Verona. This gives the instruments listed on the first page of the score their Italian names with the exception of the lines marked 'Flute', a slender hint that the copyist could have been working from a score produced in London

---

[31] I am grateful to Luca de Paolis for this observation.

[32] *Public Advertiser*, 24 Jan. 1770.

with English instrument names. A final clue is the fact that at this period of his life Guadagni was in composing mode: the pasticcio *Orfeo*, for which he provided his own 'Men tiranne', was given less than four months after Guglielmi's *Ezio*.

Guadagni had one further connection with *Ezio*. In the Carnival season of 1767, while Bertoni was presenting the première of his opera in Venice, Felice Alessandri was directing his setting of the same Metastasian text at the Teatro Filarmonico in Verona.[33] It is hardly possible that Guadagni was ignorant of Alessandri's work: within a few months they were to become brothers-in-law. Moreover, Alessandri and Guadagni were together in London in 1770 when Guadagni sang in Guglielmi's opera. Although there are no grounds for suggesting that Guadagni's aria ever found its way into performances of Alessandri's score, the various settings of the text must surely have been a topic of conversation between them. We can only presume they agreed to differ. In conspicuous contrast to Bertoni's and Alessandri's flamboyant settings of 'Pensa a serbarmi', Guadagni's aria explicitly endorses his credentials as an active protagonist in the reform of opera through its avoidance of the predictable *da capo* structure, its rejection of vocal display, its reticent lyricism and sensitive word-setting.

[33] This was Alessandri's first opera. The ms score is in the Bibliothèque Nationale, Paris, Ab.o.155 (1–3), available on line at http://gallica.bnf.fr/ark:/12148/btv1b8427210v/f1.

# 10

## At Home in Padua (1771–1782)

⌒

### SEASON OF 1771–1772

We resume the narrative of Guadagni's career with the disappointing observation that, after leaving England in the summer of 1771, he disappears from view for six months. It seems likely that he returned to Padua, but as he was paid only one salary instalment of 80 ducats that year, we must assume he spent a period of not more than three months in the city. He may have travelled to Verona in the late autumn. He was certainly there by the turn of the year when his presence at the Teatro Filarmonico was recorded by Burney,[1] and where he sang in both Carnival operas, Galuppi's *Arianna e Teseo*, and Bertoni's *Ezio*. These were revivals of works he had premièred in Venice in 1768 and 1767 respectively.

Guadagni was back in Padua by June 1772 when Maria Antonia Walpurgis, Dowager Electress of Saxony, visited the town. She heard Guadagni sing three times in two days. On Sunday 13 June the electress attended mass at the Santo and visited the relics of the saint, on which occasion Guadagni sang, as usual, Vallotti's antiphon 'O lingua benedicta'; in the evening she was entertained at an *accademia di musica* in the Giustinian palace, where Guadagni is numbered among the performers[2]; the following evening she heard him again in a performance of her own short opera, *Il trionfo della fedeltà* (first performed in Dresden, 1754) at the Palazzo Dondi Orologio. Although the latter occasion is recorded in two separate accounts, both all too typically dwell on the magnificence of the setting, the brilliance of the

---

[1] Burney, *The Present State of Music in France and Italy*, 2nd ed., p. 124.
[2] Gennari, *Notizie giornaliere,* i, pp. 104–5.

lighting and the copious profusion of the refreshments, rather than on the music and its performance.[3]

Guadagni did not hesitate to profit from Maria Antonia's visit and seized the opportunity to attach himself to her household. The Dowager Electress, widowed in 1763, kept court in Munich with her brother, the Elector Maximilian Joseph. Guadagni accompanied the electress from Padua to Munich, travelling via Verona again: according to Burney, 'Signor Guadagni came to Munich from Verona, with the Electress dowager of Saxony'.[4] Burney arrived in Munich on 16 August 1772, and found Guadagni enjoying a privileged position as house musician at the elector's palace.[5] Relations between the singer and his patrons appear to have been warm. Guadagni retained a tangible souvenir of the visit, displaying in his drawing room in his house in Padua a 'large picture' of the electoral family.[6]

Burney spent a good deal of time with Guadagni in Munich, dining frequently with him and his fellow house musicians. He recorded that 'The day after my arrival, I had the pleasure of dining with Guadagni, Rauzzini, and Ravanni, an Italian counter-tenor in the service of this court, and after dinner, of hearing them sing trios most divinely'.[7] The situation suited both scholar and singer. Burney always relished being able to claim acquaintance with celebrity, and his long friendship with Guadagni, dating from 1750, when he had given the singer English lessons and coached him in his Handelian roles, secured him a welcome into the distinguished musical establishment. It appears that Guadagni assumed the role of host. It was Guadagni who 'arranged everything' for Burney's introduction to the electress in her summer palace at Nymphenburg, and Guadagni who 'conducted [Burney] through a great number of most magnificent apartments' to be presented to her; Guadagni also thoughtfully reassured Burney that 'her highness spoke English pretty well'.[8]

Burney relates a number of incidents that shed light on Guadagni's intimacy with his illustrious employers. Burney's request to take home with him an example of the elector's compositions was only grudgingly granted, since the elector feared publication and subsequent piracy. The same request made to the electress, however, was readily acceded to, and she allowed Guadagni to look through her unpublished compositions to select items that might interest the English scholar.[9] Another episode

---

[3] Gennari, op. cit., i, p. 105; Museo Civico, Padua, Archivio Antico Q38.b, quoted in Bruno Brunelli, *I teatri di Padova*, Padua, 1921, p. 354 .

[4] Burney, *The Present State of Music in Germany*, 2nd ed., London, 1775, i, p. 126.

[5] *The Present State of Music in Germany*, i, p. 125.

[6] Inventory of Guadagni's effects at death, in Archivio di Stato, Padua, Notarile, F. Fanzago, fo. 32.

[7] *The Present State of Music in Germany*, i, pp. 128–29 (17 Aug. 1772). The versatile castrato, composer and harpsichordist Venanzio Rauzzini made his home in England from 1774.

[8] Ibid., i, pp. 135–37.

[9] Burney, op. cit., i, p. 169.

arose in a more domestic setting. It is not clear whether Burney told it to illustrate the elector's generosity or Guadagni's parsimony. After the evening concert, the elector asked Guadagni if he was planning to provide supper for Burney and the other musicians: 'Guadagni answered that he would give us bread and cheese and a glass of wine. "Here," cried the elector, emptying two dishes of game on a plate, "send that to your apartments." His Highness was implicitly obeyed. We supped together, after which I returned to Munich, abundantly flattered and satisfied with the events of the day'.[10]

During his visit to Nymphenburg, Burney heard Guadagni in several evening concerts and in rehearsals of the electress's opera *Talestri, regina delle Amazoni* (first performed at Nymphenburg in 1760), though he appears to have left Munich before the performance. He also passed on valuable evidence of Guadagni's perfect intonation, when, in a much-quoted scene, he related how he had heard Guadagni, together with Rauzzini, producing the difference tones associated with Tartini's research. The two castratos 'sung a great part of the time, particularly in the bath, where there was an excellent room for music; here they went successfully through all Tartini's experiments, in order, by sustaining with their voices two consonant intervals, to produce a *third sound*, which is generated in the air, and is their true fundamental base'.[11] It was on this visit that Burney elicited from the electress one of the most telling judgements on Guadagni's singing: 'She said [he] sung with much art, as well as feeling; and had the great secret of hiding defects'.[12]

### SEASON OF 1772–1773

Guadagni left Munich at the end of the summer. In the autumn of 1772 he was in Venice, where he was engaged to sing in San Marco for the visit of the Grand Duchess of Baden.[13] It was probably on this occasion that the doge Alvise Mocenigo, with whom he had crossed swords in 1766, awarded him the title Cavaliere di San Marco, the oldest and most distinguished order of chivalry in the Venetian republic. Like Gluck, who was awarded the more prestigious papal knighthood of the Golden Spur, Guadagni was naïvely pleased with his title, and from this point onwards he made sure he was customarily referred to as 'Cavalier Guadagni'. He presumably

[10] Ibid., i, p. 144.

[11] Ibid., i, pp. 139–40.

[12] Ibid., i, p. 136.

[13] Francesco Caffi, *Storia della musica sacra nella già cappella ducale di S Marco in Venezia*, ii, Venice: Antonelli, 1855, p. 49.

returned to Padua from time to time for the major feast days, since he received his full salary from the Santo for 1772, and four-fifths of the full sum in 1773.[14]

Back in Munich for the Carnival season of January 1773, Guadagni was joined by a former colleague, Marianna Bianchi, the Euridice of the Vienna production of *Orfeo*. Bianchi's husband, Antonio Tozzi, was newly appointed Hofkapellmeister to the court in Munich, where the Carnival season of 1773 opened on 26 January with his new opera *Zenobia*. Guadagni, who was a court musician rather than a member of the opera company, did not take part. However, although Munich normally presented only one *opera seria* in the Carnival season, this year a second opera was produced, a new pasticcio of Gluck's *Orfeo*. The enterprise was driven by Guadagni, as an informative account by an anonymous 'Saxon diplomat' makes clear:

On Friday [5 February] Maria Antonia was present at the first performance of the opera Orpheus, which Guadagni had brought with him, and which the Elector had had produced for this singer. He plays his role to perfection. There is something great in his acting, and although his voice has begun to decline, it shines in this opera, which appears to have been written expressly for him. It is an extraordinary work—I have never seen anything comparable in this genre. The action and the music are most effective, and arouse a sense of tragedy that stirs the soul, to the extent that one could entirely dispense with the poetry. It seems as if the composer, who is none other than the celebrated Gluck, decided to create a masterpiece out of a lugubrious episode, and succeeded, for without the joyful conclusion, the audience would go home in a very melancholy state. The work is very difficult to bring off. In Vienna, where it was first produced, it needed 29 rehearsals before the first night, and even then it was not entirely successful. The music is here considered more suitable to Holy Week than for Carnival. There were protests among the orchestra, and the Court intervened. Her Highness the Electress of Saxony is strongly supportive of the opera, which means that those who wish to retain the favour of this great princess are careful not to find fault with it.[15]

[14] Jolanda Dalla Vecchia, *L'organizzazione della cappella musicale antoniana di Padova nel Settecento*, Padova: Centro studi antoniani, 1995.

[15] 'Vendredi. Elles assisterent à la première representation de l'Opera, Orpheus, que Guadagni a apporté, et que l'Electeur a fait executer pour ce chanteur. Il y joue son rôle au mieux. Il y a du grand dans son action: et quoique sa voix commence à baisser, elle brille dans cet opera, qui paroit être fait exprés pour lui. C'est un spectacle tout à fait extraordinaire, et je n'ai jamais rien vu de semblable dans ce genre. Le jeu, et la musique y font un grand effét, et excitent un tristesse, qui va jusqu'a l'ame, au point, qu'on pourroit ce passer entièrement des paroles de la poesie. Il paroit, que le compositeur qui est le fameux Gluck, ce soit proposé de faire un chef

The Munich version of *Orfeo* was derived from the expanded London pasticcios of 1770–71.[16] Although the roles of Eagro and Egina were cut, it included four of the extra numbers composed by J. C. Bach, and four further Bach arias designed to expand the role of Euridice. Guadagni again included his setting of 'Men tiranne', and there were borrowings from Gluck's *Le Cadi dupé* and *Semiramide riconosciuta*. The libretto for this production reproduced Calzabigi's original text, omitting, perhaps at Guadagni's insistence, all the additional material.[17] It is probable that in the many revivals and re-adaptations of *Orfeo* in subsequent years, particularly in Padua, the published librettos do not reliably represent the exact content of the scores performed. Perhaps as a result of the expansion of Euridice's role, the part was assigned not to Bianchi but to the local prima donna Giulietta Lodi. The diplomat's comment on the deterioration in Guadagni's voice needs to be set against Burney's observation, one year earlier, that 'Guadagni sung…with his usual grace and expression, but with more voice than he had when in England'.[18]

### SEASON OF 1773–1774

Guadagni spent most of this season in Padua, where he managed to qualify to receive four-fifths of his salary for 1774. There is no record of his participation any public performances in Munich or elsewhere during the year.

### SEASON OF 1774–1775

Returning to Munich for a further Carnival season, Guadagni took part in yet another version of the Orpheus story. The new setting, which opened on 9 January 1775, was by Tozzi. Tozzi's work had two acute though far from disinterested critics, Leopold and Wolfgang Mozart, who were in Munich that season, where Wolfgang

---

d'oeuvre d'un spectacle lugubre, à quoi il n'a pas mal réussi: car dans le denouement, qui est rejouissant, les spectateurs s'en retourneroient fort melancoliquement chez eux. Au reste ce spectacle est trés difficile à executer.

'Il y en a à Vienne, où il a été produit, 29 epreuves, avant qu'on en ait pû donner une première representation, et encore n'atelle pas bien réussi. On trouve ici, que cette musique seroit plus convenable pour la Semaine Sainte, que pour le carneval; il y a des cabales dans l'Orchestre: la Cour s'en mêle: S. A. A. Madame l'Electrice de Saxe est fort portée pour cet opera, ce qui fait, que ceux qui respectent le suffrage de cette auguste Princesse, n'ont garde d'y trouver à redire.' In Moritz Fürstenau, 'Glucks Orpheus in München 1773', *Monatshefte für Musikgeschichte*, 1872–1874, p. 221.

[16] See Fürstenau, op. cit., pp. 218–24, and Alessandra Martina, *Orfeo—Orphée di Gluck: storia della trasmissione e della recezione*, Florence: De Sono, 1995, pp. 69–71.

[17] See Martina, *Orfeo—Orphée di Gluck*, p. 70.

[18] Burney, *The Present State of Music in Germany*, i, p. 142.

was preparing to direct his *buffa* opera *La finta giardiniera*. Leopold clearly saw his son's opera as being in competition with Tozzi's *opera seria*:

> You must know that a year ago Tozzi, who this year is writing the *opera seria*, wrote an *opera buffa*, and took such pains with it that it eclipsed the *opera seria* written by [Pietro Pompeo] Sales, to the extent that Sales's opera no longer pleased. Now as it happens, Wolfgang's opera is to be performed before Tozzi's opera, and when they heard the first rehearsal, everyone said that Tozzi was being paid back in his own coin, and that Wolfgang's opera would eclipse his.[19]

Leopold was mistaken. *La finta giardiniera* opened on 13 January, and fell far short of eclipsing Tozzi's opera: the latter received seven performances (a very respectable number for a Carnival opera in Munich), while *La finta giardiniera* was taken off after three.

Although there is no record of his intervention in the composition process, Guadagni must have played a role in initiating the Orpheus operas created in the 1770s. He was developing a personal identification with the role and saw to it that many aspects of original setting prevailed in the re-compositions, especially the preservation of much of Calzabigi's intensely expressive poetry, the dramatic interplay of soloist and chorus and a musical characterisation of the title role that had similar aims to Gluck's classical simplicity.

It was Coltellini (with whom Guadagni had worked on *Telemaco* in 1765) who provided the libretto for Tozzi's *Orfeo*. In a note in the libretto, Coltellini referred to the usual need to amplify the drama to provide a full evening's entertainment.[20] He rewrote the whole of the first act to revisit seventeenth-century versions of the myth, featuring the wedding of Orfeo and Euridice, and Euridice's death through a serpent's bite. The following acts retain much of Calzabigi's text, though with additional arias for Euridice, sung on this occasion by Marianna Bianchi Tozzi. Tozzi's music is largely

[19] 'Nun must Du wissen, daß der Maestro Tozi der heuer die opera Seria schreibt vorm Jahr eben um diese zeit eine opera Buffa geschrieben, und sich so bemühet solche gut zu schreiben um die opera Seria, die vorm Jahr der Maestro Sales schrieb niederzuschlagen, daß des Sales opera wirklich nicht mehr recht gefallen wollen. Nun eraignet sich der zufall, daß des Wolfgangs opera eben vor der opera des Tozi gemacht wird, und da sie die erste Probe hörten, sagte alles, nun wäre Tozi mit gleicher Münz bezahlt, indem die opera des Wolfg: die opera des Tozi niederschlage.' Leopold Mozart to his wife, 30 Dec. 1774, in *Mozart: Briefe und Aufzeichnungen*, ed. Wilhelm A. Bauer and Otto Deutsch, vol. 1, Kassel: Bärenreiter, 1962, p. 513.
[20] 'Questa amorosa Favoletta fà il soggetto del presente Drama. Il Sign. Calzabigi l'espose il primo con molto applauso all'Imperiale Teatro di Vienna con tre soli personaggi, e in un Atto cortissimo. Comparve poi sopra il Teatro di sua Maestà Britannica in Londra con non minore gradimento nella passata stagione con vari tumultary et estemporanei accrescimenti, ma in un Atto solo. Comparisa adesso, in tre atti, accresciuto di personaggi, e di scene, per accommodarsi alla durata di simili spettacoli.' In Fürstenau, 'Glucks *Orpheus* in München 1773', p. 222.

'unreformed'. In a somewhat jaundiced account of the opera, Schubart (a committed admirer of Gluck's) wrote that 'Tozzi lacked the heavenly simplicity of a Gluck...his ritornellos were intolerably lengthy, and in the bravura arias, he repeated an idea so often that all the fire in the action evaporated. All in all, this opera had all the faults of the most recent Italian opera; it raged where it should murmur'.[21] Curiously, Schubart did not mention Guadagni. However, the latter's hand in the music of the title role, where a simpler, predominantly syllabic style prevails, is unmistakable. Tozzi consulted the singer's tastes and catered to his strengths, exactly as Traetta had done in composing *Ifigenia in Tauride* some eleven years previously. Tozzi's setting of 'Men tiranne' owes much more to Guadagni's version than to Gluck's.[22] The Saxon diplomat concurred with Schubart in judging Tozzi's *Orfeo* inferior to the version of Gluck's score he had seen two years earlier: 'There are some lovely things in the music of this opera, which was composed by an Italian master called Tozzi: however it does not match that of Gluck, who was the first to set this opera in music'.[23] The last of the seven performances of Tozzi's *Orfeo* took place on 27 February. Shortly after this, Guadagni returned to Padua. He is next heard of on 29 May, singing in a private concert to honour a visit of Leopold Grand Duke of Tuscany to Padua.[24]

### SEASON OF 1775–1776

The following winter Guadagni was back in Venice. He sang in San Marco's for the Christmas services, and was engaged at San Benedetto for the Carnival season. The first Carnival opera, opening on 26 December 1775, was the première of Borghi's *Artaserse*, which presumably had little success since it was closely followed on 3 January by the première of Bertoni's *Orfeo*—Guadagni's fourth Orpheus opera in five years. Ortes gave this account of the opera:

A few nights ago I was at the Teatro San Benedetto where I again heard the little drama of *Orfeo*, preceded by a pastoral; all the music was by Bertoni, and

[21] 'Ihm fehlt die göttliche Einfalt eines Glucks.... Seine Ritornelle sind unaustehlich lang; er wiederholt in den Bravourarien einen Gedanken so oft, daß das Feuer der Handlung drunter erkaltet. Ueberhaupt hat dieser Oper den Fehler der Neuesten Italienischen Oper; sie stürmt wo sie säuseln.' Christian Friedrich Daniel Schubart, *Deutsche Chronik auf das Jahr 1775*, facsim. ed., i, Heidelberg: Schneider, 1975, pp. 239–40.

[22] See Example 9.2. Tozzi's setting is reproduced in Paolo Cattelan, 'Altri Orfei di Gaetano Guadagni', Preface to Ferdinando Bertoni, *Orfeo*, Milan: Ricordi, 1990, pp. lx–lxx.

[23] 'Il y a des belles choses dans la musique de cet opera, qui est de la composition d'un maitre Italien, nommé Tozzi: elle ne vaut cependant par celle de Gluck, qui a mis le premier cet opera en musique.' 12 Jan. 1775, in Fürstenau, 'Glucks *Orpheus* in München 1773', p. 221.

[24] 'La sera intervennero in casa Memmo sul Prato della Valle ad una privata ricreazione nella quale cantò il cavalier Guadagni.' Gennari, *Notizie giornaliere*, i, p. 131.

it pleased me greatly....As usual, the castrato Guadagni in the role of Orfeo sang well, and the music of this little opera was very fine. Gluck's setting is certainly simpler, and therefore those who have a heart will generally prefer it, but this [new] setting will give no less pleasure, and will perhaps be preferred by those who listen with their ears rather than with their heart.[25]

On his return to Padua, Guadagni found himself in dispute with the Arca. The following resolution, dated 1 February 1776, appears to refer back to his prolonged absence in Munich:

Gaetano Guadagni, contralto, is liable to lose his entire salary, for failing to appear at the five principal feasts specified in the terms of his engagement, and is also subject to penalties for failing to be present at the other musical functions. As it was considered excessive that he should suffer this double punishment, it was proposed that from today Guadagni should be exempt from penalties in connection with his musical duties, and be subject only to the loss of salary pertaining to the five principal feasts, provided that [in future] he warn the presidents fifteen days before any contemplated absence, so that a substitute can be found. The proposal was unanimously approved. Moreover, because his absence on Christmas Eve and Christmas Day was caused by his participation in serving the royal Cappella of San Marco's, a duty he could not evade, Guadagni was repaid the 80 ducats deducted on account of this absence.[26]

The records show that he received his full 400 ducats for 1776.[27] The concession by the Arca suggests that Guadagni was a valued member of the Santo choir, whom

---

[25] 'Sono stato alcune sere addietro al teatro in S Benedetto, ove ho sentito ancor qui il piccolo dramma dell'Orfeo preceduto da una pastorale, il tutto di musica del Bertoni, che mi piacquero assai...Il musico Guadagni nella parte d'Orfeo recita bene al solito e la musica di questa operetta è pure assai bella. Quella del Gluk è certemente più semplice e però piacerà generalmente più a chi ha cuore, ma questa non piacerà meno, e forse sarà preferita a quella da quei che più del cuore fan uso dell'orecchie.' Ortes to Leonilda Burgioni, 2 Feb. 1776.

[26] 'Gaetano Guadagni contralto è soggetto alla perdita dell'intero stipendio essendo mancato alle cinque principale funzioni stabilite nella parte relativa alla sua assunzione, ed è il soggetto alle pontadure essendo mancato alle altre funzioni musicali. Considerando sconveniente che egli subisca questa doppia punizione, fu proposta parte che da oggi in poi Guadagni sia esente dalle pontadure relative alle funzioni musicali, e resti soggetto solo alla perdita dello stipendio mancando alle cinque funzioni principali, à condizione però di avvertire la Presidenza 15 giorni prima delle sue eventuali assenze, in modo che si possa provvedere a un sostituto. La parte fu approvata all'unanimità. E poiche a Guadagni furono trattenuti ducati 80 per non essere intervenuto alla funzione della vigilia e del giorno di Natale, ed essendo tuttavia mancato perché occupato in pubblico servizio nella regia Cappella di S. Marco, da cui non poteva esimersi, fu ordinato all' unanimità al Cancelliere di rilasciargli il necessario mandato.' 1 Feb. 1776, see Boscolo and Pietribiasi, *La cappella musicale antoniana*, p. 285.

[27] Dalla Vecchia, *L'organizzazione della cappella musicale antoniana*.

there was no wish to penalise too harshly. It is significant that in the register of musicians whose contracts had been renewed, his name appears at the top of the singers, even though the normal process was to list sopranos, contraltos, tenors and basses in that order. It was probably this attempt to mark his pre-eminence in the choir that led to his listing as a soprano in 1774 and 1775.[28]

On 2 May 1776 he introduced Bertoni's *Orfeo* to Padua. The performance took place in the Obizzi theatre, the only occasion on which Guadagni is known to have sung there. There is some doubt as to whether this was a fully public performance. The libretto designates it as being given 'in una accademia in Padova'. Typical of an academy performance is the fact that all the singers were drawn from the Cappella. The role of Euridice was taken by the castrato Lorenzo Piatti, a piece of casting that would have raised no eyebrows in the masonic circles that dominated academy membership; the tenors Nasolini and Andreosi sang Amore and the Ombra respectively, and the bass role of Plutone was taken by Benacchio.

The performance was reprised during the summer at San Benedetto's with its original cast. It was a noted success:

*Orfeo* was the first opera to bring the name of Bertoni to the height of theatrical glory. The exquisite beauties of the music were matched with the exquisite performance of the celebrated singer Gaetano Guadagni. So great was the magnificence lavished on the production of this opera during the summer of 1776, that the management was obliged to double the entrance prices to balance the books. However, despite the extraordinary price of eight lira, the enthusiasm was such that on the evenings when it was given, those who wanted to enjoy it were obliged to take up their seats as soon as the theatre opened.[29]

At some point during the autumn of 1776 Guadagni probably travelled to Potsdam to sing before Frederick the Great. I have found no documentary evidence for the visit, but it is mentioned in the earliest dictionary entries on Guadagni. Gerber's is the first to record the event: 'In 1776 Guadagni journeyed to Potsdam to sing for King Frederick II, in recognition of which, the king presented him with a golden snuffbox set

---

[28] Contracts were renewed or cancelled following a ballot of the seven presidents of the Arca: see the *riballottazione dei musici* for 1774 and 1775 in Boscolo and Pietribiasi, op. cit., pp. 281, 283.

[29] '*Orfeo*... fu veramente la prima che il nome di Bertoni portasse all'apice della gloria teatrale. Alle squisite bellezze della musica corrispose la parimenti squisita esecuzione del celebre cantore soprano Gaetano Guadagni.... Tal fu la pompa con cui sulle scene questo drama comparve nella state del 1776, che raddoppiar si dovette il prezzo al biglietto d'ingresso per equilibrare la spesa. Malgrado però allo straordinario costo d'otto lire, l'entusiasmo tal era, che nelle tante sere di recita chi volea godere uopo era che andasse ad occuparvi un posto appena il teatri si appriva.' Caffi, *Storia della musica*, i, pp. 421–22.

with diamonds, more valuable, it was said, than any gift he had ever bestowed on any private individual'.[30]

### SEASON OF 1776–1777

Although no public performances by Guadagni are recorded for the season of 1776–77, in returning to Padua, the singer was not retiring to a backwater. The Santo was a celebrated centre of musical excellence, and the absence of fines or reprimands suggests that he played his full part in its rites and ceremonies. At this period Padua was enjoying an unprecedented phase of public building. The most notable fruit of this was the magnificent Prato della Valle, a vast elliptical space forming one of the biggest public 'squares' in Europe. The Prato, originally a Roman theatre, had by the eighteenth century degenerated into a swampy area that flooded frequently. The pool of stagnant water at its centre was full of frogs and toads, and the prolific bird life led to hunters roaming its unsavoury depths.[31] It was the scene of annual horse races or palios, less celebrated than the famous palio of Siena, but equally well supported by the citizens. In the summer of 1775, the governor of Padua, Andrea Memmo, planned to rebuild the Prato, to rectify the dangers of flooding and to maximise its commercial potential in connection with the regular fairs held in the city.

Much of his plan can still be seen today: the elliptical island, surrounded by a canal crossed with bridges, and ringed with a series of statues of local interest (the first statue to be erected, of Cicero, was criticised for its lack of local relevance, and was replaced by a statue of Antenore, whom legend identifies as the founder of Padua). An important part of Memmo's scheme was the placing of 54 temporary shops around the island, the rental income from which helped to pay for the development of the Prato. Guadagni featured among the prominent citizens who contributed financially to the building of the Prato.[32]

Visitors were drawn to the city for both its artistic and its commercial attractions. There was an abundance of theatrical activity, with comic opera at the Teatro Nuovo during Carnival, spoken drama at the Teatro Obizzi in the spring, serious opera at

---

[30] 'Noch im Jahr 1776 that Guadagni eine Reise nach Potsdam zum König Fridrich II. und liess sich vor selbigem hören. Der König beschenkte ihn darauf mit einer goldenen mit Brillanten besetzten Dose von so hohem Werthe, als sich noch keine Privatperson rühmen konnte, von ihm erhalten zu haben.' Ernst Ludwig Gerber, *Historisch-biographisches Lexicon der Tonkünstler* (Leipzig, 1790), ed. Othmar Wessely, Graz: Akademische Druck—und Verlagsanstalt, 1977, s.v.

[31] Gennari, *Notizie giornaliere*, i, pp. 132–35.

[32] Several eighteenth-century illustrations portray the Prato, including two images by Canaletto of the area before development, titled 'The Prato della Valle with Santa Giustina and the Church of Misericordia', which can be found on the second page of the collection at www.wikipaintings.org/en/canaletto/mode/all-paintings. An anonymous etching of the temporary shops erected round the central arena, titled 'Il Prato della Valle', can be

the Nuovo in June (coinciding with the trade fair), followed by performances in the little theatre in the Prato; the season concluded with comic opera at the Obizzi in August. Gennari protested at the crowded calendar: 'This is in truth too much, even for a metropolis!'[33] New roads extended the city on all sides. New buildings sprung up, including a number of substantial shops, one of them owned by Guadagni's nephew Antonio Guadagni, in addition to the temporary booths erected for the June fair. New housing included the palazzo that housed Guadagni and his patron Giuseppe Ximenes d'Aragona.

At some point in the mid-1770s, Guadagni moved into the house which was to become his home for the remainder of his life. The newly-built house he rented from the Santo stands today, one of three houses numbered 8–12 in the road now called via Melchiorre Cesarotti, adjacent to the Santo. We do not know which of the three houses was Guadagni's; each has a plain stone façade with a balcony at first-floor level. Gennari noted Guadagni's presence in 'the new houses by the Santo', fronted by a new stone pavement, where he had as neighbour the most important patron of his remaining years, Don Giuseppe Ximenes d'Aragona[34] (see Figure 10.1).

The inventory drawn up at his death provides a tantalising insight into the house and its contents.[35] It was elegantly equipped with an abundance of decorative furniture, tables small and large, sofas, armchairs, mirrors, lamps, vases, pictures and statues. There was a vast amount of tableware and cooking vessels. His itemised clothes include vestments for the performance of his church duties, silk coats and shirts, a large number of gloves and shoes and a silk umbrella. There was a pair of spectacles in every room. His theatrical trappings included thirteen stage wigs and a folder of theatrical designs. A portable stove, portable vessels for making tea, coffee and chocolate, and a portable cheese box create the picture of the travelling artist. The inventory lists a total of 369 books; no titles are mentioned, but the collection must have included many scores and librettos. Two rooms are described in particular detail. The drawing room, leading to the balcony overlooking the street, was furnished in fashionable yellow silk; it was lit by a grand chandelier and provided with a sofa and six small armchairs; a small table stood ready with a porcelain coffee service; the room was dominated by the 'large painting of the electoral family of Bavaria', a present from

---

found at www.brombin-arte.it/padova.htm. It has not been possible to reproduce these images for copyright reasons.

[33] 'O questo in verità è troppo anche per una metropoli!' Gennari, *Notizie giornaliere*, i, p. 348.

[34] 'Davanti le case nuove al Santo, abitate dal marchese Ximenes e dal cavalier Guadagni, fu fatto un bel marcepiede di macigno.' Gennari, *Notizie giornaliere*, i, p. 150. Ximenes' role in Guadagni's activities in Padua has, however, been overstated in the writings of Paolo Cattelan: see Bruno Brizi, 'Per una lettura dell'*Alceste* di Gluck', in *Mozart, Padova e la Betulia liberata*, ed. Paolo Pinamonti, pp. 260–61, Florence: Olschki, 1991.

[35] Archivio di Stato, Padua, Notarile, F. Fanzago.

FIGURE 10.1 Guadagni's house in Padua. (Photography D. L. Howard)

Guadagni's lengthy stay in Munich. Adjacent to this elegant room was his bedroom, which must have been commodious since it contained two chandeliers, a four-poster bed with curtains, a sofa and eight armchairs, several mirrors and an alarm clock. He kept a musket (*trombone*) in his wardrobe. A small room on the same floor held his harpsichord. The garden was elaborately laid out with benches, urns, statues and a fountain. Guadagni set himself up as a conspicuously prosperous resident of Padua.

## SEASON OF 1777–1778

From this point on, Guadagni's operatic performances became increasingly rare, and there are indications that, in his 50th year, his voice had begun to lose its power. However, he played a prominent role in the festivities and ceremonies of the city, organising, for Carnival 1778, a 'greatly-applauded Tyrolean masquerade' in the course of which he sang a song in praise of Padua.[36] On 5 July 1778 he gave another private performance of Bertoni's *Orfeo* with the same all-male cast as in May 1776.

---

[36] 'All'egregio signor Cav. Gaetano Guadagni che decorò il carnevale con una sua applauditissima mascherata di tirolesi, i quali facevano vedere il mondo nuovo e cantavano una leggiadra canzone in lode di Padova': see Anna

The decline of his operatic career was underlined by the engagement, in the summer of 1778, of Pacchierotti as first man in Bertoni's *Quinto Fabbio* at the Teatro Nuovo. The two singers came together to sing a duet at Vespers on 27 June in the church of the Servites. Gennari reported that a huge crowd gathered to hear the 'contest', as it was perceived.[37] A reference to the duet appears in a sonnet by the critic and dramatist Gasparo Gozzi in a letter to Giovanni Marsili, contrasting Guadagni's familiar, established status with the new brilliance of the meteoric Pacchierotti:

> You know, Guadagni, how from time to time
> A comet runs its course across the sky,
> Showering its brilliant rays of hoarded light,
> Filling with wonder every mortal eye.
> Here, there and everywhere the people gaze
> Upward, with rapt attention and in awe,
> And all because the heavenly sight on show
> Resembles nothing ever seen before.
>
> Meanwhile, our ever-faithful, constant sun
> Spreads health and wealth and treasure here on earth,
> Beaming his rays through all our neighbouring space,
> Charming our souls with beauty and with mirth.
> Yet, though he fills each dawning day with light,
> The thankless race of men longs for the night.[38]

Perhaps to assuage his feelings wounded by the comparison with Pacchierotti, Guadagni staged another civic diversion to celebrate the new Podestà (chief magistrate) Domenico Michel in August 1778. It is an example of the use made of the

---

Laura Bellina, 'Appunti sul repertorio padovano', *Mozart, Padova e la Betulia liberata*, ed. Paolo Pinamonti, Florence, Olschki, 1991, p. 187; Bruno Brizi, 'Per una lettura dell'*Alceste* di Gluck', in *Mozart, Padova e la Betulia liberata*, ed. Paolo Pinamonti, p. 262.

[37] 'Addì 27 la congregazione de' musici e suonatori solenizzò nella chiesa de' Padri serviti la festa di S. Cecilia, essendo presidente il cavalier Guadagni, e nel dopo pranzo al vespero il concorso è stato grandissimo per l'aspettazione del Pacchierotti che vi canto un duetto insieme cil signor Guadagni.' Gennari, *Notizie giornaliere*, i, p. 147.

[38] I am grateful to Brian Baldry for this elegant free translation. 'Guadagni, se talvolta in cielo piglia/Cometa il corso, e sparge accesi rai/Col non usato suo lume, ben sai,/Empie l'alme fra noi di maraviglia./Quivi le attente, e desiose ciglia/Dalla terra le genti alzar vedrai,/E studiar come ruoti, e perché mai/A null'altro del ciel segno somiglia./Intanto il sole luce feconda, e santa,/Che per eterna, e ordinata via/Empie la terra, e di ricchezza ammanta,/Che ad ogni altro pianeta il lume invia,/Ch'apre il dì, scaccia l'ombre, e l'alme incanta,/L'ingrata stirpe de' mortali obblia.'

Prato della Valle, still under construction at this period, for civic festivities. Guadagni saw it as a theatrical space, and drew up plans to transform the great piazza into an elegant garden, with trees and fountains and brilliant lighting effects; music was provided by two orchestras disposed within the spectacular setting:

> To celebrate the arrival of the new Podestà, the celebrated singer Guadagni, together with others, transformed the great piazza into an elegant garden. All the columns of the portico were delicately swathed with festoons of greenery, and the spaces between one booth and another were similarly decorated; in the niches beneath the garlands were placed statues on pedestals. Along the central avenue, and also along the other paths, orange trees were positioned, in painted wicker containers. In the four squares of the parterre, small grassy mounds were built, equipped with rising steps, and in the middle of each mound a large bay tree was planted. At the head of the piazza, opposite the stone bridge by which one enters, in the middle of a grove, was placed a rock from which a fountain continuously flowed, falling from ledge to ledge into a pool. At the foot of the rock, around a fine balustrade, were placed many musicians with string and wind instruments; a similar orchestra appeared at the entrance to the piazza. All the piazza was illuminated by wax torches, and the plants, arranged in long rows, bore empty lemon skins filled with burning oil; the four steps, already mentioned, were decorated with the shells of melons and watermelons containing lamps, and led to a plain on which stood no fewer than four rustic bay trees. At intervals along the portico were citrus trees, at the base of which were placed paper lanterns, lit from within, and decorated with the arms of His Excellency the Podestà, which made a fine show. The two orchestras carried numerous wax torches, which illuminated the great piazza as if it were day. A stand for the Podestà, made from one of the booths prepared for the Fair, was nobly adorned and situated not far from the principal orchestra. The music began [at sunset], and lasted [some four hours]; an amazing crowd of people, some of them foreigners, attended this elegant and graceful event.[39]

---

[39] Gennari, op. cit., i, pp. 149–50. Gennari dates the feast as taking place on 12 August; Bruno Brizi corrects this to 16 August in 'Per una lettura dell'*Alceste*', *Mozart, Padova e La Betulia liberata*, ed. Paolo Pinamonti, p. 262. A painting by Ignazio Colombo, of a similar nocturnal festa in the Prato to celebrate the visit of Pius VI, is reproduced as the central pages in Alessandro Prosdocimi, *Il Prato della Valle*, Padua: Comune di Padova, 1978. It has not been included here for copyright reasons.

## SEASON OF 1778–1779

Guadagni's singing career was now almost exclusively restricted to the Santo. There is no specific record of any concert or dramatic engagement in the season of 1778–79, though he probably participated in the private concert given in the palace of the new Podestà on 11 March 1779. The music was something of a side show to a magnificent ball. As usual, Gennari paid most attention to what interested him: 'In one room there was a concert, with arias and instrumental music; in another room card tables for those who wished to play. All agreed that the profusion of lights, the abundance of the refreshments and the provision of flowers were unprecedentedly splendid. The dancing lasted till dawn.'[40]

## SEASON OF 1779–1780

It must have seemed the end of an era for Guadagni on 10 January 1780, when Vallotti, for 50 years Maestro di Cappella at the Santo, died at the age of 83. Guadagni took part in a number of requiem masses, including one at the Servites' church on 2 March. Vallotti had overseen every aspect of the musical life at the Santo. His particular legacy lay in the field of instrumental music: Tartini was already in post as 'capo di concerto' when Vallotti first joined the Santo, and between them they maintained an orchestra of some reputation (though its fortunes inevitably fluctuated) for half a century. However, his preoccupation with accuracy and technique had an enduring influence on the singers who were Guadagni's colleagues during this stage of his career, and indeed on Guadagni himself. It cannot be coincidence that in their theoretical writings both Tartini and Vallotti were to a great extent concerned with intonation. Vallotti's theoretical books, the first of which was published less than two years before his death, investigated among other topics the just tuning of intervals, and a system for tuning keyboard instruments in unequal temperament. Tartini, as we have seen, devised 'experiments' to demonstrate how difference tones arise from perfectly tuned intervals. Guadagni appears to have profited from these lessons throughout his life.

Meanwhile, in the early months of 1780 Padua was enveloped in a heavy snowfall, by no means an unusual event, according to Gennari's regular weather reports, and Guadagni would have witnessed sledge races through the streets of Padua. The sledges, accompanied by mounted wind instrumentalists and drummers, and sledge-borne string players, were led by Cornelia Lezze, wife of the Podestà, scandalising 'zealous Christians' for holding such Carnival festivities after the start of

---

[40] Gennari, op. cit., i, p. 157.

Lent.[41] Even at the advanced age of 52, Guadagni may have participated in the revels: a sledge is listed in the inventory of his effects.

## SEASON OF 1780–1781

Vallotti was succeeded at the Santo by Agostino Ricci, whose oratorio *Gerusalemme trionfante* was performed on 29 May 1781 to celebrate the election of Federico Lauro Barbarigo as minister for the province of the Santo. An anonymous witness recorded that, 'after supper, in the rooms of M. Cerchiari, Father Guardian [of the Santo], was performed a magnificent oratorio called *Gerusalemme trionfante*, sung by the virtuosi Guadagni, Fanton, Nasolini and Abbate Granza. It was universally applauded'.[42] The fact that from the time of Ricci's appointment Guadagni no longer appeared at the top of the list of singers in the annual *riballottazione* for the Santo choir may indicate a less warm relationship between the new maestro and the singer. Guadagni's place at the head of the list was taken by his Euridice, Lorenzo Piatti.

## SEASON OF 1781–1782

In the autumn of 1781 Guadagni was back on stage, in a private performance of Antonio Calegari's *festa teatrale Deucalione e Pirra*, to a libretto by the Paduan poet Gaetano Sertor. No date or season has been recorded for the performance, but it was probably given as part of the celebrations for the installation on 6 November of Alvise Mocenigo as Capitano and Vice-Podestà of Padua. Mocenigo was the doge who had got the measure of Guadagni's rebellious streak in 1766 but rewarded him with a knighthood in 1772. Their relationship was now entirely affable. Gennari attended the installation, and mentioned 'a vocal and instrumental concert', but he was too distracted by the sumptuous costumes of the ladies and the copious nature of the refreshments to identify the music.[43]

In January 1782 Padua shared in the festivities surrounding the visit of the Grand Duke and Grand Duchess of Russia. The couple, supposedly travelling incognito and described as 'i conti del Nord', were received in Vienna in November 1781 where,

---

[41] Ibid., i, p. 175.

[42] 'Nella sera dopo la cena, nelle camere del p. M. Cerchiari guardiano fu fatto dal p. Agostino Ricci, Maestro di Cappella, un sontuoso Oratorio intitolato *Gerusalemme trionfante*, in cui cantarono li virtuosi Guadagni, Fanton, Nasolini e Abbate Granza, e incontrò universale applauso.' Antonio Sartori, *Documenti per la storia della musica al Santo*, p. 39 col 1, Vicenza: Pozza, 1977.

[43] 'La sera poi, nella sala dell'accademia, ci fu appunto un'accademia di suoni e canti alla quale fu invitata la nobiltà e v'intervennero 32 dame in abito di gala con moltitudine di cavalieri, e tutti partirono contenti e della copia de' rinfreschi e delle maniere affabili della moglie del signor capitano'. Gennari, op. cit., i, p. 219.

among a feast of musical entertainments, they saw Gluck's *Orfeo*. They travelled to Venice in the new year, arriving in Padua on 25 January. Two contemporary accounts of the visit indicate a discrepancy between the celebrations that were planned and those that actually took place. Angelo Nonni published a booklet that describes the arrival in Venice, and the lavish reception and colourful spectacle presented to the royal pair.[44] According to Nonni, after travelling to Padua, the couple were taken to see the Santo, and from there to the Benedictine monastery attached to the church of Santa Giustina, where, in the rooms of Father Abbot, Gluck's *Orfeo* was performed by 'the celebrated Guadagni', to the great enjoyment of the royal pair.[45] Nonni may have been writing the equivalent of an all-too-premature press release. Gennari recorded a more modest entertainment: '[In the late afternoon] the Grand Duke and Duchess arrived from Venice.... They were conducted to Santa Giustina where, in the atrium of the library the monks had arranged a concert in which Cavalier Guadagni sang a few arias, to the great pleasure of the Grand Duchess who presented him with a ring worth about 100 zecchini'.[46] It is possible that the 'few arias' were taken from Gluck's *Orfeo*, or indeed that the whole opera was performed on this occasion. Gennari's lack of interest in music, and the distractions of the no-doubt-lavish refreshments, might well have led him to record the event in such terse and uninformative terms.

On 13 May Padua welcomed Pope Pius VI. Gennari described the ceremony which appears to have been repeated whenever a high dignitary came to the Santo. A reliquary containing one of the basilica's most precious relics, the tongue of St Anthony, was placed on a special altar erected for the occasion, and while the pope venerated it, Guadagni sang the antiphon 'O lingua benedicta' 'with such devout and plaintive melodiousness that all those present were moved to tears of tenderness.'[47] No vignette could better define Guadagni's status in the Santo and in the city: his performance of the antiphon, written specially for him, was as much a part of Padua's most sacred ceremony as the veneration of the relics themselves.

[44] Angelo Nonni, *Descrizione degli spettacoli e feste datesi in Venezia per occasione della venuta delle LL AA il Gran Duca e Gran Duchessa di Moscovia, sotto il nome di Conti del Nord,* Venice, 1782.

[45] 'La sera stessa passarono a veder il famoso vicino Tempio di Sant'Antonio, che trovarono illuminato indi quello di S. Giustina con l'annesso Monastero de' Benedettini, dove nelle camere del Padre Abate, Fratello del Procurator Tron, fu fatta goder loro la Cantata dell'Orfeo, Musica del celebre Cavalier Gluck, eseguita dal famoso Cavalier Guadagni con piena soddisfazione dei Principi.' Nonni, *Descrizione degli spettacoli e feste*, p. 14.

[46] 'Alle ore 23 e mezzo, giunsero da Venezia in burchiello alla porta del Portello i conti del nord...gli condusse...a S Giustina dove que'monaci nell'atrio della libreria gli avevano apparecchiata un'accademia di musica nella quale il cavalier Guadagni cantò alcune ariette con molto piacere della granduchessa che gli regalò un anello del valore di 100 zecchini in circa.' Gennari, op. cit., i, p. 226.

[47] 'Il cavalier Guadagni cantò da coretto rimpetto al santuario l'antifona "O lingua benedetta" con sì devota e flebile melodia che tutti gli astanti si sciolsero in lacrime di tenerezza.' Gennari, op. cit., i, p. 240.

From occasional comments by visitors who saw him in Padua at this time we learn of Guadagni's hospitality. The inventory of his possessions shows him equipped to offer a well-set table, though there is no record of any specific dinner. Lord Mount Edgcumbe was only offered coffee. He was, however, one of two visitors who describe visiting the singer and being entertained by performances in Guadagni's marionette theatre. These puppet shows, which were frequent and well-attended, should perhaps be numbered among Guadagni's dramatic performances in these years.

Among the possessions catalogued in the inventory of Guadagni's possessions were a magic lantern complete with slides and a marionette theatre. We have no information about when or where he gave magic lantern shows, but his involvement in his marionette theatre is better documented. Puppet shows were enormously popular throughout Europe. These could be enacted either with glove puppets in the familiar style of Punch and Judy (*burattini*), providing popular knock-about comedy in temporary booths erected in the streets and squares, or, with greater skill and often to more discerning audiences, in miniature theatres equipped with string puppets or marionettes (*fantoccini*). The latter performances offered more varied fare, and while they, like the *burattini*, presented comedy drawn from the traditions of *commedia dell'arte*, they also included heroic drama and even opera: Alessandro Scarlatti wrote operas for Cardinal Ottoboni's marionette theatre, while Haydn provided them for Prince Nicolaus Esterházy. These private, domestic *teatrini* could rival full-sized theatres in the ingenuity and elaboration of their scenic effects. In Venice in 1746, Angelo Labia built a theatre comprising a scaled-down version of the Teatro S. Giovanni Grisostomo, complete with scenery, lighting and machines that were an exact copy of the full-sized theatre and operated by the same mechanisms. Labia even had tiny librettos printed on 24^mo-sized paper.[48]

Among the articles mentioned in the inventory, Guadagni's marionette theatre took pride of place, receiving more detailed attention than any other category of his possessions. The majority of inventory items are tersely listed: clothes and furniture, china and silverware, statues, and untitled books and paintings. In sharp

---

[48] 'Sí grande e sí generale era la inclinazione ai trattenimenti teatrali, che il patrizio Antonio [*recte* Angelo] Maria Labia... s'immaginò di far costruire nella sala di una fabbrica posta a San Gerolamo un teatrino di tavola, esattamente lavorato con le precise proporzioni dell'allora famoso Teatro di San Giovanni Grisostomo....Le scene e le decorazioni si muovono con machine e ruote allo stesso identico modo che si pratica nei maggiori teatri; e le figurine degli attori sceneggiavano senza lasciar comprendere l'artificio che produceva I loro movimenti....Vi erano perfino i libretti a stampa nella più piccolo forma del 24° e del più minuto carattere.' Gerolamo Alessandro Michiel, *Notizie ed osservazioni intorno all'origine e al progressa dei Teatri e delle Rappresentazioni teatrali in Venezia*, Venice, 1840, quoted in Roberto Leydi and Renata Mezzanotte Leydi, *Marionette e burattini*, Milan: Collana del Gallo Grande, 1958, pp. 73–74. See also Antonella Zaggia, '"La fiera delle bagatelle": Il teatro musicale per marionette di San Girolamo', *Rassegna Veneta di Studi Musicali*, 2–3 (1986–7): 133–71.

contrast, there is a meticulous description of the theatre together with its scenery and machines.[49] The inventory was drawn up in consultation with Guadagni's nephew and heir, Vincenzo Guadagni, who clearly understood the entire functioning of the theatre and shared its owner's enthusiasm. On Guadagni's death, the theatre, together with the majority of the singer's possessions, passed to Vincenzo, who unfortunately survived his uncle by less than six months. All record of the theatre then disappeared.

The theatre occupied two adjoining rooms in Guadagni's Paduan house. This was a common arrangement where marionette shows were mounted in a domestic setting. One of Goethe's earliest memories, for example, was of the theatre erected in a pair of communicating rooms in his grandmother's house in Frankfurt for a Christmas entertainment. He recreated the scene in *Wilhelm Meisters Lehrjahre*:

I can still see the moment—how wonderful it seemed—when, after receiving the usual Christmas presents, we were told to sit down in front of a door which led from one room to another. It opened, but not for the usual passing to and fro.... In the doorway a huge portal was erected, covered with a mysterious curtain. At first we stood, in wonderment, at a distance; then, becoming curious to see what glittering and rustling things might be concealed behind the half-transparent curtain, we were each given a small chair and told to wait patiently.[50]

Two surviving marionette theatres, both dating from the mid-eighteenth century and originating in the Veneto, may give some idea of the elegance and appeal of Guadagni's theatre. One example was originally built for the family of Giovanni Grimani ai Servi, installed in the Ca' Rezzonico by Ludovico Rezzonico as part of the lavish improvements made to his palazzo in the middle of the eighteenth century. From there it was moved to the Casa di Goldoni where it is currently on display (see Figure 10.2). A similar example, dating from Venice in the 1720s, can be seen in the Victoria and Albert Museum of Childhood in London. The two theatres have almost identical dimensions. Using (anachronistically) the metric scale, the proscenium arch is some two metres wide and nearly one and a half metres high; the depth of the stage is a little over a metre. Both theatres have considerable space on either side of the stage to accommodate musicians and actors.

---

[49] Archivio di Stato, Padua, Notarile, F. Fanzago, ff. 23–37.

[50] *Aus meinem Leben. Dichtung und Wahrheit*, i. i, Tübingen, 1811, and *Wilhelm Meisters Lehrjahre*, i. ii, Berlin, 1795–96.

FIGURE 10.2 Eighteenth-century marionette theatre. (Courtesy Museo Casa di Goldoni, Venice.)

The dimensions of Guadagni's theatre are not stated, but the auditorium was probably capacious. It certainly held a lot of furniture. Guadagni fitted out his auditorium with a bench running around the room and five further benches. The seating was provided with cushions of flowered silk. Two candlesticks and ten small table lamps illuminated the room. A curtain of deep blue separated the auditorium from the theatre.

We do not know when Guadagni installed his theatre; it may be significant that while he was in London between 1769 and 1771, the Italian puppeteer Carlo Perico produced regular puppet shows in the capital. It is inconceivable that Guadagni, passionate about all forms of theatre, would not have attended some of Perico's performances and fraternised with his compatriot. Perico advertised his shows frequently in the London press:

IN Panton-Street, Haymarket, the ITALIAN FANTOCINNI of Mr CARLO PERICO, will have the honour of performing THIS and every day a new representation call'd HARLEQUIN's VILLAIN, SHERIFF, JUDGE and HANGMAN. End of Act I, A Shepherdess will play a Concerto upon the Mandolino, and a Shepherd will accompany her with the Violin. End of Act II, a Black will perform sundry wonderful Balances with a Spontoon. End of Act III, a Rope-Dancer will perform upon a rope several motions, all different and quite natural, and Harlequin will second her. With a Pantomime by the large family of the jealous Pierrot. This Piece of the Italian Theatre is in Three Acts, and decorated with many agreeable changes of brilliant Scenery.[51]

As Guadagni's singing career entered its last decade his public appearances were increasingly restricted to the Santo, private concerts and civic celebrations. He received a stream of visitors, two of whom recorded seeing his marionette theatre in action. Mount Edgcumbe's account of a visit in 1784 sets Guadagni's semi-retired life in context:

In passing through Padua, I went to a grand mass in the church of St Antonio, when, it being Whit Sunday, and of course a festival, I had the good fortune to hear a *motetto*, or anthem, sung by Guadagni, of whom I had heard very much, as he had for a long time been a great favourite in England, which he left in the year 1771. When he sang as first man at our opera he was uncommonly handsome, and a remarkably good actor; Garrick himself having taken pains to instruct him. His voice was then a soprano of the finest description, and his performance, particularly of *Orfeo*, was described as having been delightful. He was now advanced in years, and sung as contralto: his voice was still full and well-toned, and his style appeared to me excellent. He belonged to the choir of the church in which I heard him, where alone he ever sung, and that only on a few particular occasions. As he retained a great partiality for England, and had been much noticed by my family, he no sooner heard I was in the town than he came to call upon me, and insisted on my taking coffee at his house, where

[51] *Daily Advertiser*, 24 Dec. 1770.

he entertained me, not with singing, which I should have liked much better, but with exhibiting fantoccini on a little stage, in which he took great delight.[52]

We need not attach too much importance to the earl's opinion of Guadagni's singing in 1771: born in 1764, Richard, 2nd Earl of Mount Edgcumbe, was, on his own evidence, too young to recall having heard Guadagni in London.[53] It is engaging to read of Guadagni's 'great partiality for England' but the opinion was probably more diplomatic than truthful, since the visit in question was the occasion not only of his appearance before the Bow Street Magistrates but also his notorious quarrels with both the opera management and the audiences at the King's Theatre.

Two years earlier he had entertained the Irish tenor Michael Kelly, who provides more useful information:

> Padua was interesting to me, as the birthplace of Tartini, and the two greatest singers of their time were living there retired, Pacchierotti and Guadagni. The latter was a Cavaliere. He had built a house, or rather a palace, in which he had a very neat theatre, and a company of puppets, which represented l'Orpheo e Euridice; himself singing the part of Orpheo behind the scenes. It was in this character, and in singing Gluck's beautiful rondo in it, 'Che farò senza Euridice', that he distinguished himself in every theatre in Europe, and drew such immense houses in London. His puppet-show was his hobby-horse, and as he received no money, he had always crowded houses. He had a good fortune, with which he was very liberal, and he was the handsomest man of his kind I ever saw.[54]

Pacchierotti did not retire to Padua till 1804, long after Guadagni's death, but he was a regular visitor, singing there in 1778, 1779 and again in 1787.[55] Kelly's visit took place in 1782, and there was probably still talk of the 'contest' between two castratos which had taken place in 1778. Guadagni may have continued to operate his theatre until 1785 when he was partially silenced by a stroke.

We owe to Kelly the information that the marionette show he saw was *Orfeo ed Euridice*. This is not surprising—Guadagni sang very little else at this time in his life. But the exact version of *Orfeo* he performed raises some interesting questions. By 1778 Guadagni had taken part in four separate Orfeo operas (see Table 10.1).

---

[52] Lord Mount Edgcumbe, *Musical reminiscences*, 4th ed., London, 1834, pp. 34–36.

[53] 'The first opera which I have the slightest recollection of having seen was that of Artaserse, in the year 1773.' Mount Edgcumbe, *Musical Reminiscences*, p. 1.

[54] Kelly, *Reminiscences*, i, p. 151.

[55] Sheila Hodges, 'Gasparo Pacchierotti', *Music Review* 55.4 (1994): 276–92; Stephen A. Willier, 'The illustrious musico Gasparo Pacchierotti: Final triumphs and retirement years', *Studi musicali* 38.2 (2009): 409–43.

TABLE 10.1

Orpheus operas performed by Guadagni

| Composer | Librettist | Location | Première |
|---|---|---|---|
| Gluck | Calzabigi | Vienna, Burgtheater | 1762 |
| Gluck, Bach, Guglielmi, Guadagni | Bottarelli, after Calzabigi, | London, King's Theatre | 1770 |
| Tozzi | Coltellini, after Calzabigi | Munich, Hoftheater | 1775 |
| Bertoni | Bertoni, after Calzabigi | Venice, Teatro S. Benedetto | 1776 |

This table is necessarily a simplification. The Bach/Bottarelli adaptation of Gluck's opera for London in 1770 proved the catalyst for a string of Orpheus operas that can be considered as direct descendents of Gluck's score of 1762, including the Munich performance of 1773. When he finally settled in Padua, Guadagni continued to sing a variety of *Orfeo* operas. From 1776 Bertoni's setting predominated: Guadagni sang in it twice that year in Venice at Carnival and in the summer, and in Padua in a private concert in May. But he also continued to perform Gluck's music in various guises, and the undated score in the Biblioteca Antoniana discussed in Chapter 9 implies that Guadagni introduced a version of *Orfeo* based on Bach and Bottarelli's additions to Padua. As we have seen, a performance of *Orfeo* with 'music by the celebrated Cavalier Gluck' was planned for the visit of the Grand Duke and Grand Duchess of Russia to Padua in January 1782, though it is not clear what was actually performed on this occasion. It is impossible to know whether the 'Orpheo e Euridice' that Kelly saw performed in the marionette theatre was drawn from Gluck's original score, some version of the Bach/Bottarelli adaptation, or even Bertoni's setting. He does not quite go so far as to say that he heard Guadagni singing 'Gluck's beautiful rondo…Che farò' on that occasion. (By a delightful irony, Gluck himself wrote of this number that 'Nothing but a change in the mode of expression is needed to turn my aria 'Che faro senza Euridice' into a dance for marionettes'.[56])

The inventory shows that Guadagni's marionette theatre was well-equipped to perform any *Orfeo* based on Calzabigi's libretto. In addition to the framework of the theatre, scenery, machines and lighting systems are listed in the inventory in some detail. Of the fourteen sets described, the first five appear to correspond exactly with Calzabigi's

---

[56] 'Non ci vuol nulla, per che la mia Aria, nell' Orfeo: 'Che faro senza Euridice', mutando solamente qualche cosa nella maniera dell'espressione, diventi un saltarello da Burattini'. Gluck to the Duke of Braganza, 30 Oct. 1770 (Preface to *Paride ed Elena*, Vienna, 1770).

TABLE 10.2

A comparison of Calzabigi's stage directions and Guadagni's scenery

| Calzabigi | Guadagni |
|---|---|
| Act I.1. A pleasant but lonely grove with laurels and cypresses | Grove with cypresses |
| Act II.1. The dreadful caverns of the Underworld; the distant view obscured with smoke, illuminated with flashes of flame | Inferno with two gauze drops (also listed in overview of apparatus: devices to raise or lower the lighting and a machine to create flame effects) |
| Act II.2. A delightful scene with verdant groves, flower-bedecked meadows and shady retreats bathed with streams and rivers | Elysian fields with three arches to create the perspective of distance (also listed: a mechanism to produce waterfalls) |
| Act III.1. A dark cave in the form of a winding labyrinth blocked by fallen rocks and covered in undergrowth and wild flowers | Dark cave |
| Act III.2. A magnificent temple dedicated to Love | Palace of Love |

requirements (see Table 10.2). Other scenery mentioned provided for a piazza, another piazza surrounded by columns, the antechamber in a royal palace and the great hall of the palace, both rooms walled with mirrors, a magnificent garden with waterfalls, a wood, an encampment with pavilions, a temple, a sea scene and a prison. Machinery was available to effect transformation scenes. The inventory describes just two of these: one that could transform a tower into a whale, and another that could cause a prison to dissolve into a bank of clouds. There is mention of 160 articulated (*movibili*) marionettes, 'suitable for comedy, tragedy and opera', twelve animal-puppets of unspecified breed, and a large chest containing properties to perform various plays, including tables, carriages, and yet more transformation devices. This was a seriously well-equipped theatre and Guadagni's shows could have included a wide range of plays and operas.

Among all this detail there is nothing to tell us how Guadagni presented his operas, and who sang in them. Some domestic performances commanded the most elaborate resources: Labia employed 'a company of select singers, hidden behind the stage, accompanied by a substantial orchestra'.[57] In an informal and spontaneous

---

[57] 'Una compagnia di scelti musici, nascosta dietro il palco e accompagnata da numerosa orchestra.' Gerolamo Michiel, in Leydi and Leydi, *Marionette e burattini*, p. 74.

performance such as the one he put on for Kelly, Guadagni probably just 'sang a few arias', perhaps even unaccompanied, to remind Kelly of former productions. But to satisfy the 'crowded houses', and do justice to the well-equipped theatre, something more elaborate must have been attempted. When Guadagni performed Bertoni's *Orfeo* in private performances in Padua, he was part of an all-male cast drawn from fellow members of the Santo, with Piatti taking the part of Euridice, Nasolini as Amore, and the bass Giambattista Benacchio as Plutone. A similar all-male cast, drawn from the Santo, could easily have been assembled for his house performances. Although there is no record of any performance of the Bach/Botarelli *Orfeo* employing a castrato Euridice, a precedent for the interchangeability of male and female singers was established in the original London production in which the part of Amore, a soprano in Vienna, was assigned to the castrato Giuseppe Giustinelli. The indispensability of the chorus in performing any of the settings of Calzabigi's libretto raises another question. More than the three cast members of Gluck's score would have been needed to perform the choruses, though any version of the opera involving Bottarelli's extra characters would have furnished a quorum. Again Guadagni could presumably have invited reinforcements from the choral forces of the Santo.

As far as instrumental forces are concerned, Guadagni probably distinguished between purely private performances for his personal guests and the 'crowded houses' mentioned by Kelly. The inventory notes the presence of a harpsichord in the house and this may have sufficed for the intimate private shows. (We do not know whether Guadagni would have played the harpsichord himself, but the training of singers always involved some instrumental skills, even if few attained the virtuosity of a Rauzzini, who often performed solo keyboard items in his vocal recitals.) For larger audiences, a small string ensemble could have been recruited from the Santo which regularly employed eight violins, five violas, three cellos and two violoni at this date. A variety of wind players were on the payroll in any one year; in 1782, Guadagni could have called upon a single oboe player and two corni da caccia. The instrumentalists from the Santo were not unwilling to perform outside their ecclesiastical sphere. Between 1785 and 1790 they organised and presumably played in the popular Teatro Vacca in the Prato della Valle.[58] Such was Guadagni's prestige and, it seems, popularity among his colleagues, that he would

---

[58] 'I "suonatori della Cappella del Santo" … tennero il monopolio per cinque anni consecutive, dal 1785 al 1790'. Girolamo Polcastro, in Franco Mancini, Maria Teresa Muraro, Elena Povoledo, *I teatri del Veneto: Padova, Rovigo, e il loro territorio*, vol. 3, Venice: Corbo e Fiore, 1988, p. 162.

probably have had no difficulty in assembling adequate forces, limited only by the space available.

A more puzzling question is, who operated the puppets? As far as public marionette shows were concerned, there was normally a clear division of labour between those who provided the voices for the puppets (spoken or sung) and those who pulled the strings. One account of a London show identifies a master-of-ceremonies (the 'Conjurer') who 'stood on one side of the scene' and told the story, entirely separate from the puppet operators who would have taken their places on an iron bridge above the stage, hidden from the audience by the superstructure of the proscenium arch:

> Dear cousin Ap Shinkins—last Saturday night,
> I went with Joe Jenkins to see a great sight;
> 'Twas a fine raree show all of puppets so gay,
> You'd have thought they were fairies performing a play.
> The man beat his drum, and said gem'men walk in,
> The fam'd Fantoccini will shortly begin;
> So in we both squeezed, where the folks in a row
> Sat patiently waiting to see the fine show.
> Before us was hung up a curtain of green,
> And the Conjurer stood on one side of the scene;
> On the opposite side the musicians were sitting,
> With their books and their candles before them befitting,
> Where two fiddles squeak'd, and a grunting bassoon,
> By way of an overture, scrap'd an old tune.
> Then the curtain drew up, and the man with a bow
> Said, ladies and gem'men, attend to me now....[59]

Very little has been recorded about the considerable numbers of marionette masters in Italy at this time. It was a highly skilled trade. Many marionette plays included fights and even beheadings, involving techniques of articulation and manipulation that it is difficult to imagine. It is not surprising that some moves required two operators for a single character. One nineteenth-century traveller in Sicily described a scene in which

Ferrain cut off the Duca d'Anela's head, which rolled about on the stage. Immediately there came three Turks. Ferrain stabbed each as he entered, one,

---

[59] *The Fantoccini OR The Great Public Puppet-Show as exhibited by Signior Tintaraboloso, described in a poetical epistle from Griffith Llewellyn to his cousin, Rice ap Shinkins,* London, 1809, pp. 9–10.

two, three, and their bodies encumbered the ground as the curtain fell…There came three knights in armour; Ferrain fought them all three together for a very considerable time and it was deafening. He killed them…a bloody sight.[60]

Surviving examples of eighteenth-century puppets show a considerable variety in the degree of complexity with which they are equipped. The most elaborate were controlled by eight strings attached to three rods, one string each for the head and the middle back, with a further string to control each hand, leg and foot. (Early in the nineteenth century, the knees were also articulated.) The simplest and perhaps the most common system, however, was to have only three strings for each figure, one for the head and one for each hand, as seen in Figure 10.2. Control of such a puppet would not have been beyond the scope of an amateur.[61]

The puppet masters' skills were usually quite distinct from those of the actors who read (or sang) their parts, or the narrators who provided a commentary. Descriptions of performance practice distinguish between *manovratori* and *parlatori*. According to Pasqualini: 'The speakers are different people [from those who manipulate the puppets], taking their place in the wings, on the spectators' left.'[62] The practice, though, seems to vary from region to region, and Pasqualini conceded that in Naples the roles of *manovratori* and *parlatori* were performed by the same people. One celebrated English puppet master (or mistress) who may have combined the roles was the writer and actress Charlotte Charke, the youngest daughter of Colley Cibber. In the course of her colourful career, Charke owned a puppet company and sang and acted on stage, and, although her memoirs do not put the matter beyond doubt, it seems highly probable that she played the combined roles of operator and speaker.[63]

With his well-documented enthusiasm for everything to do with the theatre, it is certainly possible that Guadagni might have taken a hand in operating the character with whom he identified so closely, particularly if his puppets were the three-string type—and in fact it is hard to imagine him refraining from taking part. Other candidates are his valet Girolamo Gambaro, whose 'faithful service' was recognised in Guadagni's will, and his 'most beloved' nephew Vincenzo Guadagni. If casual visitors were treated to presentations in Guadagni's theatre, as Mount Edgcumbe and Kelly imply, a few people capable of operating the marionettes must have been on

---

[60] Henry Festing Jones, *Diversions in Sicily*, p. 72, London, 1909, p. 72.

[61] Diagrams showing the variety of ways in which a marionette might be strung and operated appear in John McCormick and Bennie Pratasik, *Popular Puppet Theatre in Europe, 1800–1914*, Cambridge: Cambridge University Press, 1998, pp. 134–35.

[62] Antonio Pasqualini, *Opera dei pupi,* Palermo: Sellerio, 1978, p. 78.

[63] Charlotte Charke, *A Narrative of the Life*, London, 1755.

hand to mount the impromptu performances, even if Guadagni called upon more professional collaborators when playing to his 'crowded houses'. Perhaps the most salient fact to emerge from the incomplete evidence of Guadagni's marionette theatre is the dominant role played by *Orfeo*, in one version or another, in his repertory during the last decade of his professional life.

# 11

The Last Decade (1782–1792)

$\sim$ ─────────────────────────────────────────────

IN JULY 1783 Guadagni took part in the festivities marking the retirement of Alvise Mocenigo, Podestà (chief magistrate) of Padua. On 6 July he sang in an allegorical cantata, *Le virtù rivali*, composed by his brother-in-law Felice Alessandri to a poem by Francesco Piombiolo degli Enghelfreddi. The performance was in the prestigious Teatro Nuovo. Guadagni was paired with a young rising singer, the castrato Luigi Marchesi. Despite Marchesi's brilliance, Guadagni did not on this occasion appear to suffer from adverse comparisons, and in Gennari's account (as usual, long on decor but short on musical detail) he is the only singer who did not need to be identified by role:

> This evening, the nobility of the city, wanting to give a public testimonial of their gratitude to His Excellency Signor Cavalier Mocenigo at the end of his period in office, arranged to have a cantata of the most splendid and solemn nature performed in their theatre. Starting work after the opera had finished, at dawn on the morning of 6 July all the benches were quickly removed from the stalls and in their place five rows of seats were put in place. The boxes were decorated in matching silks; on either side of each one was placed a great candle, in the centre, at varying heights, five crystal chandeliers.... From the floor of the theatre there rose two staircases leading to two glazed doors at the top. Between these doors the musicians were disposed, one section above another on an inclined floor. On the first level appeared Signor Luigi Marchesi (first man in the opera company), Signora Anna Morichelli Bosello (first woman), Cavalier Guadagni, and Mengozzi (tenor); the instrumentalists were on the second and third levels and on the fourth level, behind a blind, the chorus.

The whole stage was furnished with large mirrors and pillasters, and brightly illuminated…as the hour struck, Cavalier Mocenigo arrived with his wife and the Bishop and took their places in three special chairs; behind them assembled a crowd of ladies and gentlemen from Padua, Venice, Vicenza, Ferrara, Lombardy and beyond: their finery was a marvel to behold.…While a sinfonia was played, sixty waiters descended the staircases, bearing copious refreshments…and then the first scene of the cantata was performed. The two singers, Marchesi and Guadagni, sang with great bravura, and received a good deal of applause from the crowd of spectators, noble and civil, who listened to them in complete silence, whether from the boxes or from the stalls.[1]

Gennari noted that the performance with all its trappings cost the nobles more than 700 zecchini, but that it 'succeeded to everyone's satisfaction'. Guadagni may have sung at another tribute to Mocenigo a few days later in the Sala del Consiglio, but he is not mentioned by name among the musicians.[2]

There are occasional references in Gennari to remind us that Guadagni continued to be an esteemed figure in Paduan musical life. In the summer of 1784 (the year of Michael Kelly's visit) he was engaged on at least two occasions to sing the antiphon 'O lingua benedicta', accompanied by 'a few instruments', while distinguished visitors visited the relics at the Santo. On 12 May, the visitor was the Duke of Parma, on 24 June, the Grand Duke of Tuscany.[3] His operatic career was now exclusively concerned with the role of *Orfeo*, performing (probably) Gluck's score in his marionette theatre and Bertoni's setting on stage. On 17 May an entertainment was prepared for the visit of the King of Sweden:

Signor Professor Baglioni [the Provveditore of Padua] had had the Great Hall of the Palazzo Pretorio and some adjacent rooms lavishly adorned in preparation for a performance of *Orfeo* to which all the nobility was invited. The Deputies had contrived magnificent lighting of candles and torches in the Sala della Ragione, as had been done in 1709 for the visit of the King of Denmark.…In the Sala della Podestà, in the presence of ladies and gentlemen and university professors, Cavalier Guadagni and [Cecilia] Zuliani from Venice performed *Orfeo*; His Excellency the Provveditore dispensed copious refreshments.[4]

---

[1] Gennari, *Notizie giornaliere*, i, pp. 295–96.
[2] 12 July 1783, Gennari, op. cit., i, p. 297.
[3] Gennari, op. cit., i, p. 336, p. 341.
[4] Gennari, op. cit., i, pp. 336–37. The libretto, in the Museo Civico, Padua, BP 3.2377, establishes beyond doubt that the performance on 17 May 1784 was of Bertoni's score.

In the summer of 1784 Giuseppe Millico came to Padua and presented his dramatic cantata *La pietà d'amore* in a Paduan academy. Unfortunately there is no record of a meeting between Guadagni and his successor in the role of Orfeo, which Millico first sang in Parma in 1769. It is inconceivable that the two singers did not meet. Of more interest to the diarist Gennari was the building work continuing in the Prato area. Guadagni again sponsored a part of this, dedicating his profits from a lottery to the completion of the bridge opposite the monastery of the Misericordia.[5]

The summer of 1785 saw the last occasions on which Guadagni is known to have sung in concert. Both recitals were given in Padua as part of civic festivities. On 26 July the supporters of Andrea Memmo, 'of whom Guadagni was the foremost', celebrated Memmo's recent appointment as Procurator at San Marco with a concert given at Pedrani's coffee house, accompanied by fireworks and special lighting effects.[6] Three days later he sang at a private concert in Memmo's palace to mark the visit of Emperor Leopold II and his brothers Ferdinand and Maximilian.[7]

It is not recorded exactly when he suffered a stroke. The inventory of his effects records his physical decline, with a cupping glass, a lancet and a copper basin for bleeding, a traditional treatment for stroke victims. He appears to have lost status at the Santo before the end of 1785, since in that year's *riballottazione* he is listed below all the sopranos, and in December 1786 he is the last named contralto, a change in practice which probably indicated his inability to play a full part in services. Even this catastrophe, however, did not silence him. The nature of his illness was unusual: having lost his ability to speak, Guadagni was nevertheless able to 'vocalise' wordlessly.

On 17 June 1787, Gennari described 'an extraordinary crowd that assembled at the Santo to hear the castrato [Carlo] Conciolini, the tenor [Matteo] Babbini and Cavalier Guadagni, the latter having lost his use of language a year ago as the result of an apoplectic stroke. The curiosity of hearing him sing a versicle attracted an incredible number of people'.[8] According to Gennari's obituary notice, Guadagni continued to play a part in the services until his death.

---

[5] 'Nel seminario si è continuata la fabbrica al lato che guarda il mezzodì e nel Prato della Valle fu terminato quasi del tutto il muro del canale elittico co' denari mandati da Roma dal nobiluomo signor Andrea Memmo. Presto sarà murato il ponte da lato delle monache della Misericordia, lavoro promosso dal musico cavalier Guadagni chi ha tratto denaro da un lotto e in altre maniere.' Gennari, op. cit., i, p. 353. See also p. 387: 'Nella erezione di questo ponte ebbe molto merito il signor cavalier Guadagni'.

[6] Gennari, op. cit., i, p. 387.

[7] See Bellina, 'Appunti sul repertorio padovano', in *Mozart, Padova e la Betulia liberata*, ed. Paolo Pinamonti, p. 188, n. 53.

[8] 'Ci fu straordinario concorso alla musica nella quale cantarono il musico Conciolini, il tenore Babbini, e il cavalier Guadagni il quale, per un colpo di apoplessia, è già un anno che ha perduto l'uso della parola. La curiosità di sentirlo cantare un versetto vi attrasse un numero incredibile di persone.' Gennari, op. cit., i, p. 459.

Guadagni remained on the payroll at the Santo, even though he was unable properly to carry out his duties. Since his return to the Cappella in 1768, his salary had fluctuated between the maximum 400 ducats when he fulfilled all his duties including the five principal feasts, to receiving nothing in 1770 when he was in England throughout the year, and a mere 80 ducats for 1771 when he was in Padua for only one of the feasts. In the first years of his illness, 1785 and 1786, he received 320 ducats. This may have caused some hardship, for his brother-in-law Nasolini intervened to request that his usual salary be paid.[9] Nasolini's petition was successful, and the maximum salary was restored in 1787, dipping to 320 ducats in 1788, and thereafter continuing at or close to 400 ducats until his death—evidence of the esteem in which his remarkable service at the Santo was held. On 29 December 1790 he petitioned the governing body to receive his salary in more frequent instalments and to ensure that his rent was paid:

> The misfortune that has befallen Gaetano Guadagni, contralto, has deprived him of the honour of continuing to perform his duties in the Cappella. Since the Doge has granted him the same salary determined by the authorities, Guadagni petitions the Presidency that it might be paid at a rate of 25 ducats per month and that from the remaining 100 ducats the sum of 50 ducats is disbursed at Easter, and 50 ducats on the feast of Santa Giustina to Father Procurator of the Convent of the Santo, as payment for the rent of the house in which Guadagni resides.[10]

The implication is that his legendary extravagance had tempted him to set aside insufficient funds for his daily needs.

His poverty at the end of his life is rumoured in the obituaries, though it is difficult to discover whether he was actually in debt. In 1786 his nephew, Antonio Guadagni, draper, died, leaving his uncle a legacy of 500 ducats a year for life, to be paid monthly, with the significant proviso that he would lose the legacy if his

---

[9] 'Rilevata, dalla richiesta fatta a voce da Antonio Nasolini, cognato di Gaetano Guadagni, la grave malattia di cui soffre quest'ultimo, malattia che comunque è risaputa e a cause della quale egli non è potuto intervenire alla funzione di Natale, fu ordinato all'unanimità al Cancelliere il rilascio del solito mandato di £496.' 31 Dec. 1786, see Boscolo and Pietribiasi, *La cappella musicale antoniana*, p. 331. The sum of 496 Venetian lire mentioned was the equivalent of 80 ducats, the amount necessary to bring his salary up to the maximum of 400 ducats.

[10] 'La disgrazia successa a Gaetano Guadagni contralto lo ha privato dell'onore di poter continuare a svolgere il suo dovere in Cappella. Il Doge gli ha concesso il beneficio di percepire lo stesso stipendio fissato dalle ducali, e Guadagni chiede alla Presidenza che gli sia ripartito in ducati 25 al mese e che l'avanzo dei ducati 100 sia consegnato in ragione di ducati 50 per la S. Pasqua e di ducati 50 per la festa di S. Giustina al Padre Procuratore del Convento del Santo, come pagamento dell'affitto casa in cui Guadagni abita', see Boscolo and Pietribiasi, op. cit., pp. 341–42. Santa Giustina's feast day is 7 October.

co-heirs discovered that he was spending it in advance.[11] This amount more than doubled his income. By 1790 we hear no more of his attendance in the Cappella, but the Arca continued his salary, as they were accustomed to do for failing and aged members. He received a further augmentation of his income when, in the early months of 1791, he made, somewhat preposterously, a successful petition to the Portuguese court for compensation for the disturbance to his career caused by the Lisbon earthquake 36 years previously.[12] He received the generous sum of 96,000 reals, approximately 900 ducats.

His style of living gives no indication of penury. The inventory lists a great number of beautiful and valuable objects which he must have owned outright, since they formed part of his estate. It does, however, conclude with a much shorter list of gold and silver articles, tableware, snuffboxes, a clock and so forth, that he had pawned, some through an official pawnbroker, other items were lodged with friends. There was a flurry of such pawning activity in August 1792, which might indicate real hardship or, more probably, the paranoia of age and infirmity.[13]

On 27 September 1792 Guadagni made his will. The circumstances were unusual:

This is the solemn testament of Signor Cavalier Gaetano Guadagni, [son] of the late Sebastiano, delivered in the evening of Saturday 27 September in the presence of seven witnesses, whose signatures follow. Seven lighted candles were placed on a table in full view of the above-mentioned testator, who was lying on a sofa, suffering in his body but of sound and lucid mind. Because he had difficulty in speaking, on account of his misfortune, I asked him, in the presence of the seven witnesses, if it was his testament, written and countersigned in his own hand, to which he replied 'Yes'.[14]

The will itself was written, as testified, by Guadagni himself, in a careful, ponderous hand, far removed from the elegant script of earlier samples of his handwriting.

---

[11] 'Lascia 500 ducati annui al cavalier Gaetano suo zio, sua vita durante, da essergli pagati di mese in mese colla comminatoria di perdere il legato se constasse agli eredi che lo avesse ippotecato'. Gennari, op. cit., i, p. 404.

[12] Two petitions were made on 2 Feb. and 21 Mar. 1791. De Brito, *Opera in Portugal*, p. 31.

[13] Archivio di Stato, Padua, Notarile, F. Fanzago, fo. 35.

[14] 'Questo è il solenne testamento del S. Kᵛ Gaetano Guadagni fu Sebastiano, a me sottoscritto Notᵒ: lott ᶜ: consegnato alle ore tre di notte alla presenza degli oltrescritti sette testimoni con n. 7 candele accese poste sopra un tavolino in prospetto al sudetto Sigʳ Testatore il quale si assiede giacente sopra un soffà aggravato di malle di corpo ma di sincero e lucido intelletto; e siccome ha difficoltà di parlare per la disgrazia accadutagli, così interrogato da me Notᵒ alla presenza degli oltrascritti sette testimoni quali sottoscrissero e sigliarono se sia esso testimento: tutto scrisso e sottoscrisso di suo proprio pugno e carattere rispose alla presenza degli stessi di sì.' Archivio di Stato, Padua, Notarile, F. Fanzago, fo. 19.

It is an articulate if formulaic document, and shows Guadagni in full command of his faculties, choreographing the theatre of ritual to the last:

26 September 1792: Padua

I, Cavalier Gaetano Guadagni, believing that there is nothing in this world as certain as death, nor nothing more uncertain than the hour of it, being of sound and lucid mind, have decided to arrange for the disposal of my possessions, and to set out my last wishes in my own hand, guaranteeing its validity by my signature on each page.

First I commend my soul to God, to the Blessed Virgin, to St. Anthony, to the saint whose name I bear, and to the whole Heavenly Court that they may intercede for me at the hour of my death that I may be worthy of eternal bliss. After my death, I wish my body to be interred in the church of the glorious St Anthony, beseeching the Noble Fathers to receive me into that church and have me buried in the most suitable tomb.

I charge my executor and heir to fulfil faithfully my wishes as to the conduct of my funeral, namely to disburse two lire to each of twelve priests and one lira each for a candle; also four lire to the four institutions for the Orphans and the Mendicants, with the customary alms, and with a candle worth half a lira to each member of the institutions. In addition, two candles are to be given to each of twelve Reverend Fathers of St Anthony's, and round my bier eight torches, at four lire each, borne by eight priests. A hundred masses are to be said for me, at a cost of two lire each, and one sung mass in the presence of my body.

I leave as reimbursement to the distinguished Signor Giovanni Sografi [my doctor] the furnishings of the two rooms on the first floor that overlook the garden, with all the contents therein on the day of my death, in gratitude for all he has done for me during my illness. I likewise leave my entire wardrobe to my valet Girolamo Gambaro as reimbursement and recompense for the faithful service he has always rendered me.

After my death, my executor and heir will arrange for Signor Francesco Fanzago, Notary, to make an exact inventory of my possessions, as security for my creditors. I intend and desire Signor Vincenzo Guadagni, my beloved nephew, to be my universal heir, inheriting the remainder of all my goods, effects, furniture, deeds, rights and credits that I hold both with His Excellency the Marchese Carlo Spinola and with the Guadagni shop, and settling my accounts with any other person, my legatees, and my funeral expenses; if he were to die before me, I name [as heir] in his stead the holy Ospedale degli Infermi in this town.

I entreat the distinguished Giovanni Sografi to act as my executor of this, my last will and testament....

Cavalier Gaetano Guadagni.[15]

Some six weeks after making his will, Guadagni died. The official record of his death contains the following information and misinformation: 'On 11 November 1792, after suffering from leucophlegmatica, Signor Gaetano Guadagni died, aged sixty-three years less two months, attended by Dr Sografi of the parish of San Lorenzo'[16] (see Figure 11.1). The cause of death, leucophlegmatica, is sometimes known as anasarca, or dropsy, an accumulation of fluid in various cavities and organs of the body. The death certificate contains an erroneous attempt at establishing his age, describing the singer as being two months short of 63 years of age, information that led Paolo Cattelan mistakenly to conclude that he was born in 1729. Cattelan also misread the month of death, attributing it to October rather than November.[17] Guadagni was in fact some three months short of his sixty-fifth birthday when he died, but it was by no means uncommon in earlier centuries for people to be vague about their exact age, since in a less bureaucratic era accuracy was rarely required. The Arca sent news of his death to the Council of Ten in Venice, stating his salary at 400 ducats per annum. The information was necessary since the Council had recently determined to prohibit changes to the personnel of the Cappella without notification of the death, sacking, or absence that required a new appointment and an explanation of the financial implications of the substitution, hence the need to mention Guadagni's exceptional salary.

Cattelan's misreading of the date of Guadagni's death has given rise to a number of unnecessary theories. Taking the erroneous October date as accurate, Jolanda Dalla Vecchia has argued that confusion over the date of Guadagni's death might have been an attempt to enhance the payment due to his heir. But her calculations depend on the assumption that Guadagni was still being paid in five instalments for the five

---

[15] Archivio di Stato, Padua, Notarile F. Fanzago, ff. 20–22. A transcription of the will appears in Appendix C.

[16] '1792…Novembre…11 ditto, Il Sig. Gaetano Guadagni, ammalato da una affezione leucoflegmazia, d'anni 63 a mesi 2, visitato dal P. P.r Sografi, Parr[occhi]a San Lorenzo.' Archivio di Stato, Padua, Ufficio Sanità, Morti 1792, folder 509. The date is confirmed in the briefer record in folder 461: 'Guadagni—Kr. Gaetano, 1792 11 novembre'. I am grateful for the assistance of Lorenzo Bianconi and Stefano Arieti in reading this document. The document is transcribed incorrectly in Paolo Cattelan, 'La musica della "omnigena religio"', p. 162, n. 34, where Cattelan substitutes 'ottobre' for 'novembre' and misreads the description of Guadagni's illness; moreover when he quotes Gennari's diary, Cattelan alters Gennari's date to harmonise with his misreading of the date in the death certificate: Cattelan, 'La musica', p. 158, n. 18.

[17] Cattelan, 'La musica', p. 162.

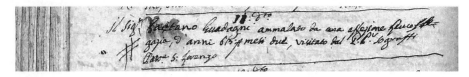

FIGURE 11.1 Record of Guadagni's death, Archivio di Stato, Padua. (Photography F. M. Howard Whitaker)

compulsory festivals, and ignore the new arrangements in place at the end of 1790 to pay his salary monthly.[18] There is, nevertheless, a discrepancy. In 1790, Guadagni had successfully petitioned the Arca to be paid at the rate of 25 ducats per month with an extra payment of 50 ducats at Easter and the remaining 50 ducats to be paid direct to the Santo on Santa Giustina's day (7 October) in lieu of rent. At the point of his death, he had been paid 375 ducats, that is, his full annual salary, including the Easter bonus and a year's rent, less one month. The Arca should have paid the full 400 ducats, since it was customary, if someone died in service, to pay their stipend up to the end of the quarter. No explanation has been found for this curtailment.

The funeral took place the day after his death: 'Yesterday, among others, died Gaetano Guadagni…he was buried today in the church of the Santo'.[19] Padua's diarists produced two obituaries, covering much the same ground:

> This November saw the melancholy end of a theatrical celebrity, dying in obscurity and in poverty, despite the great riches he acquired in the years of his triumphs. The celebrated musician Cavalier Gaetano Guadagni had here received much approbation and much success both as an artist and as a man, until, just at the moment when he found himself opposed by a jealous rival in the person of Pacchierotti, an unhappy fate robbed him of his physical powers so that he was restricted to singing only in the choir of the Santo, and his throat and lips which used to enchant us with melodies and such divine art could not even pronounce the words of the motets, and was scarcely able to produce a note.[20]

---

[18] Jolanda Dalla Vecchia, 'Cantanti e strumentisti nei Settecento. La Cappella Antoniana a Padova', *Rassegna veneta di Studi Musicali*, 9–10, (1993–94), pp. 142–44.

[19] 'Addí 12. Ieri è passato tra' più il cavalier Gaetano Guadagni…e oggi fu seppellito nella chiesa del Santo'. Gennari, op. cit., ii, p. 683.

[20] 'Quello stesso novembre vedeva la malinconica fine di una celebrità del teatro, spentasi nell'ombra e nella miseria, malgrado le ricchezze accumulate negli anni dei trionfi. Moriva in Padova il K.r Gaetano Guadagni, il celebro musico, che pure quì aveva raccolto tanti applausi e tanta fortuna come artista e come uomo, finchè il destino avverso, mentre faceva sorgere di contro a lui un rivale invidiato, il Pacchierotti, gli menomara le forze fisiche, in modo da obbligarlo a cantare soltanto nella cappella del Santo, e a costringere la gola, le labbra, che avevano ammaliato un giorno colle melodie e l'arte sovrana, a non pronunciare nemmeno le parole dei mottetti, appena vocalizzati.' Girolamo Polcastro, *Raccolta dei più singolari avvenimenti accaduti nel corso*

12 [November]. Yesterday, among others, died Gaetano Guadagni, an excellent singer, among the finest of the century. Today he was buried in the church of the Santo, where for many years he was employed by the Cappella. He earned great wealth through his exceptional contralto voice, his great vocal ability and his acting upon the operatic stage, but squandered it all and died in debt. It is several years since, as the result of an apoplectic stroke, he lost the power of speech, and he could only manage to pronounce two or three words. Despite this, on holy days he sang in the services as best he could, not uttering the words but, as it were, 'vocalising'. Besides being a skilful musician, he was also very handsome, and without those bodily defects that are usually seen in castratos.[21]

He was buried in the north aisle of the Santo. The exact location of his grave is not recorded.

*d'anni 22, cioè dall'anno 1764 fino a tutto il 1786, tratti dalle memorie postume di Santo Pengo*, in Brunelli, *I teatri di Padova*, p. 311.

[21] 'Addì 12. Ieri è passato tra' più il Cavalier Gaetano Guadagni, musico eccellente e tra i primi di questo secolo, e oggi fu seppellito nella chiesa del Santo, dove da molti anni era salariato per la Cappella. Egli guadagnò grandi ricchezze colla sua rara voce di contralto, colla sua perizia nel canto e coll'azione sullo scene treatrali, ma sprecò tutto e morendo lasciò de' debiti. Erano alcuni anni passati dacché per un colpo apopletico aveva perduto la loquela e non poteva profferire che due o tre parole. Con tutto ciò ne' giorni delle musiche solenni cantava il mottetto come meglio poteva, non profferendo le parole ma, per così spiegarmi, vocalizzando. Oltre ad essere valente musico, era anche bello della persona, e senza que' difetti nel corpo che ne' castrati ordinariamente si vedono.' Gennari, op. cit., ii, p. 683.

# 12

## Guadagni the Singer

To discover the quality of Guadagni's voice is triply denied us. Not only is the sound unavailable to us in the same way that Bach's organ playing, or Paganini's violin playing or Chopin's piano playing are, but while physical instruments survive, from which certain deductions about timbre, tonal range and volume can be made, singers leave no instruments.[1] And beyond this, the castrato voice is especially elusive. Even though the technique of voice production and singing styles have changed radically over the centuries, we have an understanding of the nature of the soprano or bass voice that enables us to make imaginative contact with a soprano or bass from an earlier age, but the actual sonority of the castrato remains inaccessible.

Few think that the recordings of Alessandro Moreschi, the so-called last castrato, represent the sound of the greatest eighteenth-century castratos, though the remote and infinitely melancholy charm of his voice may be the best clue we have.[2] Its appeal is not universal. Listeners much closer to the era of the castrato found both the quality of voice and the style of singing an acquired taste. An account by Gounod of hearing the music of Palestrina sung by the choir of the Sistine Chapel (where Moreschi sang throughout his life) in 1839 conveys both fascination and repulsion:

> I went to the Sistine Chapel as often as possible. This austere, ascetic...passionless music, with an intensity of contemplation that bordered on ecstasy, at first

---

[1] Though at least one, Brigida Banti, was subjected to a post mortem examination to investigate her larynx, which was found to be exceptionally large. Bruce Carr, 'Brigida Giorgi Banti', *The New Grove Dictionary of Music and Musicians*, London: Macmillan, 1980.

[2] Two sets of recordings were made: in 1902 with the producer Fred Gaisberg, and in 1904 with W. Sinkler Darby; these were issued by Opal in 1993 (OPAL CD 9823). Tracks from the recordings are readily accessible online. The recordings are discussed in an important article by Joe K. Law, 'Alessandro Moreschi Reconsidered: A castrato on Records', *Opera Quarterly* 2.2 (1984): 1–12.

produced in me a strange and almost disagreeable effect. Was it the style of the compositions themselves, an entirely new experience for me, or was it the distinctive sonority of those special voices that I was hearing for the first time, or rather the firm attack, verging on harshness, the striking accent which shaped the performance, underlining the different entries of the voices....I was not dismayed by my first impressions, bizarre as they were. I returned again and again until at last I could not stay away.[3]

The 'firm attack, verging on harshness' is conspicuous in Moreschi's recordings. Joe Law describes him as 'launching himself into the head voice...[with] recourse to an *acciaccatura,* sometimes as much as an octave below the note he wishes to gain'.[4] Law points out that the 'most disagreeable' effect of attack by *acciaccatura* was also described by Mendelssohn who visited the Sistine Chapel in 1813.[5] The effect appears to have a long history. Law traces it back to an early fourteenth-century source, but, more relevantly, it appears to have been known to Caccini, who, writing around 1602, clearly disapproved: 'There are indeed some who in attacking the first note [of a phrase] begin a third below....I should say it were rather unpleasant to the ear and ought to be used but seldom.'[6] The effect clearly persisted into the early twentieth century, and does little to render more attractive the only recorded examples of the castrato voice.

Although we are unable to discover how Guadagni's voice would sound like to us twenty-first-century listeners, there is plenty of evidence to suggest how it sounded to his contemporaries. From the outset of his career, the quality of his voice was widely praised: 'full and well toned', 'pleasing and expressive', 'delicate, polished and refined', 'a passionate singer who faithfully represents Nature', 'Guadagni sings and charms all ears'.[7] For Mrs Thrale, he was 'soft Guadagni', whom she cites as an example

---

[3] 'J'allais donc le plus possible à la chapelle Sixtine. Cette musique, sévère, ascétique...antisensuelle, et néanmoins d'une intensité de contemplation qui va parfois à l'extase, me produisait d'abord un effet étrange, presque désagréable. Ètait-ce le style même de ces compositions, entièrement nouveau pour moi, était-ce la sonorité particulière de ces voix spéciales que mon oreille entendait pour la première fois, ou bien cette attaque ferme jusqu'à la rudesse, ce martèlement si saillant qui donne un tel relief à l'exécution en soulignant les diverses entrées des voix...cette impression, pour bizarre qu'elle fût, ne me rebuta point. J'y revins encore, puis encore, et je finis par ne pouvoir plus m'en passer.' Charles Gounod, *Mémoires d'un artiste,* pp. 99–100, Paris, 1896.

[4] Joe K. Law, 'Alessandro Moreschi Reconsidered', p. 9.

[5] Ibid., p. 10.

[6] Giulio Caccini, *Le nuove musiche* (1602), trans. H. Wiley Hitchcock, cited in Michael Scott, *The Record of Singing: To 1914,* London: Duckworth, 1974, pp. 48–49. Discussed in Law, op. cit., pp. 9–10.

[7] Burney, *General History,* ii, p. 875; *Mercure de France,* May 1754, p. 184; Burney, op. cit., p. 876; Alessandro Pepoli, introduction to *Meleagro,* Venice, 1790 in Paolo Cattelan, 'Giovanni Ferrandini, musicista Padovano', in *Mozart, Padova e la Betulia liberata,* ed. Paolo Pinamonti, p. 220; Edward Poore to James Harris Jr, March 1770, in Burrows and Dunhill, *Music and Theatre in Handel's World,* p. 585.

of the singer with the greatest power to move an elderly and jaded opera-goer.[8] These subjective judgements are supported by the evidence of his earnings: the fees he received from his operatic performances were at the highest level, and the exceptional salary he drew at the Santo marked his star status.

There are some negatives, not least the unspecified 'defects' that Maria Walpurgis detected in his singing and claimed he had the art to conceal.[9] It appears that his voice was not powerful: Burney described it not only as 'delicate', but also 'thin and feeble',[10] and there is some confirmation of this in that the singer himself said it was too small for the San Carlo in Naples, where he sang for one season only. More surprisingly, he was never praised for his virtuosity, though the evidence is unclear. Although in Ortes' opinion, Guadagni 'always pleases but never astonishes',[11] some of the roles he undertook contain formidable passages of vocal fireworks, from Handel's dazzling middle section of 'But who may abide' (*Messiah*, 1750), to Guglielmi's powerful 'Nel suo dolor ristretto' (*Ezio*, 1770). To deliver these numbers even adequately he must have commanded a degree of agility, but there is a conspicuous lack of comment on this aspect of his performance. There is so much that we cannot know. It would be good, for example, to discover Croce's meaning when he reported that Guadagni's 'very beautiful voice…negotiates the registers cleanly'. This could imply either that he aimed to disguise the break between chest and head registers, a growing trend in eighteenth-century vocal technique, or that he preserved the distinction while producing equally attractive tone in both.[12]

When Burney described the young Guadagni as 'a wild and careless singer',[13] it is not entirely clear whether he was referring to his style of singing or to his behaviour, but the charge of caprice recurs, and a number of sources implied that he could be unreliable. Croce quoted the accusation that he was 'capricious, and rarely gives of his best', and Elizabeth Harris declared he should be 'whipt for laziness and impertinence'.[14] Guadagni was, as we have seen, a notoriously difficult character; although what was judged as his laziness could have been either a disinclination or an inability to bring off virtuosic passages and his refusal to give encores may have been a principled stand to uphold the integrity of his role.

[8] 'In Theatro', Samuel Johnson, trans. Mrs Thrale, London, 1771. The references to living actors and musicians were inserted by Mrs Thrale into Johnson's classical parody.

[9] Burney, *The Present State of Music in Germany*, i, p. 136.

[10] Burney, *General History* ii, p. 876.

[11] Ortes to Hasse, 31 Dec. 1768.

[12] Croce, *I teatri di Napoli*, p. 751.

[13] Burney, *General History*, ii, p. 875.

[14] Croce, *I teatri di Napoli*, p. 749; Elizabeth Harris to James Harris Jr, 8 Mar. 1771, Burrows and Dunhill, *Music and Theatre*, p. 626.

The longest and most detailed description of his singing comes, inevitably, from Burney. It is instructive to look at the complete passage, already partially quoted throughout this book:

> He acquired great reputation as first man, in all the principal theatres in Italy, and the year [*recte* years] before his return to England, he excited great admiration by his talents, as well as disturbance, by his caprice, in Vienna. The highest expectations of his abilities were raised by rumour, before his arrival here for the winter season.… But though his manner of singing was perfectly delicate, polished, and refined, his voice seemed, at first, to disappoint every hearer. Those who remembered it when he was in England before, found it comparatively thin and feeble. For he had now changed it to a soprano, and extended its compass from six or seven notes, to fourteen or fifteen. And let a fluid of six feet in depth be spread over more than double its usual surface, and it will necessarily be shallower, though of greater extent. The Music he sung was the most simple imaginable; a few notes with frequent pauses, and opportunities of being liberated from the composer and the band were all he wanted. And in these seemingly extemporaneous effusions, he proved the inherent power of melody totally divorced from harmony and unassisted even by unisonous accompaniment. Surprised at such great effects from causes apparently so small, I frequently tried to analize the pleasure he communicated to the audience, and found it chiefly arose from his artful manner of diminishing the tones of his voice, like the dying notes of the Æolian harp. Most other singers captivate by a swell or *messa di voce*; but Guadagni, after beginning a note or passage with all the force he could safely exert, fined it off to a thread, and gave it all the effect of extreme distance.[15]

There is useful detail here. Burney was intent on comparing Guadagni's singing in 1769 with his memory of it on the occasion of the singer's earlier London visit in 1748–1755. His criticism seems to depend on the erroneous perception that Guadagni's voice had migrated to the soprano register. On the evidence of the roles he sang, Guadagni had available to him, throughout his life, a range of two octaves, from g to g″. Individual composers exploited different areas of this range, and his tessitura changed with his roles rather than at different periods of his life.[16] Burney's next comment contains a surprising implication. His reference to Guadagni being 'liberated from the composer and the band' suggests that the great beauty of Guadagni's

---

[15] Burney, *General History*, ii, p. 876.
[16] See Patricia Howard, 'Did Burney Blunder?' *Musical Times* 139 (1998): 29–32.

singing lay in his improvised cadenzas—this in a singer who identified closely with Gluck's stand against excessive ornamentation. It is difficult to evaluate the comment in the light of the very small number of authentic instances of Guadagni's written ornamentation and the unavailability of his extempore embellishments (see Chapter 9). The most substantive information in Burney's account is his description of Guadagni's diminuendos. A number of his roles provide opportunities for this technique. The effect would have been to maximise the dynamic range of a small voice, truly the art of 'hiding defects'.

Another assessment of his singing stems from to the same period. Shortly after Guadagni's London visit of 1769–1771, he was succeeded at the King's Theatre by Giuseppe Millico, who had taken the role of Orfeo in Gluck's adaptation of the opera for Parma in 1769, and brought this version to London in 1773.[17] Comparisons between the two singers were inevitable. Unusually informative reporting in the London press attempted a diplomatic impartiality: *The Morning Chronicle* preferred Millico's singing but Guadagni's acting: 'Millico…exceeded Guadagni in the favourite air of *che farò senza Euridice*, etc, although he did not play the character so well'.[18] *The General Evening Post* drew a further distinction between the two: 'Millico sung the famous air *che farò* in a taste different from Guadagni, but with equal success; it would be difficult to draw a parallel between these two great performers; yet it must be acknowledged that Guadagni has an evident superiority in the infernal part.'[19] Among the public, the general consensus was that while Millico's voice was the 'sweeter',[20] Guadagni was the more impassioned singer. According to one opera-goer:

> In the Line of Spectacle, great disputes subsist at present about the Superiority of Millico and Guadagni in 'che faro' in the Orfeo: But it seems rather to be given in favour of the former, without any just reason I think, because the whole comes to this Point whether a Man should be affected by a sudden Event of distress, passionately and hastily, or with despondency and dejection. These are their two ways of Singing it, and that must depend upon the constitution and temper of each person, both may be equally just.[21]

---

[17] See Patricia Howard, 'For the English: a reconstruction of Gluck's 1773 *Orfeo*', *Musical Times* 137 (1996): 13–15.

[18] *Morning Chronicle*, 10 Mar. 1773.

[19] *General Evening Post*, 9–11 Mar. 1773.

[20] See for example Fanny Burney, *The Early Journals and Letters*, ed. Lars E. Troide, i, Oxford: Oxford University Press, 1988, pp. 236, 238–39, 260.

[21] George Bussy Villiers to Lady Spencer, 16 Mar. 1773. I am grateful to Ian Woodfield for drawing this source to my attention. The ambiguity of the wording is discussed in Ian Woodfield, *Opera and Drama in Eighteenth-Century London*, Cambridge: Cambridge University Press, 2001, p. 50.

Unfortunately the wording of this important assessment is far from clear. The writer apparently intended to challenge public opinion, which had judged in favour of 'the former', presumably (and grammatically) Millico. However, 'the former' could be read as referring to Guadagni, who both created the role and was first to sing it in London. Certainly 'passionately and hastily' are hallmarks of Guadagni's style, while 'despondency and dejection' are compatible with Millico's 'sweet' singing and more passive acting.

We know nothing about Guadagni's initial training as a singer. He arrived in Padua in 1746 already sufficiently skilful to be elected unanimously into the prestigious choir at the Santo. Bearing in mind the singing careers of his three sisters and brother, it is probable that he learned his technique at home, perhaps singing in the cathedral at Lodi as a boy. The brief duration of his first engagement at the Santo introduced him to the demanding standards of Vallotti and Tartini, both overwhelmingly concerned with precision and intonation, and whose lessons remained with him throughout his life. (If Guadagni and Rauzzini successfully tested Tartini's experiments with difference tones, their intonation must have been excellent.[22]) Beyond this, we have Burney's puzzling references to a period of study with Gizziello immediately after his involvement in the Lisbon earthquake of 1755. According to Burney, the 'musical counsel' which he obtained from Gizziello transformed him 'from a young and wild singer of the second and third class' into 'the first singer of his time'.[23] There is no evidence to support this story. Heriot states that Gizziello left Lisbon in 1753, and so missed both the earthquake and Guadagni's debut there,[24] but Winton Dean claims that Gizziello was employed by the Lisbon court theatre from 1752 to 1755 and could have coincided both with Guadagni and the earthquake.[25] Whatever the truth of Burney's assertion, the years 1755–56 marked a turning point in Guadagni's career. From this moment he abandoned comic opera and, for the most part, oratorio, and rapidly built his career on the continent, winning *primo uomo* roles in prestigious *opera seria* premières in leading theatres throughout Italy and beyond.

We can learn more about the character of his voice and the nature of his technique by examining the music written specifically for him or adapted to suit him. Appendix A lists the dramatic roles Guadagni is known to have undertaken. While a considerable quantity of the music is lost, enough remains for us to be able to form an impression of the range and character of Guadagni's singing throughout his

---

[22] Burney, *The Present State of Music in Germany*, i, 139–40. See Chapter 10.
[23] Burney, *General History*, ii, pp. 800 and 876.
[24] Heriot, *The Castrati in Opera*, p. 116.
[25] Winton Dean, 'Conti', *The New Grove Dictionary of Music and Musicians*, London: Macmillan, 1980.

career. The majority of Guadagni's roles can be described as 'romantic leads'. While he occasionally played a son (Telemaco), a friend and brother (Oreste), or a god (Apollo, Bacchus), for the most part he is a star-crossed lover who woos and eventually wins his girl. It goes without saying that, throughout the century, there was no reluctance to cast either a castrato or a female soprano as a male lover, and Guadagni was never mocked for any physical inadequacy to discharge a romantic role. On the contrary, as we have seen, in the later Enlightenment period, the ideal of masculinity became 'dangerously effeminate',[26] and the cult of sensibility made the gracefully nuanced emotional range of the high voice particularly appropriate to express the tender effusions of a lover.

The conventions of eighteenth-century opera provided composers with a practical guide to matching aria style to character or situation, prompting them to select certain metres, keys and instrumental colour to distinguish the class and function of a role. A king or victorious hero, for example, might well sing in common time, in C or D major, and the instrumentation would often include horns or trumpets, while airs for a maid or peasant girl would be likely to be in compound time, in G major, with string accompaniment. The music assigned to a romantic lead would frequently be in simple duple or triple time, often in E flat or E major, featuring wind instruments, particularly clarinets and horns, and characterised by a sweet, lyrical melody. An aria of this type was identified as an *aria cantabile* or *aria d'affetto*. Unfortunately the classifications are inconsistent and the definitions emanate from philosophers rather than composers. One of the most complete attempts to define eighteenth-century aria types appears in John Brown's *Letters upon the Poetry and Music of Italian Opera*.[27] Brown defined the *aria cantabile* as 'the only kind of song which gives the singer an opportunity of displaying at once, and in the highest degree, all his powers'; such arias do, nevertheless, avoid wide leaps and prolonged passages of vocal athletics, though gentle flights of conjunct triplets are a common decorative device. According to Brown, 'the proper subjects for this Air are sentiments of tenderness'. These arias are usually relatively short and often avoid the formality of a full-length da capo structure.

As romantic lead, Guadagni was allotted a good number of *arie cantabili* by a variety of composers throughout his career. The style suited everything we know about his voice: the refined tonal beauty, the delicacy of phrasing and the appropriate ('judicious') expression of the emotion represented. None of the roles that Guadagni sang in his first London seasons was written specially for him, and the fact that many

---

[26] Chloe Chard, 'Effeminacy and pleasure', in *Femininity and Masculinity in Eighteenth-century Art and Culture*, ed. Gill Perry and Michael Rossington, Manchester: Manchester University Press, 1994, p. 158.

[27] Edinburgh, 1789, pp. 36–40. See Chapter 9, note 20.

EXAMPLE 12.1  Ciampi, 'Felice io sono', from *Bertoldo* (1754)

of the items that have survived display the characteristics of the *aria cantabile* cannot be taken to prove that he was assigned such or such a role because his voice was considered suitable to perform it; it is far more likely that he was charged with a role because he was available. Many revivals, however, included new airs, designed to suit the singer, and we learn from Burney that an *aria cantabile* inserted into Ciampi's *Bertoldo* in 1754 was composed specifically for Guadagni. Burney described the music as 'natural and elegant', terms which he also applied to Guadagni's voice[28] (see Example 12.1).

The romantic lead was not restricted to the lyrical style of an *aria cantabile*. For moments of heightened emotion—anger, despair, the frustration of his amatory ambitions—the character might resort to an *aria parlante*, a predominantly syllabic setting that delivers the text without embellishment. According to Brown, 'the *aria parlante*, or speaking Air, is that which…admits neither of long notes in the composition nor of many ornaments in the execution. The rapidity of motion in this air is proportioned to the violence of the passion which is expressed by it.' The skill involved in singing an *aria parlante* is akin to the declamation of recitative, though the interpretation is governed more strictly by the notation, and the singer is allowed

---

[28] Burney, *General History*, i, p. 863.

few freedoms of tempo or rhythm. The prime requisite is clear diction, but feeling, expression, spirit and nature are all qualities referred to in vocal tutors as being essential for this style of singing. For Vincenzo Manfredini, a theoretician whose views command particular respect since his brother was the noted castrato Giuseppe Manfredini, defined it as 'singing with feeling and with spirit; varying the voice with light and shade; and above all expressing every piece of music according to its true meaning and character'.[29] It is not easy to establish, from the meagre comments of his contemporaries, precisely how Guadagni delivered this aria style. The strongest clues are bound up in the comparisons between him and Millico in the London performances of *Orfeo*: Guadagni 'played the character' more effectively than Millico, and he delivered his airs 'more passionately', especially in the Underworld scene. The increasing number of *parlante* arias written for him after 1762 (for example, in Gluck's *Telemaco* and Traetta's *Ifigenia in Tauride*) suggests that *Orfeo* was a catalyst, and that it was as a result of Gluck's or Calzabigi's coaching that the *parlante* style became one of Guadagni's acknowledged strengths. Example 12.2 is an *aria parlante* taken from Piccinni's setting of *Olimpiade*, which Guadagni premièred in Rome in 1768 and repeated in London the following season.

The *aria di bravura* or *aria di agilità* was usually allocated to kings, princes and victorious soldiers. According to Brown it was 'composed *chiefly*, indeed, too often, *merely*, to indulge the singer in the display of certain powers in the execution, particularly extraordinary agility or compass of voice'. Guadagni was not usually cast as a power figure, nor did he ever, apparently, seek opportunities to display the 'extraordinary agility', which he may or may not have commanded. In the opera *Ezio*, however, the title role unites the lover and the victorious soldier, and an *aria di bravura* was therefore called for. As we have seen, in Guglielmi's *Ezio,* given in London in 1770, where Metastasio had provided the text 'Pensa a serbarmi, o cara', which Guadagni himself later set, Guglielmi substituted a more turbulent aria, providing a vigorous, *bravura* setting that focused on the word 'combattono', characterising Ezio as soldier rather than lover (see Example 12.3).

Inevitably, Guadagni's vocal development was nurtured by the composers with whom he worked. While the system of single-season engagements and the consequent perpetual itinerancy of leading singers was not conducive to the formation of lasting relationships between singer and composer, Guadagni did enjoy a few more permanent bonds with a handful of composers. The composer with whom he had the longest association is Handel. With one exception, in each of the six Lenten seasons

---

[29] 'Cantar con sentimento, con anima; sostenere e ombreggiare la voce; e sopratutto esprimere ogni pezzo di musica secondo il suo vero senso e carattere.' Vincenzo Manfredini, *Regole armoniche o sieno precetti ragionati per apprender la musica*, p. 57, Bologna, 1775.

**Andante sostenuto**

Se cer - ca, se di - ce l'a - mi - co dov'
è, l'a - mi-co dov' è, l'a-mi-co in-fe - li- ce, l'a-mi-co in fe-
li - ce ri-spon-di mo - rì,
mo - rì, ah nò, si gran duo-lo, si gran duo-lo non
dar - le, non dar - le per me, non dar - le, non dar - le per me.

EXAMPLE 12.2  Piccinni, 'Se cerca, se dice', from *Olimpiade* (1768)

between 1750 and 1755 Guadagni's repertory featured a wide range of Handel's oratorios. Apart from the London seasons, further performances in Salisbury and one
Lent spent in Dublin (1752) expanded the tally (see Table 12.1).

Because their collaboration came at so early a period in Guadagni's career, it
is hard to see how Handel's music could fail to have had a powerful influence on
forming the voice of the 'young and wild performer', building his technique and
developing his approach to dramatic expression. Moreover, in the two roles Handel
wrote specifically for the singer, Didymus in *Theodora* and Hercules in *The Choice of
Hercules*, we have a coherent picture of how Handel heard Guadagni's voice and how
he exploited his strengths. One thing that distinguishes Handel's understanding of
Guadagni's voice from that of any other composer writing for him in the 1750s is
that Handel clearly regarded Guadagni as an alto. The roles he sang in comic opera
during this period lie in a compass we would now describe as mezzo soprano: there
are plenty of top Fs and F sharps, and in the role of Lysander in J. C. Smith's *The
Fairies* he was required to sing a number of top Gs; at the bottom end, his range
rarely dropped below middle D in these roles. Handel's approach was markedly
different. Guadagni's numbers in *Theodora* lie within an alto tessitura. The range
is from low A to high E flat (a–e flat"), and most of the role lies between middle D
and the C above (d'–c"), the 'six or seven notes' Burney identified as characteristic of

EXAMPLE 12.3  Guglielmi, 'Nel suo dolor ristretto', from *Ezio* (1770)

Guadagni's voice. Handel occasionally took Guadagni down to a low G (g) in, for example, 'For He is like a refiner's fire' (*Messiah*), written for Guadagni in 1750. It is, moreover, significant that when he adapted for Guadagni roles originally designed for female altos, he sometimes put the music down a tone. An instance of this is the aria 'Fly from the cleaving mischief': this aria, created for a revival of *Samson* in 1745 for a Miss Robinson, was originally in E major; when Guadagni took over the role of Micah in 1750, the aria was transposed down to D major.

The roles of both Didymus and Hercules demonstrate a restrained lyricism. Despite occasional brief excursions into mild athleticism, the prevailing style is the *aria cantabile*. In *Theodora*, the only role Handel composed from scratch for Guadagni, the composer immediately hit upon the flowing, conjunct style that came to be Guadagni's preferred vehicle for his 'refined' and 'well toned' voice. The opening of his first air, 'The raptur'd soul', even provides an opportunity (on the second note) for his famous

TABLE 12.1

Handel's oratorios and odes performed by Guadagni between 1750 and 1755

| | |
|---|---|
| **1750** | *Saul* |
| | *Judas Maccabaeus* |
| | *Theodora* |
| | *Samson* |
| | *Messiah* |
| | *L'Allegro, il Penseroso ed il Moderato* |
| **1751** | *Belshazzar* |
| | *Alexander's Feast* and *The Choice of Hercules* |
| | *Esther* |
| | *Judas Maccabaeus* |
| | *Messiah* |
| **1752** | ? *L'Allegro, il Penseroso ed il Moderato* |
| | ? *Joshua* |
| | *Judas Maccabaeus* |
| | *Samson* |
| **1753** | *Alexander's Feast* and *The Choice of Hercules* |
| | *Jephtha* |
| | *Judas Maccabaeus* |
| | ? *Samson* |
| | *Messiah* |
| **1755** | *Alexander's Feast* and *The Choice of Hercules* |
| | *L'Allegro, il Penseroso ed il Moderato* |
| | *Samson* |
| | *Joseph* |
| | *Theodora* |
| | *Esther* |
| | *Judas Maccabaeus* |
| | *Messiah* |

diminuendo, the 'effect of extreme distance' that later became his trademark (see Example 12.4). In the duets, especially 'To thee, thou glorious son of worth', the need to interweave the voices leads Handel to combine *cantabile* and *parlante* styles.

Different circumstances apply in Guadagni's contribution to *The Choice of Hercules*, which Handel reworked from music he had prepared earlier to accompany

EXAMPLE 12.4 Handel, 'The raptur'd soul', from *Theodora* (1750)

Smollett's play *Alceste*, never performed. Although the music was not written for Guadagni in the first instance, Handel appears to have selected Hercules' airs with the special qualities of Guadagni's voice in mind. The music is a feast of cantabile lyricism, notably in the memorable portrayal of Hercules seduced by Pleasure, 'Yet can I hear that dulcet lay', surely the most sensuous celebration of legato singing in Guadagni's repertory.[30] Elsewhere, Handel chose to challenge the 'wild and careless singer' with the demanding *bravura* of 'For He is like a refiner's fire'. (See Example 12.5.) In adapting the score of *Messiah* for Guadagni in 1750, Handel replaced the florid, conjunct runs of his earlier setting for bass voice with one of the most technically demanding passages Guadagni was called upon to deliver. We know nothing of the success of this, though if Guadagni had failed to bring it off, Handel would surely have removed the setting from Guadagni's later performances in 1751, 1753 and 1755. He did not, though it may be significant that he later wrote an alternative to bar 72, transposing the three notes up an octave, avoiding the low G.

---

[30] 'Yet can I hear that dulcet lay' can be heard on 'Arias for Guadagni'.

EXAMPLE 12.5 Handel, 'For he is like a refiner's fire', from *Messiah* (1750)

However sympathetically Handel created and adapted roles for Guadagni, it was Gluck who changed the whole focus of Guadagni's career by creating in *Orfeo* a vehicle of expression that entirely coincided with the singer's strengths and limitations. There are no *bravura* numbers. The arias 'Chiamo il mio ben così' and 'Che farò' relate in style to the *aria cantabile*. The vocal lines display an effusion of tender emotions expressed in the balanced rising and falling of lyrical phrases. The word-setting, however, is more straightforward than in traditional *opera-seria cantabile* arias; Gluck's aim of simplifying operatic language in the interests of telling the story more directly led him to write in an almost exclusively syllabic style. This *parlante* style is particularly prominent in the short airs in Act II scene 1, 'Mille pene' and 'Men tiranne', whose declamatory settings gave full scope for Guadagni's expressive delivery of the words (Example 12.6).

Gluck was never reluctant to set out his principles of word-setting. His dramatic aims are voiced here by Calzabigi:

In the new scheme of drama…carried out for the first time in *Orfeo*…nature and feeling prevail.…Compressed to the form of Greek tragedy, the drama

EXAMPLE 12.6 Gluck, 'Men tiranne', from *Orfeo ed Euridice* (1762)

has the power to arouse pity and terror, and to act upon the soul to the same degree as spoken tragedy does…the music expresses nothing but that which arises from the words; consequently the words are not buried in notes, and are not used to prolong the performance inappropriately. I consider that a note should never have the value of more than one syllable: it is ridiculous to extend the pronunciation of 'amore' (for example) to a hundred notes when nature has limited it to just three.[31]

It is, as we noted above, all the more unaccountable that the next role Gluck wrote for Guadagni contained the *aria di bravura* 'Se il fulmine', an aria reworked from an earlier opera and designed for a more agile singer. According to one critic, Guadagni failed to do it justice, and it is clear that the style suited neither his voice nor his temperament.[32] See Example 12.7.

Despite his importance for the singer's career, Gluck worked with Guadagni on just four operas, only two of which were written specially for him. Traetta wrote five roles for Guadagni, all of them sympathetically shaped to exploit his talents.

[31] 'Nel nuovo piano di drammi…il primo eseguito in *Orfeo*…qui tutto è natura, tutto è passione…ridotti alla contestura delle tragedie greche, hanno il privilegio d'eccitare il terrore e la compassione, e di agir sull'anima al pari d'una tragedia declamata…non entra altra musica che la semplice d'espressione che nasce dalla parola; sì perché non la seppellisca fralle note, sì perché non prolunghi impropriamente lo spettacolo, essendo ridicolo il sentire prolungar la voce d'amore (per esempio) da cento note quando e tre sole l'ha ristretto la natura, parendo a me che la nota non abbia mai da valere più d'una sillaba.' Calzabigi to Kaunitz, 6 Mar. 1767, in Vladimir Helfert, 'Dosud Neznámy dopis Ran. Calsabigiho z r. 1767', *Musikologie* 1 (1938): 116–17.

[32] *Wienerisches Diarium*, 7 Jan. 1764.

EXAMPLE 12.7  Gluck, 'Se il fulmine sospendi', from *Ezio* (1763)

Traetta's *Ifigenia in Tauride* appeared in Vienna in the season after *Orfeo* and the role of Oreste was clearly crafted for the same voice for which the music of Orfeo had been 'tailor-made'. It is apparent from Oreste's music throughout the opera that Traetta appreciated Guadagni's strengths as a declamatory singer-actor. There is a telling contrast between the vocal writing for the four main characters.[33] Three of them were allotted brilliant *bravura* writing. In the first act alone, Pilade ('Stelle irate'), Toante ('Frena l'ingiuste lagrime') and Ifigenia ('Sò che pietà de' miseri') display their virtuoso credentials, but none of Oreste's music approaches this level of agility. His role is highly expressive throughout, with impassioned *accompagnati* and short declamatory airs. A conspicuous feature of his music is that much of the melodic interest is transferred to the orchestra. In 'Qual destra', turbulent strings represent Oreste's tormented mental state, while in 'Ah, per pietà' Oreste's plea for mercy to the Eumenides, his declamatory line is supported by a lyrical solo cello in a dialogue between voice and instrument that owes much to the second act of Gluck's *Orfeo* (see Examples 12.8 and 12.9).

For a final piece of evidence in our attempt to deduce how his contemporaries understood Guadagni's voice, it is worth looking at Vallotti's antiphon 'O lingua benedicta'. This piece was written especially for Guadagni's re-entry to the Santo in 1768, and because of the part it played in the Santo's ceremonies it was the item

[33] See Traetta, *Ifigenia in Tauride* (in facsimile), ed. Howard Mayer Brown, New York: Garland, 1978.

EXAMPLE 12.8 Traetta, 'Qual destra omicida', from *Ifigenia in Tauride* (1763)

he performed more often than any other in his repertory. The range is in the alto register, from low A to D (a to d″). The voice enters with a sustained note suitable for Guadagni's trademark *messa di voce*. The word-setting is in the cantabile style throughout, with modest melismas and minimal trills at conventional cadence points. The fact that Guadagni sang this antiphon over a great many years, probably even after he had lost the power of enunciating words, suggests that it fitted his voice every bit as sympathetically as his more famous role of Orfeo. See Example 12.10.

But it is as the voice of Orpheus that Guadagni's fame has been perpetuated. His role in Gluck's opera contains some of the most familiar and best-loved castrato arias

EXAMPLE 12.9 Traetta, 'Ah, per pietà placatevi', from *Ifigenia in Tauride* (1763)

EXAMPLE 12.10  Vallotti, 'O lingua benedicta' (1768)

performed today. *Orfeo ed Euridice* was, remarkably, the first *opera seria* to achieve repertory status, the first opera to engage audiences decades (and subsequently centuries) after it was written. Even today the role of Orfeo is the earliest castrato role that many modern listeners encounter. And, I would argue, much of the enduring appeal of that role results from Guadagni's input into its concentrated passion and memorable lyricism.

## Conclusion

GUADAGNI HAS A powerful claim to be regarded as a modern castrato—if not the first modern castrato (though it is difficult to see who could contest the title), then certainly a prominent representative of the post-Farinelli generation who flourished in the second half of the eighteenth century. Guadagni and his coevals had the advantage of living in a period when audiences had become used to the castrato persona. Distaste, satire and ridicule had gradually fallen away, and the singers found themselves increasingly accepted into all levels of society. Guadagni, always popular with fellow performers, appears to have mixed on easy, if not equal, terms with scholars such as Burney, patrons like Maria Antonia Walpurgis, and an influential circle of brother Freemasons, who numbered not only practical men of the theatre like Durazzo, Gluck and Calzabigi but theorists, among them Giuseppe Ximenes and Algarotti, whose writings he came to know through the librettist Frugoni. In such company he could not fail to absorb a good deal of the current debate on dramatic theory. It was fortunate coincidence that placed Guadagni at the centre of the new operatic age, but it was his own talents and abilities that enabled him to play a leading part in the reform.

Guadagni was the first and perhaps the only eighteenth-century singer fully to realise what was at stake. He was quick to identify with the reform. Selected to create the one role that came to symbolise the new approach, Orpheus in Gluck's *Orfeo ed Euridice* of 1762, he built his subsequent career around it (mirroring Gluck's own mid-life change of direction). Understanding the demands and opportunities of the role, he recognised that it perfectly suited his skills, and just as importantly his limitations. In the words of one of his fellow reformers, it fitted him like a glove. Having found this perfect vehicle for his talents, he promoted the opera, in sometimes approximate or distorted reincarnations, in London, Munich, Venice and Padua: he could hardly have been a more pro-active propagandist. And when he became too old to enact it on the stage, he recreated it in his celebrated marionette theatre.

The new operatic age challenged the traditions and conventions of heroic opera and promoted of a new style of music drama whose keywords were 'nature' and 'feeling'. It achieved far more than the transformation of vocal delivery. Embracing realism in costume and asymmetry in stage design, it encouraged the assimilation of dance and chorus into the narrative, and accorded an enhanced role to the orchestra. But the most immediate effect was on the performance of solo vocal music. Pronouncing against closed forms, virtuosity and static delivery, it gave primacy to the expression and enunciation of words and a vocabulary of eloquent gestures. These requirements suited Guadagni in every respect, and it is apparent that a degree of self-knowledge shaped his response to the reform. Where his vocal limitations guided him to endorse the 'noble simplicity' called for by Gluck, his skills equipped him to deliver the *parlante* style to perfection. His talents as an actor were formed by the leading exponents with whom he had worked. Even his combative personality was put to the service of the reform when he challenged audiences to respect the integrity of an opera. Guadagni was in every department of his life a modern castrato, fully in tune with his age.

*Appendix A*

GUADAGNI'S DRAMATIC ROLES

TABLE A.1 IS necessarily provisional and almost certainly incomplete. The information has been assembled from librettos (not all of which include a cast list), some scores, Sartori's index of *Libretti italiani a stampa dalle origini al 1800* (1990–1994), and the *Almanacco dramattico*, edited by Roberto Verti (1996). A * denotes a première, with the important implication that the role was composed expressly to fit Guadagni's voice; it is a moot point whether pasticcios count as premières, and for the purpose of this list I have not marked them as such. A ? denotes works in which Guadagni's participation is presumed but not proven. Some of the works were repeated in subsequent seasons and these revivals are not listed. More detailed information on the opera seasons and actual dates of performances, where known, is to be found in the body of the book.

TABLE A.1

Guadagni's dramatic roles

| Title | Role | Composer | Location | Date / Season |
|---|---|---|---|---|
| *Cesare in Egitto* | Achilla | Colombo | Venice (San Moisè) | autumn 1746 |
| *Zenobia* | Mitrane | Michieli | Venice (San Moisè) | autumn 1746 |
| ?*La fiametta* | | pasticcio | Parma (Reale) | summer 1747 |
| *La comedia in comedia* | Celindo | Da Capua | London (King's) | 8 Nov. 1748 |
| *Orazio* | Leandro | Auletta | London (King's) | 29 Nov. 1748 |
| ?*La finta frascatana* | | pasticcio | London (King's) | 31 Dec. 1748 |

(*Continued*)

TABLE A.1 (CONTINUED)

| Title | Role | Composer | Location | Date / Season |
|---|---|---|---|---|
| *Don Calascione* | Filandro | Latilla | London (King's) | 21 Jan. 1749 |
| *?Il giramondo* | | pasticcio | London (King's) | 14 Feb. 1749 |
| *?La maestra* | | Cocchi | London (King's) | 28 Feb. 1749 |
| *? I tre cicisbei ridicoli* | | Resta / Ciampi | London (King's) | 14 Mar. 1749 |
| *? Peace in Europe* ('A new serenade') | | pasticcio | London (King's) | 29 Apr. 1749 |
| *?Il negligente* | | Ciampi | London (Little Theatre) | 21 Nov. 1749 |
| *?Madama Ciana* | | Latilla | London (King's) | 13 Jan. 1750 |
| *\*Adriano in Siria* | Farnaspe | Ciampi | London (King's) | 20 Feb. 1750 |
| *Saul* | David | Handel | London (Covent Garden) | 2 Mar. 1750 |
| *Judas Maccabaeus* | Israelite Man and Messenger | Handel | London (Covent Garden) | 9 Mar. 1750 |
| *\*Theodora* | Didymus | Handel | London (Covent Garden) | 16 Mar. 1750 |
| *\*Il trionfo di Camilla* | Prenesto | Ciampi | London (King's) | 31 Mar. 1750 |
| *Samson* | Micah | Handel | London (Covent Garden) | 4 Apr. 1750 |
| *Messiah* | | Handel | London (Covent Garden) | 12 Apr. 1750 |
| *L'Allegro ed il Penseroso* | | Handel | Salisbury (Assembly Rooms) | 5 Oct. 1750 |
| *\*La forza d'amore* | Tirsi | Paradies | London (Little Theatre) | 19 Jan. 1751 |
| *?Nerina* | | ?Paradies | London (Little Theatre) | 16 Feb. 1751 |
| *Belshazzar* | Cyrus | Handel | London (Covent Garden) | 22 Feb. 1751 |
| *Alexander's Feast* and *\*The Choice of Hercules* | Hercules | Handel | London (Covent Garden) | 1 Mar. 1751 |

*(Continued)*

TABLE A.1 (CONTINUED)

| Title | Role | Composer | Location | Date / Season |
|---|---|---|---|---|
| *Esther* | Assuerus | Handel | London (Covent Garden) | 15 Mar. 1751 |
| ?*Joshua* | Othniel | Handel | Dublin (Fishamble Street) | 3 February 1752 |
| *Jephtha* | Hamor | Handel | London (Covent Garden) | 16 Mar. 1753 |
| *\*Alfred* | Prince Edward | Arne | London (King's) | 12 May 1753 |
| *Didone abbandonata* | Enea | Hasse | Versailles | 13 Oct. 1753 |
| *L'Arcadia in Brenta* | Giacinto | Galuppi | London (Covent Garden) | 18 Nov. 1754 |
| *Bertoldo, Bertoldino e Cacasenno* | Alboino | Ciampi | London (Covent Garden) | 9 Dec. 1754 |
| *\*The Fairies* | Lysander | J. C. Smith | London (Drury Lane) | 3 Feb. 1755 |
| *Joseph* | Joseph | Handel | London (Covent Garden) | 28 Feb. 1755 |
| *\*Antigono* | | Mazzoni | Lisbon (Do Tejo) | Oct. 1755 |
| *Artaserse* | Arbace | Galuppi | Vicenza (Delle Grazie) | Aug. 1756 |
| *\*Catone in Utica* | Arbace | Ciampi | Venice (San Benedetto) | 26 Dec. 1756 |
| *\*Adriano in Siria* | Farnaspe | Brusa | Venice (San Benedetto) | Jan. 1757 |
| *\*Nitteti* | Sammete | Traetta | Reggio Emilia (Pubblico) | 29 Apr. 1757 |
| *Alessandro Severo* | Alessandro | pasticcio (Lotti) | Parma (Ducale) | Carnival 1758 |
| *\*Ricimero re di Goti* | Ricimero | Ferradini | Parma (Ducale) | Carnival 1758 |
| *Artaserse* | Arbace | Scolari | Venice (San Salvatore) | 4 May 1758 |
| *\*Olimpiade* | Licida | Traetta | Verona (Filarmonico) | Nov. 1758 |
| *\*Adriano in Siria* | Farnaspe | Borghi | Turin (Regio) | 26 Dec. 1758 |
| *\*Eumene* | Eumene | Mazzoni | Turin (Regio) | 27 Jan. 1759 |

(*Continued*)

TABLE A.I (CONTINUED)

| Title | Role | Composer | Location | Date / Season |
|---|---|---|---|---|
| *Alessandro nell'Indie* | Poro | Hasse | Lucca (Pubblico) | 14 Sept. 1759 |
| *Prologo: Li prodigi di Atlanta* | Apollo | De Majo | Naples (San Carlo) | 10 July 1760 |
| *Le feste d'Imeneo* | Amore, Cromi, Alceo | Traetta | Parma (Ducale) | 3 Sept. 1760 |
| *Artaserse* | Arbace | J. C. Bach | Turin (Regio) | 26 Dec. 1760 |
| *Tigrane* | Tigrane | Piccinni | Turin (Regio) | 10 Jan. 1761 |
| *Enea e Lavinia* | Enea | Traetta | Parma (Ducale) | 1 May 1761 |
| *L'isola disabitata* | Gernando | Jommelli | Ludwigsburg (Schloß) | 4 Nov. 1761 |
| *Semiramide* | Scitalce | Jommelli | Stuttgart (Herzoglichestheater) | 11 Feb. 1761 |
| *Il trionfo di Clelia* | Orazio | Hasse | Vienna (Burgtheater) | 27 Apr. 1762 |
| *Arianna* | Bacco | pasticcio (Gluck) | Laxenburg | 27 May 1762 |
| *Orfeo ed Euridice* | Orfeo | Gluck | Vienna (Burgtheater) | 5 Oct. 1762 |
| *Artaserse* | Arbace | G. Scarlatti | Vienna (Burgtheater) | 4 Jan. 1763 |
| *La Betulia liberata* | Ozia | Holzbauer | Vienna (Burgtheater) | 27 Feb. 1763 |
| *Il sogno di Scipione* | Scipione | Bonno | Vienna (Burgtheater) | 13 Mar. 1763 |
| *L'isola disabitata* | Gernando | Bonno | Vienna (Burgtheater) | 12 May 1763 |
| *Ifigenia in Tauride* | Oreste | Traetta | Vienna (Schönbrunn) | 4 Oct. 1763 |
| *Ezio* | Ezio | Gluck | Vienna (Burgtheater) | 26 Dec. 1763 |
| *Egeria* | Mercurio | Hasse | Vienna (Burgtheater) | 24 Apr. 1764 |
| *Alcide negli orti Esperidi* | Alcide | De Majo | Vienna (Burgtheater) | 7 June 1764 |
| *Olimpiade* | Megacle | Gaßmann | Vienna (Burgtheater) | 18 Oct. 1764 |
| *Il trionfo d'Amore* | Apollo | Gaßmann | Vienna (Schönbrunn) | 25 Jan. 1765 |

(*Continued*)

TABLE A.I (CONTINUED)

| Title | Role | Composer | Location | Date / Season |
|---|---|---|---|---|
| *Telemaco | Telemaco | Gluck | Vienna (Burgtheater) | 30 Jan. 1765 |
| *Romolo ed Ersilia | Romolo | Hasse | Innsbruck (Schloßtheater) | 6 Aug. 1765 |
| *Olimpiade | Megacle | Guglielmi/ Pampani/ Brusa | Venice (San Benedetto) | 26 Dec. 1766 |
| *Ezio | Ezio | Bertoni | Venice (San Benedetto) | Feb. 1767 |
| *Cantata a quattro voci | Apollo | Lucchesi | Venice (San Benedetto) | 11 Feb. 1767 |
| *Olimpiade | Megacle | Piccinni | Rome (Argentina) | Carnival 1768 |
| *Artaserse | Arbace | Sacchini | Rome (Argentina) | Carnival 1768 |
| *Narciso al fonte | | Mysliveček | Padua (Palazzo Abate Vigodarzere) | 1 Sept. 1768 |
| *Alessandro in Armenia | Alessandro | Borghi | Venice (San Benedetto) | 26 Nov. 1768 |
| Arianna e Teseo | Teseo | Galuppi | Venice (San Benedetto) | 26 Dec. 1768 |
| *Demofoonte | Timante | Mysliveček | Venice (San Benedetto) | Jan. 1769 |
| *Ruggiero | Ruggiero | Guglielmi | Venice (San Salvatore) | 3 May 1769 |
| Il re pastore | Aminta | Galuppi | Venice (San Salvatore) | summer 1769 |
| *Il trionfo di Clelia | Orazio | Bertoni | Padua (Nuovo) | 10 June 1769 |
| Olimpiade | Megacle | pasticcio (Piccinni) | London (King's) | 11 Nov. 1769 |
| *Ezio | Ezio | Guglielmi | London (King's) | 13 Jan. 1770 |
| La passione | Pietro | Jommelli | London (King's) | 1 Mar. 1770 |
| Acis and Galatea | | Handel | London (Drury Lane) | 16 Mar. 1770 |
| *Gioas re di Giuda | Gioas | J. C. Bach | London (King's) | 22 Mar. 1770 |
| Orfeo ed Euridice | Orfeo | pasticcio (Gluck) | London (King's) | 7 Apr. 1770 |
| Ruth | | Giardini | London (Lock Hospital) | 24 Apr. 1770 |

(Continued)

TABLE A.1 (CONTINUED)

| Title | Role | Composer | Location | Date / Season |
|---|---|---|---|---|
| *Artaserse | Arbace | Vento | London (Carlisle House) | 24 Jan. 1771 |
| The Death of Abel | | Piccinni | London (Covent Garden) | 6 Mar. 1771 |
| *The Resurrection | | Arnold | London (Covent Garden) | 15 Mar. 1771 |
| Il trionfo della fedeltà | Tirsi | Maria Antonia Walpurgis | Padua (Palazzo Dondi Orologio) | 14 June 1772 |
| Talestri, regina delle Amazoni | | Maria Antonia Walpurgis | Munich (Nymphenberg) | August 1772 |
| *Orfeo ed Euridice | Orfeo | Tozzi | Munich (Hoftheater) | 9 Jan. 1775 |
| *Artaserse | Arbace | Borghi | Venice (San Benedetto) | 26 Dec. 1775 |
| *Orfeo ed Euridice | Orfeo | Bertoni | Venice (San Benedetto) | 3 Jan. 1776 |
| *Gerusalemme trionfante | | Ricci | Padua (Convento del Santo) | 29 May 1781 |
| *Deucalione e Pirra | Deucalione | Callegari | Padua (accademia privata) | 6 Nov. 1781 |
| *Le virtù rivali | Clemenza | Alessandri | Padua (Nuovo) | 5 July 1783 |

*Appendix B*

GUADAGNI'S SALARY AT THE SANTO

---

THE MOST COMPLETE sequence of Guadagni's earnings comprises the payments made to him while he was employed at the Santo. (Information on his theatre salaries and *ex gratia* payments is patchy and inconsistent; the available details have been noted in the course of the biography.) His salary from the Santo does not merely establish his basic income during the years in question. Because the structure of the payments was based on his attendance at the five principal feasts, it shows what portion of each year he spent in Padua; the record is, therefore, helpful in tracking his travels across the continent, indicating the years in which he was predominantly in Padua (from 1776) and marking the years in which he was partly or wholly absent.

The sources for Guadagni's income from the Santo are taken from two manuscript sources. The *Libri di Atti e Parti dell'Archivio Antico dell'Arca* contains the deliberations of the governing body of the Santo—essentially the minutes of their meetings; a useful summary of these minutes is excerpted in *La cappella musicale antoniana di Padova nel secolo XVIII*, Boscolo and Pietribiasi (1997). A more complete listing of salaries is found in the *Giornali di cassa*, a day-by-day record of expenditure; this material has been investigated by Jolanda Dalla Vecchia, in *L'organizzazione della cappella musicale antoniana di Padova nel settecento* (1995).

The *Libri di Atti* give his salary in ducats; the daybooks cite it in Venetian lire. There was no unified currency in use throughout Italy in the eighteenth century. The most frequently-quoted currency units in the Veneto are the gold coins (zecchino, scudo, ducat), silver coins (lira, cassetto, soldo) and copper coins (denaro).

Some approximate equivalents:

1 zecchino = 1.5 ducats
1 ducat = 6.2 lire

TABLE B.1

Guadagni's salary at the Santo

| Year | Salary in ducats | Notes |
| --- | --- | --- |
| 1746 | 75 | Guadagni entered the Santo, July 1746 |
| 1747 | 37 | Salary reduced because of unauthorised absences |
| 1748 | 112 | Guadagni left the Santo and travelled to London |
| 1768 | 240 | Guadagni rejoined the Santo with a salary exceeding that of Vallotti and Tartini |
| 1769 | 320 | |
| | | In 1770 Guadagni received no salary as he was in England |
| 1771 | 80 | |
| 1772 | 400 | |
| 1773 | 320 | Guadagni's salary was reduced in 1773–1775 because of his visits to Munich |
| 1774 | 320 | |
| 1775 | 240 | |
| 1776 | 400 | |
| 1777 | 400 | |
| 1778 | 400 | |
| 1779 | 400 | |
| 1780 | 400 | |
| 1781 | 400 | |
| 1782 | 400 | |
| 1783 | 400 | |
| 1784 | 400 | |
| 1785 | 320 | In 1785 Guadagni suffered a stroke and was unable to fulfil his duties at the Santo. His salary would normally continue to be paid in full. However there were fluctuations. |
| 1786 | 320 | |
| 1787 | 400 | |
| 1788 | 320 | |
| 1789 | 430 | |
| 1790 | 400 | Guadagni petitioned the Santo to receive his salary in monthly instalments. |
| 1791 | 400 | |
| 1792 | 375 | The salary should have been paid in full up to the end of the year. |

*Appendix C*

A SELECTION OF DOCUMENTS

—

BAPTISMAL RECORD

Cosmus Guadagnus. Anno Domini millesimo septingentesimo vigesimo octavo, die lune, decima sexta mensii Februarii. Ego Camillus Bonius canonicus parochus ecclesie Cathedralis Laude baptizavi infantem hodiem manem natus ex Sebastiano Guadagno et Catharina Maura coniugibus huius parochie maiorii cui impositum fuit nomen Cosmus Caetanus. [16 February 1728]
In *Liber baptismatorum ab anno 1719 usque ad anno 1732,* xii, p. 106r, Archivio Parrocchio, Lodi

ADMISSION TO THE CAPPELLA MUSICALE ANTONIANA, 1746

Sentito in prova sugli Organi il Signor Gaetano Guadagni contralto, che desidera esser assunto al servizio della V[eneran]da Arca, ed essendo stato riconosciuto idoneo per parere anche del Maestro di Cappella, fu proposta parte di assumerlo in Cappella come contralto con uno stipendio di ducati 150 annui, e di rimborsagli le spese di viaggio da Cremona a Padova. La parte fu approvata all'unanimità. [5 July 1746]
In *Atti e Parti,* vol 30, fo. 124v–125r, Archivio Antico della Veneranda Arca del Santo

ADMISSION TO THE CAPPELLA MUSICALE ANTONIANA, 1768

(1) Fu letta la supplica con cui Gaetano Guadagni contralto chiede di essere assunto in Cappella con lo stesso stipendio annuale di Mariano Nicolini, morto recentemente, di d.ti 400 pagabili in 5 rate di d.ti 80 l'una. Egli si impegna a cantare nelle cinque principali funzioni dell'anno e in quelle con l'intervento orchestrale, di avvisare la Presidenza nel caso fosse invitato a cantare nelle corti estere e, in caso di sua mancanza, si contenta di perdere un'intera rata per ciascuna

delle funzioni principali, e di soggiacere alle solite pontadure. Avendo i Presidenti riflettuto sulla fama e virtù del musicista, attestata dal Maestro di Cappello, sarebbero intenzionati a riceverlo, ma non lo possono eleggere senza il permesso pubblico, tanto più che, accordandogli i suddetti d.ti 400, la somma di d.to 4000 fissata dai pubblici decreti per la musica verebbe oltrepassata di d.ti 18. Fu perciò proposta parte di incaricare i Presidenti alla Chiesa di sottoporre la supplica al Provveditore perché la trasmetta al Consiglio dei Dieci e si conoscano quindi le pubbliche deliberazioni. La parte fu approvata all'unanimità. [30 April 1768]

*Atti e Parti*, vol. 32, fo. 152r–153r.

(2) Essendo stata concessa alla Presidenza con le ducali del Consiglio dei Dieci del 4 maggio 1768, la facoltà di assumere in Cappella il célèbre contralto Gaetano Guadagni, fu approvata all'unanimità la proposta di assumerlo con uno stipendio annuo di d.ti 400, pagabili in 5 rate di d.ti 80 ciascuna, ognuna dopo ciascuna delle principali funzioni. In caso di assenza dale principali funzioni, per ciascuna di esse perderà una rata, che dovrà restare nella cassa della V. Arca, e se mancherà alle alter funzioni musicali con intervento orchestrale sarà soggetto alle solite pontadure; e come si ricava dalla sua supplica del 30 aprile scorso, comincerà a percepire il suo stipendio a partire dal 10 maggio corrente. [16 May 1768]

*Atti e Parti*, vol. 32, fo. 155r–156r.

(3) Il 16 maggio scorso fu assunto in Cappella Gaetano Guadagni contralto, con l'obbligo di cantare nelle cinque principali funzioni, come nella sua supplica del 30 aprile scorso. Ma non essendo stato precisato quail sono tali funzioni a scanso di equivoci i Presidenti dichiarono che si tratta del giorno della S. Lingua, della Pasqua, della Pentecoste, della domenica fra l'ottava del Santo, tutti mattina (messa) e dopopranzo (vespro); della sera della vigilia di Natale (messa) e della mattina del giorno di Natale (messa). Riguardo poi al suo stipendio, che in ordine alla supplica suddetta dovrebbe essere pagato in cinque rate di d.ti 80 ciascuna, i Presidenti stabilirono che esso sia pagato ogni tre mesi come agli altri salariati, con d.ti 80 al trimestre e con d.ti 160 nell'ultimo trimestre, per un totale di d.ti 400 annui. In caso di mancanza alle principali funzioni, gli verranno trattenuti d.ti 80 per ciascuna di esse, e nell'ultimo trimestre gli saranno anche le pontadure relative a tutte le funzioni dell'anno con l'intervento orchestrale. [6 August 1768]

*Atti e Parti,* vol. 32, fo. 161r–162r.

### GUADAGNI'S WILL

26 settembre 1792: Padova. Considerando io Kavalier Gaetano Guadagni non esservi a questo Mondo cosa più certa della Morte, né più incerta dell'ora di quella; perciò sino attanto mi ritrovo di sincero e lucido intelletto, ho pensato di voler disporre delle cose mie, e di scrivere le mie ultime volontà di propria mia mano, lo quale sarà vinco da me sottoscritto a facciata per facciata debba in qualunque tempo, e caso da riportare la sua inviolabile esecuzione.

E prima di ogni cosa raccomando l'anima al Signore Dio, alla B.V.M., a Sant'Antonio, al Santo del mio nome, e a tutta la Corte Celestiale acchioché m'intercedano grazie verso sua Divina Maestà nel momento estremo della mia morte d'esser fatta degna dell'eterna Beatitudine. Il mio corpo fatto cadavere intendo e voglio sii posto nella Chiesa del glorioso Sant'Antonio pregando li N.N.P.P. [Nobili Padri] di volermi accogliere in detta chiesa, e farmi posare in quell'Arca che crederanno più opportuna.

Il mio Funeral dovrà esser fatto nel modo seguente: incaricando il mio commissario et erede di eseguirlo fedelmente, cioè avante dodeci preti con l'elemosine di L.2 per cadauno, e una candella di L.1 per ciasche d'uno; così pure L.4 Ospitali, cioè Orfani, Orfane, Mendicanti e Mendicante con la solita elemosine e con una candella di mezza lira per ciasche d'uno e ciasche d'una di ogni Ospitale. Così pure dodici dei R.R.P.P. [Reverendi Padri] di detta chiesa di Sant'Antonio, alli quali dovranno esser due candelle per cadauno, al Cataletto 8 torce di L.4 l'una che saranno portate da 8 preti.

Mi saranno celebrate Messe 100 con Elemosine di L.2 l'una, e una Massa cantata alla presenza del mio cadavere. Lascio per ragione di pagato all'illustrissimo Signor Giovanni Sografi, Publ.° professore li fornimenti delle due camere di primo solaro riguardanti il giardino con tutto ciò che si trova esser nelle stesse il giorno della mia morte in grata riconoscenza di quanto fece per me nella mia malattia. Idem lascio per ragion di pagato a Girolamo Gambaro mio cameriere tutto il mio vestiario in premio della fedele servitù sempre portatami.

Seguita la mia Morte sarà dal mio commissario ed erede fatto fare dal Signor Francesco Fanzago Notaio un esatto inventario di tutto per cauzione dei miei creditori. Erede poi universale residuario di tutti i miei beni, effetti, mobili, azioni, ragioni e crediti che tengo tanto da S. E. il Marchese Carlo Spinola, e dal Negozio Guadagni, e da qualunque altra persona suppositi tutti li miei debiti, e Legati, e Funerale, intendo e voglio che sia il Signor Vincenzo Guadagni mio carissimo Nipote, e se mancasse di vita avanti di me, sostituisco il pio Ospedale degli Infermi di questa Città.

Commissario esecutore di questa mia disposizione prego essere l'illustrissimo Sig. Giovanni Sografi, Publico Professore. E questo intendo e voglio sia il mio ultimo Testamento, e ultima volontà, annulando qualunque altro disposizione che [?] fatta volando che la [?] abbia per causo di morta riport[?] la sua occasione cioè a Gloria di Dio. [26 September 1792]

In Notarile F. Fanzago, ff. 20–22, Archivio di Stato di Padova.

# BIBLIOGRAPHY

Alfieri, Benedetto. *Il nuovo teatro di Torino*. Turin: Stamperia Reale, 1761.

Algarotti, Francesco. *Saggio sopra l'opera in musica* (Liverno, 1763), translated (anon.) as *An Essay on the Opera* (London, 1768). Edited by Robin Burgess. Lampeter and New York: Edwin Mellen Press, 2005.

Anon. *Dei magnifici spettacoli, altre feste, e spezialmente della sontuosa regatta del 3 giugno 1767 istituita ad onorare il soggiorno in Venezia di Sua Altezza Sereniss. Carlo Eugenio Duca di Vittemberga, Teck ecc*. Venice, 1767.

Arnold, Denis. 'Charity music in 18th-century Dublin.' *Galpin Society Journal* 21 (1968): 62–174.

Balatri, Filippo. *Frutti del mondo*. Edited by Karl Vosser. Naples: Sandron, 1924.

Barbier, Patrick. *Histoire des Castrats*. Paris: Grasset, 1989. Translated by Margaret Crosland as *The World of the Castrati*. London: Souvenir Press, 1988.

Barbier, Patrick. *La Maison des Italiens*. Paris: Grasset, 1998.

Barbieri, Patrizio. 'The acoustics of Italian opera houses and auditoriums, ca. 1450–1900.' *Recercare* 10 (1998): 263–328.

Baretti, Giuseppe Marc' Antonio. *An Account of the Manners and Customs of Italy; with observations on the mistakes of some travellers, with regard to that country*. 2 vols. Dublin, 1769.

Barezzani, Maria Teresa Rosa. 'L'opera in musica.' In *La musica a Brescia nel settecento*. Edited by Attilio Mazza. Brescia: Grafo, 1980.

Barnett, Dene. 'The Performance Practice of Acting: the Eighteenth Century.' *Theatre Research International* 2 (1977): 157–86, 3(1977): 1–19, 4(1977): 79–93, 5(1978–1980): 1–36, 6(1980–81): 1–32.

Barnett, Dene. *The Art of Gesture: the Practices and Principles of 18th century Acting*. Heidelberg: Winter, 1987.

Basso, Alberto. *Storia del Teatro Regio di Torino.* 5 vols. Turin: Cassa di Risparmio di Torino, 1976–1988.

Basso, Alberto. *Musica in scena: storia dello spettacolo musicale.* 6 vols. Turin: Unione Tipografico-Editrice Torinese, 1995–1997.

Bauman, Thomas. 'The Eighteenth Century: Serious Opera.' In *The Oxford Illustrated History of Opera.* Edited by Roger Parker. Oxford: Oxford University Press, 1994, pp. 47–83.

Bellina, Anna Laura. 'Appunti sul repertorio padovano.' In Paolo Pinamonti (ed.), *Mozart, Padova e la Betulia liberata: Committenza, interpretazione e fortuna delle azioni sacre metastasiane nel '700. Quaderni della Rivista italiana di musicologia* 24. Florence: Leo S. Olschki, 1991, pp. 173–90.

Bérard, Jean-Antoine. *L'Art du Chant.* Paris, 1755.

Bianconi, Lorenzo, and Giorgio Pestelli, eds. *Opera Production and Its Resources.* Translated by Lydia G. Cochrane. Chicago and London: University of Chicago Press, c. 1998.

Bianconi, Lorenzo, and Giorgio Pestelli, eds. *Opera on Stage.* Translated by Kate Singleton. Chicago and London: University of Chicago Press, 2002.

Bianconi, Lorenzo, and Giorgio Pestelli, eds. *Opera in Theory and Practice, Image and Myth.* Translated by Kenneth and Mary Whittall. Chicago and London: University of Chicago Press, 2003.

Boscolo, Lucia, and Maddalena Pietribiasi. *La capella musicale antoniana.* Padua: Centro studi antoniani, 1997.

Bouquet, Marie-Thérèse. *Il teatro di corte dalle origini al 1788. (Storia del Teatro Regio di Torino, vol. 1.)* Turin: Cassa di Risparmio di Torino, 1976.

Boydell, Brian. *A Dublin Musical Calendar 1700–1760.* Blackrock: Irish Academic Press, 1988.

Boydell, Brian. 'The Dublin musical scene 1749–50 and its background.' *Journal of the Royal Musical Association* 105 (1978–79): 77–89.

Brito, Manuel Carlos de. *Opera in Portugal in the Eighteenth Century.* Cambridge: Cambridge University Press, 1989.

Brizi, Bruno. 'Per una lettera. dell'Alceste di Gluck.' In Paolo Pinamonti (ed.), *Mozart, Padova e la Betulia liberata: Committenza, interpretazione e fortuna delle azioni sacre metastasiane nel '700. Quaderni della Rivista italiana di musicologia* 24. Florence: Leo S. Olschki, 1991, pp. 245–71.

Brosses, Charles de. *Lettre d'Italie sur les spectacles et la musique.* Paris: Librairie La Flute de Pan, 1980.

Brown, Bruce Alan. *Gluck and the French Theatre in Vienna.* Oxford: Clarendon Press, 1991.

Brown, Bruce Alan. ' "Mon opéra italien": Giacomo Durazzo and the genesis of *Alcide al bivio'.* In *Pietro Metastasio: uomo universale (1698–1782), Festgabe der Österreichischen Akademie der Wissenschaften zum 300. Geburtstag von Pietro Metastasio.* Edited by Andrea Sommer-Mathis and Elisabeth Theresia Hilscher. Vienna: Verlag der Österreichischen Akademie der Wissenschaften, 2000, pp. 115–42.

Brumana, Biancamaria. 'Fortuna e modelli compositivi della Passione tra Jommelli, Paisiello e Morlacchi.' *Musica e stori,* 9.1 (2001): 199–224.

Brunelli, Bruno. *I teatri di Padova dalle origini alla fine del secolo XIX.* Padua: Draghi, 1921.

Burden, Michael. 'Metastasio's "London Pasties": Curate's egg or pudding's proof?' In *Pietro Metastasio uomo universale (1698–1782), Festgabe der Österreichischen Akademie der Wissenschaften zum 300. Geburtstag von Pietro Metastasio.* Edited by Andrea Sommer-Mathis and Elisabeth Theresia Hilscher. Vienna: Verlag der Österreichischen Akademie der Wissenschaften, 2000, pp. 293–309.

Burden, Michael. 'Metastasio on the London Stage, 1728 to 1840: A Catalogue.' *Royal Musical Association Research Chronicle* 40 (2007): 1–365.

Burney, Charles. *Music, Men and Manners in France and Italy*. London, 1771.

Burney, Charles. *The Present State of Music in France and Italy*. 2nd ed. London, 1773.

Burney, Charles. *The Present State of Music in Germany, the Netherlands, and United Provinces.* 2nd ed. London, 1775.

Burney, Charles. *A General History of Music*. Edited by Frank Mercer. New York: Dover, 1957.

Burney, Charles. *Dr Burney's Musical Tours in Europe*. 2 vols. Edited by Percy Scholes. Oxford: Oxford University Press, 1959.

Burney, Charles. *Memoirs of Dr. Charles Burney 1726–1769*. Edited by Slava Klima, Garry Bowes and Kerry S. Grant. Lincoln and London: University of Nebraska Press, 1988.

Burrows, Donald, and Rosemary Dunhill. *Music and Theatre in Handel's World: The Family Papers of James Harris, 1732–1780*. Oxford: Oxford University Press, 2002.

Buschmeier, Gabriele. 'Ezio in Prag und Wien: Bemerkungen zu den beiden Fassungen von Glucks Ezio.' In *Gluck in Wien: Kongressbericht Wien 1987*. Edited by Gerhard Croll and Monika Woitas. Kassel: Bärenreiter, 1989, pp. 85–88.

Busi, Leonida. *Il padre G. B. Martini… Notizie raccolte da L. Busi*. Bologna: Zanichelli, 1891.

Butler, Margaret R. *Operatic Reform at Turin's Teatro Regio*. Lucca: Libreria Musicale Italiana, 2001.

Caffi, Francesco. *Storia della musica sacra nella già cappella ducale di S Marco in Venezia*. Venice: Antonelli, 1855.

Calzabigi, Ranieri de'. 'Dissertazione di Ranieri de' Calzabigi, dell'Accademia di Cortona, su le poesie drammatiche del sig. Abate Pietro Metastasio'. In *Poesie del Signor Abate Pietro Metastasio*, Paris, 1755.

Cappelletto, Sandro. 'Un astro del belcanto.' *Nuova rivista musicale italiana* 27.2 (1993): 195–204.

Casanova, J. de Seingalt. *Histoire de ma vie*. 12 vols. Paris: La Sirène, 1924.

Cattelan, Paolo. 'La musica della "omnigena religio": accademie musicali a Padova nei secondo Settecento.' *Acta musicologica* 59.2 (1987): 152–86.

Cattelan, Paolo. 'Altri Orfei di Gaetano Guadagni.' Preface to Ferdinando Bertoni, *Orfeo*. Milan: Ricordi, 1989, ix-cxliv.

Cattelan, Paolo. 'G. Ferrandini, musicista Padovano.' In Paolo Pinamonti (ed.), *Mozart, Padova e la Betulia liberata: Committenza, interpretazione e fortuna delle azioni sacre metastasiane nel '700. Quaderni della Rivista italiana di musicologia* 24. Florence: Leo S. Olschki, 1991, pp. 217–44.

Chard, Chloe. 'Effeminacy, pleasure and the classical body', in *Femininity and Masculinity in Eighteenth-century Art and Culture*. Edited by Gill Perry and Michael Rossington. Manchester: Manchester University Press, 1994, pp. 142–61.

Cibber, Colley. *A Critical Edition of An Apology for the Life of Mr. Colley Cibber, Comedian*. Edited by John Maurice Evans. New York and London: Garland, 1987.

Cicali, Gianni. *Attori e ruoli nell'opera buffa italiana del settecento*. Florence: Le Lettere, 2005.

Clapton, Nicholas. *Moreschi: The Last Castrato*. London: Haus, 2004.

Collé, Charles. *Journal et Mémoires*. Edited by Honoré Bonhomme. Paris: Firmin Didot, 1868.

Cooper, Anthony Ashley. *Letters of the Earl of Shaftesbury, author of The Characteristicks, collected in one volume*. Glasgow[?], 1746.

Corri, Domenico. *A Select Collection of the Most Admired Songs, Duetts, etc from Operas in the Highest Esteem*. Edinburgh: J. Corri, 1779.

Corri, Domenico. *The Singer's Preceptor*. London, 1810.

Cramer, Carl Friedrich, ed. *Magazine der Musik*. Hamburg, 1786.

Croce, Benedetto. *I teatri di Napoli, secolo XV–XVIII*. Naples: L. Pierro, 1891.

Croll, Gerhard. 'Musiker und Musik in der Privatkorrespondenz von Wenzel Anton Fürst von Kaunitz.' In *Staatskanzler Wenzel Anton von Kaunitz-Rietberg 1711–1794*. Edited by Grete Klingenstein and Franz Szabo. Graz: Schneider, 1996, pp. 341–59.

Cumberland, Richard. *Memoirs of Richard Cumberland*. London, 1806.

Dalla Vecchia, Jolanda. 'Cantanti e strumentalisti nei Settecento: La Cappella Antoniana a Padova.' *Rassegna Veneta di Studi Musicali* 9–10 (1993–94): 131–68.

Dalla Vecchia, Jolanda. *L'organizzazione della cappella musicale antoniana di Padova nel settecento*. Padua: Centro studi antoniani, 1995.

Dean, Winton. *Handel's Dramatic Oratorios and Masques*. London: Oxford University Press, 1959.

Dean, Winton. *Handel and the Opera Seria*. London: Oxford University Press, 1970.

Delany, Mary. *The Autobiography and Correspondence of Mary Granville, Mrs Delany*. Edited by The Right Honourable Lady Llanover. London: Richard Bentley, 1861.

De La Platière, Roland. *Lettres écrites de Suisse, d'Italie, de Sicile et de Malthe. Par M\*\*\*, Avocat en Parlement. à Mlle. \*\* à Paris, en 1776, 1777 & 1778*. Amsterdam, 1780.

Diderot, Denis. *Paradoxe sur le comédien*. Edited by Frantz André Burguet. Paris: Gallimard, 1966.

Durante, S. and Pietro Petrobelli. *Storia della musica al Santo di Padova*. Vicenza: Pozza, 1990.

Fanzago, Francesco Luigi. *Elogi di G. Tartini, Vallotti, e Gozzi*. Padua, 1792.

Feldman, Martha. *Opera and Sovereignty: Transforming Myths in Eighteenth-Century Italy*. Chicago and London: University of Chicago Press, 2007.

Fétis, Francois Joseph. *Biographie universelle des musiciens, et bibliographie generale de la musique*. Paris, 1833; 2nd ed., Paris, 1860–1866; *Supplement et complement* edited by Arthur Pougin. Paris, 1878–1880.

Findlen, Paula, Wendy Ryworth and Catherine Sama, eds. *Italy's Eighteenth Century: Culture and Gender in the Age of the Grand Tour*. Stanford: Stanford University Press, 2009.

Fiske, Roger. *English Theatre Music in the Eighteenth Century*. 2nd ed. Oxford: Oxford University Press, 1986.

Forkel, Johann Nicolaus. *Musikalischer Almanach für Deutschland*. Leipzig, 1783.

Frati, Vasco, ed. *Il teatro grande di Brescia*. 2 vols. Brescia: Il Teatro, 1985.

Freitas, Roger. 'The Eroticism of Emasculation: Confronting the Baroque Body of the Castrato.' *Journal of Musicology*, 20 (2003): 196–249.

Freitas, Roger. *Portrait of a Castrato: Politics, Patronage, and Music in the Life of Atto Melani*. Cambridge: Cambridge University Press, 2009.

Fürstenau, Moritz. 'Glucks *Orpheus* in München 1773.' *Monatshefte für Musikgeschichte* 4 (1872): 218–24.

Gennari, Giuseppe. *Notizie giornaliere di quanto avvenne specialmente in Padova dall'anno 1739 all'anno 1800*. 2 vols. Edited by Loredana Olivato. Cittadella: Rebellato, 1982.

Gerber, Ernst Ludwig. *Historisch-biographisches Lexicon der Tonkünstler* (Leipzig, 1790). Edited by Othmar Wessely. Graz: Akademische Druck und Verlagsanstalt, 1977.

Goldoni, Carlo. *Mémoires*. 3 vols. Paris, 1787.

Goring, Paul. *The Rhetoric of Sensibility in 18th-century Culture*. Cambridge: Cambridge University Press, 2005.

Grant, Kerry S. 'Dr Burney, the Bear, and the Knight: E. F. Burney's *Amateurs of Tye-Wig Music*.' In *Opera and the Enlightenment*. Edited by Thomas Bauman and Marita Petzoldt McClymonds. Cambridge: Cambridge University Press, 1995, pp. 43–60.

Gratton Flood, W. H. 'Fishamble St. Music Hall, Dublin, 1741–1777.' *Sammelbände der Internationalen Musikgesellschaft* 14 (1912–13): 51–57.

Grossato, Elisa. 'Le accademie musicale a Padova.' In Paolo Pinamonti (ed.), *Mozart, Padova e la Betulia liberata: Committenza, interpretazione e fortuna delle azioni sacre metastasiane nel '700. Quaderni della Rivista italiana di musicologia* 24. Florence: Leo S. Olschki, 1991, pp. 191–208.

Gumpenhuber, Philipp. 'Repertoire de tous les Spectacles qui ont été donné au Theatre pres de la Cour depuis le 1er Janvier jusqu'au dernier Decembre de l'An 1761.' Band b: 1762, Band c: 1763. *Ms.* Österreichische Nationalbibliothek, Vienna, Musiksammlung Mus. Hs. 34580 a–c.

Haböck, Franz. *Die Kastraten und ihre Gesangskunst. Eine gesangsphysiologische, kultur- und musikhistorische Studie.* Edited by Martina Haböck. Berlin and Leipzig: Deutsche Verlagsanstalt, 1927.

Hadamowsky, Franz. 'Leitung, Verwaltung und ausübende Künstler des Deutschen und Französichen Schauspiels.' *Jahrbuch der Gesellschaft für Wiener Theaterforschung* 12 (1960): 113–33.

Hansell, Sven H. 'Stage deportment and scenographic design in the Italian opera seria of the settecento.' *International Musicological Society Congress Report* 1 (1972): 415–24.

Hasse, Johann Adolf, e Giammaria Ortes. *Lettere (1760–1783)*. Edited by Livia Pancino. Turnhout: Brepols, 1998.

Heartz, Daniel. 'Orfeo ed Euridice: Some criticisms, revisions, and stage-realizations during Gluck's lifetime.' *Chigiana* 9–10 (1975): 383–94.

Heartz, Daniel. 'Nicolas Jadot and the building of the Burgtheater.' *Musical Quarterly*, 68.1 (1982): 1–31.

Heartz, Daniel. 'Traetta in Vienna: *Armida* (1761) and *Ifigenia in Tauride* (1763).' *Studies in Music*. Ontario: University of Western Ontario Press, 1982.

Heartz, Daniel, *Music in European Capitals*. New York: Norton, 2003.

Heartz, Daniel. *From Garrick to Gluck*. Edited by Daniel Heartz and John A. Rice. Hillsdale, NY: Pendragon, 2004.

Heier, Edmund. *L. H. Nicolay (1737–1820) and His Contemporaries*. The Hague: Martinus Nijhoff, 1965.

Helfert, Vladimir. 'Dosud Neznámý Dopis Ran. Calsabigiho z r. 1767.' *Musikologie* 1 (1938): 114–22.

Heriot, Angus. *The Castrati in Opera*. London: Calder, 1960.

Highfill, Philip H. Jr, Kalman A. Burnim, and Edward A. Langhans, eds. *A Biographical Dictionary of Actors, Actresses, Musicians, Dancers, Managers & Other Stage Personnel in London, 1660–1800*. Carbondale and Edwardsville: Southern Illinois University Press, 1973–1993.

Holmes, William C. *Opera Observed: Views of a Florentine Impresario in the Early Eighteenth Century*. Chicago and London: University of Chicago Press, 1993.

Howard, Patricia. *Gluck: An Eighteenth-century Portrait in Letters and Documents*. Oxford: Clarendon Press, 1995.

Howard, Patricia. 'For the English. *Orfeo* in London in 1773: A reconstruction.' *Musical Times* 137 (1996): 13–15.

Howard, Patricia. 'Did Burney Blunder?' *Musical Times* 139 (1998): 29–32.

Howard, Patricia. 'Guadagni in the Dock.' *Early Music*, 27.1 (1999): 87–95.

Howard, Patricia. '"Mr Justice Blindman" and the "Priestess of Fashion".' *Il Saggiatore musicale* 7.1 (2000): 47–59.

Howard, Patricia. *In Defence of Modern Music and Its Celebrated Performers: A Translation and Critical Edition of Vincenzo Manfredini, 'Difesa della music moderna' (1788)*. Lampeter and New York: Edwin Mellen Press, 2002.

Howard, Patricia. 'Happy birthday, Cosimo Gaetano Guadagni!' *Musical Times* 148 (2007): 93–96.

Howard, Patricia. 'No equal on any stage in Europe: Guadagni as Actor.' *Musical Times* 151 (2009): 9–21.

Howard, Patricia. 'Orpheus on a Shoestring: Guadagni's Marionette Theatre.' *Il Saggiatore musicale* 17.1 (2010): 5–18.

Howard, Patricia. 'The castrato composes: Guadagni's setting of "Pensa a serbarmi, o cara".' *Musical Times* 154 (2012): 3–30.

Howard, Patricia. 'Castrato.' In *Oxford Bibliographies in Music*. Edited by Bruce Gustafson. New York: Oxford University Press (forthcoming).

Ivaldi, Armando Fabio. '"Magnificenza, e buon gusto inarrivabili": La villa e il teatrino di Giacomo Durazzo a Mestre.' *Nuova Rivista Musicale Italiana* 2 (2012): 181–204.

Ivaldi, Armando Fabio. 'Un problematico *Orfeo* "cantato" a Genova nel 1780'. *Encomium Musices: Contribuiti di musicologia, bibliografia, e di varia umanità. Studi per Saverio Franchi*. Rome: Ibimus (forthcoming).

Kelly, Michael. *The Reminiscences of Michael Kelly*. 2 vols. London: Colburn, 1826.

King, Richard G. and Saskia Willaert. 'Giovanni Francesco Crosa and the first Italian comic operas in London'. *Journal of the Royal Musical Association* 118 (1993): 246–75.

Klingenstein, Grete and Franz Szabo, eds. *Staatskanzler Wenzel Anton von Kaunitz-Rietberg 1711–1794*. Graz: Schneider, 1996.

Korsmeier, Claudia Maria. *Der Sänger Giovanni Carestini (1700–1760) und 'seine' Komponisten: die Karriere eines Kastraten in der ersten Hälfte des 18. Jahrhunderts*. Eisenach: Wagner, 2000.

Kunz, Harald. 'Höfisches Theater in Wien zur Zeit der Maria Theresia.' *Jahrbuch der Gesellschaft für Wiener Theaterforschung* (1953–54): 3–113.

Lalande, Joseph Jérôme le Français de. *Voyage d'un français en Italie, fait dans les années 1765 et 1766*. 8 vols. Paris and Venice: Desaint, 1769.

Law, Joe K. 'Alessandro Moreschi Reconsidered: A Castrato on Records.' *The Opera Quarterly* 2.2 (1984): 1–12.

Lee, Vernon. *Althea*. London: Bodley Head, n.d.

Leopold, Silke. '"Not Sex but Pitch": Kastraten als Liebhaber—einmal über der Gürtellinie betrachtet.' In *Provokation und Tradition: Erfahrungen mit der Alten Musik*. Edited by Hans-Martin Linde and Regula Rapp. Weimar: J. B. Metzler, 2000, pp. 219–40.

Liebrecht, Henri. *Histoire du théâtre français à Bruxelles au XVIIe et XVIIIe siècles*. 2 vols. Paris: Edouard Champion, 1923.

Liesenfeld, V. J. *The Licensing Act of 1737*. Madison: University of Wisconsin Press, 1988.

Loewenberg, Alfred. *Annals of Opera, 1597–1940*. 2nd ed. New York: Rowman and Littlefield, 1970.

Lonsdale, Roger. 'Dr Burney's "Dictionary of Music".' *Musicology Australia* 5.1 (1979), p. 167.

Mamy, Sylvie. *Les grands Castrats napolitains à Venise au XVIIIe siècle*. Liege: Mardaga, 1994.

Mancini, Franco, Maria Teresa Muraro, and Elsa Povoledo. *I teatri del Veneto: Padova, Rovigo, e il loro territorio.* Vol. 3. Venice: Corbo e Fiore, 1988.

Mancini, Giambattista. *Pensieri e riflessioni pratiche sopra il canto figurato* (Vienna, 1774, 1777). Translated and edited by Edward Foreman as *Practical Reflections on Figured Singing.* Champaign, Ill.: Pro Musica Press, 1967.

Mangini, Nicola. *I teatri di Venezia.* Milan: Mursia, 1974.

Martina, Alessandra. *Orfeo—Orphée di Gluck: storia della trasmissione e della recezione.* Florence: De Sono, 1995.

Massaro, Maria Nevilla. 'La cappella musicale del Santo nella seconda metà del settecento.' In Paolo Pinamonti (ed.), *Mozart, Padova e la Betulia liberata: Committenza, interpretazione e fortuna delle azioni sacre metastasiane nel '700. Quaderni della Rivista italiana di musicologia* 24. Florence: Leo S. Olschki, 1991, pp. 209–16.

Mazza, Attilio, ed. *La musica a Brescia nel settecento.* Brescia: Grafo, 1980.

Mazzacani, Claudio. 'Lo stato degli studi dell'opera di F. G. Bertoni (1725–1813).' Brescia: Comunità Montana Parco Alto Garda Bresciano, 1997.

McCormick, John, and Bennie Pratasik. *Popular Puppet Theatre in Europe, 1800–1914.* Cambridge: Cambridge University Press, 1998.

McGeary, Thomas. 'Verse epistles on Italian opera singers.' *Royal Musical Association Research Chronicle* 33 (2000): 29–88.

Mellace, Raffaele. 'Il pianto di Pietro: Fortuna del tema e strategie drammaturgiche tra gli oratori viennesi e la Passione metastasiana.' *Musica e storia* 9.1 (2001): 145–75.

Metastasio, Pietro. *Lettere.* In *Tutte le opere di Pietro Metastasio,* vols. 3–5. Edited by Bruno Brunelli. Verona: Mondadori, 1951–1965. Also online at www.liberliber.it/mediateca/libri/m/metastasio/lettere_edizione_brunelli/pdf/letter_p.pdf

Mondroit, Isabelle. *L'opéra seria, ou, Le règne des castrats.* Paris: Fayard, 1993.

Mount Edgcumbe, Lord. *Musical Reminiscences.* 4th ed. London, 1834.

Mowl, Timothy. *Horace Walpole: The Great Outsider.* London: John Murray, 1996.

Nalbach, Daniel. *The King's Theatre, 1704–1867.* London: Society for Theatre Research, 1972.

Nicolay, Ludwig Heinrich von. *L. H. Nicolay, 1737–1820, and His Contemporaries.* Edited by Edmund Heier. The Hague: Martinus Nijhoff, 1965.

Nonni, Angelo. *Descrizione degli spettacole e feste datesi in Venezia per occasione della venuta delle LL. AA. Il Gran Duca e Gran Duchessa di Moscovia … nel mese di gennaio 1782.* Venice: Vincenzo Formaleoni, 1782.

Oldrini, Gasparo. *Storia della coltura laudense.* Lodi: Giulio Oldani, 1885.

Ortes, Gian Maria. [Letters to Hasse]. *Ms.* Museo Civico Correr, Venice: Cod. Cicogna 2658. A selection of the letters to Hasse and his family is published in Livia Pancino, *Johann Adolf Hasse e Giammaria Ortes: lettere (1760–1783),* Turnhout: Brepols, 1998.

Parke, William Thomas. *Musical Memoirs.* London: Colburn and Bentley, 1830.

Pepoli, Alessandro. 'Lettera ad un uomo ragionevole sul melodrama detto serio', preface to Pepoli, *Meleagro.* Venice, 1790.

Petrobelli, Pierluigi. *Giuseppe Tartini. Le fonti biografiche.* Venice: Fondazione Giorgi Cini, 1968.

[Pickering, Roger.] *Reflections upon Theatrical Expression in Tragedy.* London, 1755.

Pierre, Constant. *Histoire du Concert-Spirituel (1725–1790).* Paris: Heugel, 1975.

Pietrantoni, Laura. *Il palcoscenico ritrovato. Storia del teatro musicale a Lodi dal XVII al XX secolo.* Lodi: Il Papiro Editrice Altra Storia, 1933.

Pilot, A. *Feste e spettacoli per l'arrivo dei conti del Nord a Venezia nel 1782.* Venice: Scarabellin, 1914.

Pinamonti, Paolo, ed. *Mozart, Padova e la Betulia liberata: Committenza, interpretazione e fortuna delle azioni sacre metastasiane nel '700. Quaderni della Rivista italiana di musicologia* 24. Florence: Leo S. Olschki, 1991.

Planelli, Antonio. *Dell'opera in musica.* Fiesole: Discanto, 1981.

Rees, Abraham, ed. *The Cyclopaedia; or, Universal Dictionary of Arts, Sciences, and Literature.* London, 1802–1820, 39 vols.

Reid, Douglas J. and Brian Pritchard. 'Some festival programmes of the eighteenth and nineteenth centuries. I. Salisbury and Winchester.' *Royal Musical Association Research Chronicle* 5 (1965): 51–79.

Ricci, Giuliana. *Teatri d'Italia.* Milan: Bramante, 1971.

Robins, Brian. *Catch and Glee Culture in Eighteenth-Century England.* Woodbridge: Boydell Press, 2006.

Romagnoli, Sergio, and Elvira Garbero. *Teatro a Reggio Emilia.* 2 vols. Florence: Sansoni, 1980.

Rosenfeld, Sybil. *Foreign Theatrical Companies in Great Britain in the 17th and 18th Centuries.* London: Society for Theatre Research, 1955.

Rosselli, John. *The Opera Industry in Italy from Cimarosa to Verdi.* Cambridge: Cambridge University Press, 1984.

Rosselli, John. 'The castrati as a professional group.' *Acta musicologica* 60 (1988): 143–79.

Rosselli, John. *Singers of Italian Opera.* Cambridge: Cambridge University Press, 1992.

Sartori, Antonio, and Elisa Grossato. *Documenti per la storia della musica al Santo e nel Veneto.* Vicenza: Neri Pozza, 1997.

Sartori, Claudio. *I libretti italiani a stampa dalle origini al 1800.* 7 vols. Cuneo: Bertola and Locatelli, 1990–1994.

Savage, Richard. 'Staging an opera: Letters from the Cesarian poet.' *Early Music* 26.4 (1998): 583–95.

Schindler, Otto and Margret Dietrich. 'Das Publikum des Burgtheaters in der Josephinischen Ära.' In *Das Burgtheater und sein Publikum*, i, 1976 , pp. 11–95.

Scholderer, Hans-Joachim. *Das Schloßtheater Ludwigsburg: Geschichte, Architektur, Buhnentechnik.* Berlin: Gesellschaft für Theatergeschichte, 1994.

Scott, Alexander. Preface to *Alfred.* In *Musica Britannica* vol. 47. London: Stainer and Bell, 1981.

Scott, Michael. *The Record of Singing: To 1914.* London: Duckworth, 1974.

Selfridge-Field, Eleanor. *Song and Season: Science, Culture and Theatrical Time in Early Modern Venice.* Stanford: Stanford University Press, 2007.

Sharp, Samuel. *Letters from Italy, describing the Customs and Manners of that Country in the Years 1765 and 1766.* London, 1766.

Simek, Ursula. *Das Berufstheater in Innsbruck im 18. Jahrhundert.* Vienna: Verlag der Österreichischen Akademie der Wissenschaften, 1992.

Sittard, Josef. *Zur Geschichte der Musik und des Theaters am Württembergischen Hofe, 1458–1793.* Hildesheim and New York: Georg Olms, 1970.

Sonnenfels, Joseph von. *Briefe über die Wienerische Schaubühne.* Edited by Hilde Haider-Pregler. Graz: Akademische Druck- und Verlagsanstalt, 1988.

Tartini, Giuseppe. *Trattato di musica secondo la vera scienza dell'armonia.* Padua: Stamperia del Seminario, 1754.

Tenducci, Dora. *A True and Genuine Narrative of the Marriage and subsequent Proceedings of Mr and Mrs Tenducci*. London: Pridden, 1768.

Tocchini, Gerardo. *I fratelli d'Orfeo*. Florence: Olschki, 1998.

Tosi, Pier Francesco. *Opinioni de' cantori antichi e moderni* (Bologna, 1723). Translated by John Ernest Galliard as *Observations on the Florid Song* (London, 1743). Edited by Michael Pilkington. London: Stainer and Bell, 1987.

Tufano, Lucio. *I viaggi di Orfeo: Musiche e musicisti intorno a Ranieri Calzabigi*. Rome: Edicampus Edizioni, 2012.

Vallotti, Francescantonio. *Della scienza teorica e pratica della moderna musica*. Padua: Stamperia del Seminario, 1779.

Verti, Roberto, ed. *Un almanacco dramattico* [sic]: *Indice de' teatrali spettacoli*. Pesaro: Fondazione Rossini, 1996.

Victor, Benjamin. *The History of the Theatres of London and Dublin, from the Year 1730 to the Present Time*. Dublin, 1761.

Volkov, Nikolai. *La Secte russe des castrats*. Paris: Les Belles Lettres, 1995.

Walker, Frank. 'Orazio: The history of a pasticcio.' *Musical Quarterly* 38 (1952): 369–83.

Walpole, Horace. *Horace Walpole's Correspondence: The Yale Edition of Horace Walpole's Correspondence*. 48 vols. Edited by Wilmarth Sheldon Lewis. London: Oxford University Press, 1937–1983.

Walsh, T. J. *Opera in Dublin 1705–1797*. Dublin: Allen Figgis, 1973.

Wilkes, Thomas. *A General View of the Stage*. 2nd ed, London: Williams, 1762.

Woodfield, Ian. *Opera and Drama in 18th-c London*. Cambridge: Cambridge University Press, 2001.

Wurzbach, Constant von. *Biographisches Lexicon des Kaiserthums Oesterreich enthaltend die Lebenskizzen der denkwurdigen Personen, welche 1750 bis 1850 im Kaiserstaate und in seinen Kronlandern gelebt haben*. Vienna: K. K. Hof- und Staatsdruckerie, 1856–1891.

Yorke Long, Alan. *Music at Court*. London: Weidenfeld and Nicolson, 1954.

Zechmeister, Gustav. *Die Wiener Theater nächst der Burg und nächst dem Kärntnerthor von 1747 bis 1776*. Vienna: Böhlau Verlag, 1972.

Zinzendorf, Karl, Graf von. *Aus den Jugendtagebüchern 1747, 1752 bis 1763*. Edited by Maria Breunlich and Marieluise Mader. Vienna: Böhlau Verlag, 1997.

Zinzendorf, Karl, Graf von. 'Journal du Comte Charles de Zinzendorf et Pottendorf'. *Ms*. Haus- Hof- und Staatsarchiv, Vienna.

Zobel, Konrad and Frederick Warner. 'The old Burgtheater: a structural history 1741–1888.' *Theatre Studies* 19 (1972–73): 19–53.

# INDEX

Abel, Carl Friedrich, 132
Alessandri, Felice (husband of Lavinia Guadagni), 113, 116, 154, 183
Algarotti, Francesco, 70, 73, 74, 81, 211
Andreoni, Giovanni Battista, 45
Angiolini, Gasparo [Domenico Maria Angiolo Gasparini], 66, 100
Arne, Thomas Augustine, 52, 55–56, 124
Arnold, Samuel, 125, 133, 134
Auletta, Pietro, 30, 147

Bach, Johann Christian, 82, 90–91, 125, 126, 132, 139, 146, 159, 177, 179
Balatri, Filippo, 19
Barthélémon, François-Hippolyte, 124
Bath, 9, 48–49, 51, 53
Bertoni, Ferdinando Gasparo, 31, 45, 112–113, 121, 167
   *Ezio*, 152–154, 155
   *Orfeo ed Euridice*, 142, 144, 161, 163, 166, 177, 179, 184
Bianchi, Marianna (wife of Antonio Tozzi), 80, 88, 93, 98, 101, 102, 158, 159, 160
'Bologna score', 147, 148, 150
Bonno, Giuseppe, 103
Borghi, Giovanni Battista, 86, 120, 161
Bottarelli, Giovanni Gualberto, 126, 142, 177, 179

Brescia, 20, 81, 85
Brown, John, 150, 198–199, 200
Brusa, Giovanni Francesco, 82, 112
Burney, Charles, 4, 8–9, 16, 17, 29–30, 42, 45, 46, 64, 98, 118, 124, 125, 126, 155, 199, 211
   on Garrick, 65, 66, 69
   on Guadagni, 7, 8, 10, 11, 22, 43, 47, 56, 71, 74–75, 76, 78, 79, 80, 128, 135, 138, 139, 151, 152, 156–157, 159, 194, 195–196, 197, 201
   on theatres, 43–44, 81, 85, 87, 89, 92, 95
Burney, Fanny, 37, 131

Caffarelli, 1, 19, 33, 38, 59, 60, 61, 79, 80
Calegari, Antonio [Callegari], 170
Calzabigi, Ranieri de', 2, 56, 75, 81, 99, 127, 139, 142, 159, 177, 178, 179
   and the reform of opera, 1, 66, 96–7, 98, 100, 108, 128, 160, 200, 205–206, 211
Capua, Rinaldo da [di], 30,
Carestini, Giovanni, 1, 7, 138
Casanova, Giacomo, Chevalier de Seingalt, 39, 67, 131
castration
   church's attitude to, 18, 34
   effect on character of, 8, 34
   practice of, 17–18, 19

castrato
    in operatic roles, 38–39, 40–41, 197–8
    physical appearance of, 3, 36, 37, 191
    satirical treatment of, 34–35
    sexual appeal of, 34–36, 37–38, 39
    sexual performance of, 33–34. 35–36
Catch Club (The Noblemen and Gentlemen's
    Catch Club), 124, 130
Charke, Charlotte, 181
Chiabrano [Chabran], Carlo, 54, 57–59
Ciampi, Vincenzo, 28, 29, 31, 42, 43, 49, 51, 54,
    57–59, 61, 82, 199
Cibber, Colley, 42, 181
Cibber, Susanna, 47, 97
Clement XIII (Carlo Rezzonico), 85
Collé, Charles, 69
Coltellini, Marco, 1, 104, 106, 107, 160, 177
Cornelys, Teresa (Teresa Imer), 130–132
Corri, Domenico, 69, 101, 138–139
Croce, Benedetto, 88, 89, 194
Crosa, Giovanni Francesco [John Francis
    Croza], 26, 27–30
Cuzzoni, Francesca, 50, 51

De Amicis, Anna Lucia, 120, 121
Decayed Musicians' Fund, 31, 51, 54, 59,
    64, 124
Delany, Mary, 10, 52,
Delaval, Francis Blake, 32
Devizes, 47, 48, 51, 53
Diderot, Denis, 66, 72
Dublin, 2, 9, 10, 52–53, 56, 64, 201
Durastanti, Margherita, 39
Durazzo, Count Giacomo, 1, 15, 90, 94, 96, 97,
    98, 99, 102, 103, 104, 106–107, 110, 111, 211

Farinelli [Carlo Broschi], 1,10, 13, 34–35, 41, 46,
    74, 75, 84, 106
Ferrradini, Giovanni Battista, 84
Fétis, François-Joseph, 13, 16, 17, 26
Fielding, Sir John, 2, 4, 131–133
Francis I, Holy Roman Emperor and Grand
    Duke of Tuscany, 105
Frasi, Giulia, 4, 10, 28, 29, 31, 42, 43, 44, 45, 50,
    57–58, 64, 129, 134
Frugoni, Carlo Innocenzo, 66, 89, 90, 211

Gabrielli, Caterina, 4, 40, 84, 90
Galli, Caterina, 44, 48, 50
Galliari, Bernardino, 66

Galliari, Fabrizio, brother of Bernardino, 66
Galuppi, Baldassare, 61, 80, 84, 85, 106, 120,
    121, 155
Garrick, David, 28, 56, 62–3, 65, 66, 69–73, 98,
    129, 175
Gaßmann, Florian Leopold, 107, 108,
Giardini, Felice de, 54, 129, 131, 134
Giordani, Tommaso, 138
Gizziello [Gioacchino Conti] , 1, 19, 78–80, 197
Gluck, Christoph Willibald, Ritter von, 1, 8, 27,
    57–58, 66, 157, 196, 211, 212
    *Arianna*, 96
    *Enea e Ascanio*, 106
    *Ezio*, 7, 81, 105, 151, 152, 206–207
    *Le feste d'Apollo*, 127
    *Orfeo ed Euridice*, 2, 7, 13, 75–76, 96, 97, 98,
        99, 100–101, 103, 104, 125–126, 127, 137, 138,
        140–145,146, 158, 159, 162, 171, 176, 177, 179,
        184, 205, 207, 208–209, 211
    and the reform of opera, 94, 98, 128, 129, 139,
        151–152, 160, 161, 205
    *Il parnaso confuso*, 107
    *Telemaco*, 7, 107, 200
    *Tetide*, 89
Goethe, Johann Wolfgang von, 39, 74, 105, 173
Goldoni, Carlo, 42, 61, 67–68, 69, 84, 91, 116
Grassi, Cecilia, 121, 128
Guadagni, Angiola (older sister of Gaetano), 4,
    19, 20, 23, 80, 85, 113, 116
Guadagni, Anna (older sister), 19, 20, 23
Guadagni, Antonio (nephew), 117, 165, 186
Guadagni, Caterina (mother), 16, 19
Guadagni, Gaetano
    birth, 16–17
    admission to Santo, 20–21
    his house in London, 123
    his house in Padua, 116, 156, 166, 172–173,
        175–176
    knighthood, 157
    marionette theatre, 172–182
    participation in civic feasts, 4, 6, 85, 164–165,
        166–170, 171, 183–185
    return to Santo, 117–118, 155–156
    death, 189–191
Guadagni, Giuseppe (older brother), 19, 20, 23,
    25, 117
Guadagni, Lavinia (younger sister), 19, 20, 23, 75,
    106, 113, 116, 123
Guadagni, Sebastiano (father), 16, 19, 20, 187
Guadagni, Vincenzo (nephew), 117, 173, 181, 188

Guglielmi, Pietro Alessandro, 112, 121, 126, 135, 139, 146, 177
   *Ezio*, 124, 152–154, 194, 200, 202

Handel, George Frideric, 4, 31, 39, 40, 41, 48, 49, 50–51, 52, 54, 57–60, 62, 63, 138
   as formative influence on Guadagni, 2, 97–98, 127, 200–201
   on Guadagni's voice, 44–47, 194, 201–205
Hasse, Johann Adolf, 57, 60, 88, 89, 94,
   roles created for Guadagni, 75, 91, 93, 95, 104, 106, 108
Haydn, Joseph, 33, 96, 172
Hobart, George, 20, 121, 123–124,129, 130–133, 134
Holzbauer, Ignaz, 102

Jommelli, Nicolò, 1, 30, 31, 45, 92, 93, 96
   *L'isola disabitata*, 91
   *La passione*, 125
   *Semiramide*, 92

Kelly, Michael, 3, 67, 81, 86, 176, 177, 179, 181, 184

Laschi, Filippo, 28, 29, 42, 43, 66–67, 69, 75, 76
Latilla, Gaetano, 29, 31, 43
Le Gros, Joseph, 75–76, 81
Le Texier, Antoine, 74, 77, 129
Lisbon, 2, 78–80, 91, 113, 187, 197
Lodi, 2, 16–17, 20, 21, 28, 197
London
   Almack's Rooms, 134
   concert life in, 31, 54–55
   Covent Garden Theatre, 43, 44, 45, 46, 50, 54, 55, 56, 61, 78, 125, 133, 134
   Drury Lane Theatre, 43, 56, 62, 125,
   Foundling Hospital, 51, 56, 59, 64
   Great Room, Dean Street, 54, 56, 64
   Hickford's Room, Brewer Street, 50, 64
   King's Theatre, Haymarket, 20, 27, 29, 30, 31, 42, 43, 50, 54, 56, 59, 64, 66, 85, 101, 121, 123, 124, 125, 126, 127, 129, 130, 131, 134, 135, 152, 176, 177, 196
   Licensing Act and, 29, 130–134
   Little Theatre, Haymarket, 32, 42, 43, 44, 50, 62, 64
   Lock Hospital, 129, 134
   pasticcio operas in, 125–127, 141–142, 177, 179
   puppet shows in, 174–175, 180
   theatre prices in, 43–44, 85
Lucca, 84, 88

Lucchesi, Andrea, 113

Majo, Gian Francesco de, 88, 107
Mancini, Giambattista, 68, 71
Marchesi, Luigi, 1, 6, 183, 184
Maria Antonia Walpurgis, Dowager Electress of Saxony, 11, 155, 156–158, 194, 211
Maria Josepha of Saxony, Dauphine of France, 59
Maria Theresia, Empress of Austria, 95, 100, 103, 107, 108
Mazzoni, Antonio, 79, 86
Memmo, Andrea, 164, 185
Metastasio, Pietro [Antonio Domenico Bonaventura Trapassi], 23, 43, 56, 79, 80, 81, 86, 91, 93, 101–102, 103, 106, 107, 108, 121, 125, 146, 152, 153, 200
   as dramatist, 70, 73
   on singers, 10, 75, 84, 106
Migliavacca, Giovanni Ambrogio, 96, 104
Millico, Giuseppe, 37, 81, 127, 138, 141, 185, 196–197, 200
Moreschi, Alessandro, 18, 192–193
Mount Edgcumbe, Richard, 2nd Earl, 172, 175, 176, 181
Mozart, Leopold, 159
Mozart, Wolfgang Amadeus, 96, 159
Munich, 2, 7, 10, 11, 14, 76, 135, 143, 156–157, 158–159, 160, 162, 166, 177, 211
Mysliveček, Josef, 118, 119, 121

Naples, 18, 23, 30, 31, 81, 82, 86, 88–89, 115, 181, 194
Nasolini, Antonio (husband of Angiola Guadagni), 20, 113, 116, 163, 170, 179, 186
Nicolini, Carlo, 95, 103
Noverre, Jean-Georges, 66, 92

opera seasons, 81, 87, 91, 95

Pacchierotti [Pacchiarotti], Gasparo, 8, 13, 167, 176, 190
Padua, 4, 16–17, 85, 86, 155, 158, 159, 169
   Prato della Valle, 164, 185
   private concerts in, 118–119, 122, 142, 161, 169, 170, 171, 177, 179, 184, 185
   Santo, 20, 21, 116, 162, 164, 171, 184, 186, 190–191
   Teatro Nuovo, 81, 84, 121, 164, 183–184
   Teatro Obizzi, 163, 164
Palomba, Antonio, 30
Pampani, Antonio Gaetano, 112
Paradies, Domenico, 50

Paris, 11, 56, 61, 68, 75–76, 78–79, 81, 83, 99,
    107, 137
    castratos in, 60
    Concert Spirituel, 60, 61
Parma, 9, 26, 84, 89, 91, 96, 141, 196
Passerini, Christina (wife of Giuseppe),
    54, 63–64
Passerini, Giuseppe, 54, 55, 58–59,
Pergolesi, Giovanni Battista, 30, 43, 52, 59, 60,
    61, 125
Pertici, Pietro, 28, 29, 30, 31, 42, 66, 67, 68,
    69, 75, 98
Philidor, François-André-Danican, 55, 57, 61
Piatti, Lorenzo, 163, 170, 179
Piccinni, Niccolò, 82, 91, 106, 116, 123, 124, 133,
    200–201
Pickering, Roger, 74, 76
Pirker, Franz, 27, 28, 30, 31, 66,
Planelli, Antonio, 73
Porpora, Nicola, 19, 146

Quaglio, Giovanni Maria, 100
Quin, James, 70

Rameau, Jean-Philippe, 21, 90, 135
Rauzzini, Venanzio, 1, 22, 156, 157, 179, 197
Reggio Emilia, 25, 81, 82–83, 88
Ricci, Agostino, 170
Rousseau, Jean-Jacques, 56

Sacchini, Antonio, 116, 121, 138
Salisbury, 9, 47–48, 51, 53, 201
Scarlatti, Giuseppe, 101–102
Scolari, Giuseppe, 84
Senesino [Francesco Bernardi], 1, 7, 35, 39, 138
Sirmen, Maddalena Laura, 134
Smith, John Christopher jr, 62–63, 125, 201
Stanley, John, 125
Stuttgart, 90–92, 93, 95, 96

Tartini, Giuseppe, 22, 85, 118, 134, 157, 169, 176, 197
Tenducci, Giusto Ferdinando, 1, 33, 124, 125, 130
Tibaldi, Giuseppe, 4, 80, 82, 88–89, 93, 95, 104,
    105, 106, 107
Toms, Edward, 125, 133
Tozzi, Antonio, 142, 158, 159–161, 177

Traetta, Tommaso, 1, 66, 90, 92, 93, 94, 104,
    107, 206
    *Enea e Lavinia*, 91
    *Le feste d'Imeneo*, 89, 90, 96
    *Ifigenia in Tauride*, 103–104, 161, 200,
        207–209
    *Nitteti*, 25, 82, 88
    *Olimpiade*, 86
Treviso, 23
Turin, 9, 23, 81, 82, 86, 90–91,

Vallotti, Francesco Antonio, 21, 22, 103, 117–118,
    169–170, 197
    'O lingua benedicta', 117–118, 155, 207, 210
Vanneschi, Francesco, 30, 42, 50
Venice, 10, 15, 20, 23, 26, 28, 40, 107, 110, 113, 115,
    130, 154, 155, 171, 172, 173, 189, 211
    San Marco, 110–112, 157, 161
    Teatro San Benedetto, 23, 82, 112–113, 120–121,
        152, 161, 177
    Teatro San Moisè, 23, 24, 113
    Teatro San Salvatore, 84
Vento, Matthia, 124, 131, 134
Verona, 11, 86, 152, 153, 154, 155, 156
    'Verona score', 147–150, 153
Versailles, 61
Vicenza, 16, 17, 20, 80, 82, 90
Vienna, 66, 76, 80, 89, 93–109
    Burgtheater, 91, 94–95, 96, 98–99, 103,
        104, 106
    concerts in, 95–96, 102–103
    Freemasonry in, 100
    Kärntnertortheater, 95
    Laxenburg, 95, 103
    Schönbrunn, 91, 107
Vittori, Loreto, 19

Walpole, Horace, 28, 32, 43, 44, 63, 66, 131
Walpurgis, *see* Maria Antonia
Wynn, Watkin Williams, 4th Baronet, 50,
    129–130, 134

Ximenes d'Aragona, Giuseppe, 100, 165, 211

Zinzendorf and Pottendorf, Count Johann Karl,
    93, 94, 99, 100, 101, 103, 104, 105